Gender Theory in Troubled Times

In memory of Annette Fitzsimons

Gender Theory in Troubled Times

KATHLEEN LENNON &
RACHEL ALSOP

polity

Copyright © Kathleen Lennon & Rachel Alsop 2020

The right of Kathleen Lennon & Rachel Alsop to be identified as Authors of this Work has been asserted in accordance with the UK Copyright, Designs and Patents Act 1988.

First published in 2020 by Polity Press

Polity Press
65 Bridge Street
Cambridge CB2 1UR, UK

Polity Press
101 Station Landing
Suite 300
Medford, MA 02155, USA

All rights reserved. Except for the quotation of short passages for the purpose of criticism and review, no part of this publication may be reproduced, stored in a retrieval system or transmitted, in any form or by any means, electronic, mechanical, photocopying, recording or otherwise, without the prior permission of the publisher.

ISBN-13: 978-0-7456-8301-0
ISBN-13: 978-0-7456-8302-7 (pb)

A catalogue record for this book is available from the British Library.

Library of Congress Cataloging-in-Publication Data
Names: Lennon, Kathleen, author. | Alsop, Rachel, author.
Title: Gender theory in troubled times / Kathleen Lennon & Rachel Alsop.
Description: Cambridge, UK ; Medford, MA : Polity, 2020. | Includes bibliographical references and index. | Summary: «This timely and necessary intervention revisits gender theory for contemporary times. The authors explore the multiple strands which go into making our gendered identities and refuse a singular ‹truth about gender›, resulting in the ideal critical overview»-- Provided by publisher.
Identifiers: LCCN 2019024006 | ISBN 9780745683010 (hardback) | ISBN 9780745683027 (paperback) | ISBN 9780745683058 (epub)
Subjects: LCSH: Gender identity. | Queer theory. | Sex (Psychology)
Classification: LCC HQ18.55 .L46 2020 | DDC 305.3--dc23
LC record available at https://lccn.loc.gov/2019024006

Typeset in 11 on 13pt Scala
by Fakenham Prepress Solutions, Fakenham, Norfolk NR21 8NL
Printed and bound in Great Britain by CPI Group (UK) Ltd, Croydon

The publisher has used its best endeavours to ensure that the URLs for external websites referred to in this book are correct and active at the time of going to press. However, the publisher has no responsibility for the websites and can make no guarantee that a site will remain live or that the content is or will remain appropriate.

Every effort has been made to trace all copyright holders, but if any have been overlooked the publisher will be pleased to include any necessary credits in any subsequent reprint or edition.

For further information on Polity, visit our website: politybooks.com

Contents

Preface vi

Introduction 1
1 The Data of Biology 20
2 Gendered Psyches: Psychoanalysis and Sexual Difference 44
3 Historical Materialism 71
4 Simone de Beauvoir: Becoming Woman 96
5 Intersectionality 122
6 Judith Butler: Performativity, Precariousness and Queering 151
7 Making Sense of our (Gendered) Selves 176
Conclusion: The 'Truth about Gender' 199

Questions for Further Reflection 211
Notes 218
References 228
Index 251

Preface

This book began as a second edition of our *Theorizing Gender* (2002) and then morphed into a new work that revisits many of the same concerns, but in a changed political and social, as well as theoretical, context. The original *Theorizing Gender* was written in collaboration with Annette Fitzsimons and Ros Minsky. Both are sadly no longer with us, but we remain informed by their knowledge and insights. Regretfully also gone is the Hull Centre for Gender Studies, which for thirty-five years sustained and supported the research of many scholars and activists, including our own. We pay tribute to the commitment and expertise of those who made Hull an important centre of excellence for gendered research, maintained close links with activist groups in the local community, and established and perpetuated a set of international networks. Collectively they/we promoted a commitment to internationalism and localism as key to any feminist agenda, interweaving feminist and LGBTQI+ concerns internationally with those of migration and borders. The legacy of the centre burns bright, however, in the transfer of the Erasmus Mundus GEMMA Masters of Excellence to the Centre for Women's Studies at the University of York and the ongoing research and teaching of the centre's alumni across the world, including within the inspiring Global Grace Project. We would also like to thank each other for many years of fruitful and enjoyable collaboration in both teaching and research.

Introduction

What is gender?

This book is about theorizing gender. So, what is *gender*? When we were writing *Theorizing Gender*, at the end of the 1990s, the term gender was associated primarily with the psychological, behavioural and social aspects of being a man or a woman, or someone who refuses that binary. It was contrasted with the term *sex*, which, by many, was taken to be a marker of biological difference. In terms of the famous sex/gender distinction (which we discuss in chapter 1), sexed difference was considered as something biological (often characterized as being male or female) but gender was viewed as socially constructed, variable historically, as well as cross- and intra-culturally, and susceptible to change.

Much has happened to all the terms since then.

Theoretically, the sex/gender distinction has been further problematized (see chapter 1). The apparent givenness of biology in some accounts has been destabilized by feminist biologists, among others, and the necessity of a binary biological division into male and female challenged as itself mediated by cultural assumptions about gender and by norms of heterosexuality. On the other side, the body has been seen as central to the psychological, behavioural and social aspects of being a man or a woman. Gender cannot be pruned off as simply a matter of *style*. What might be considered a question of style is femininity and masculinity. Femininity would here be considered the modes of appearance and behaviour which are normatively linked, in a specific context, to being a woman, masculinity what is normatively linked to being a man.

Secondly, widely, within English-speaking countries, the term 'gender' has come to stand for a positioning of oneself or others as a 'man' or a 'woman', or as 'non-binary', without reference to the sex/gender distinction and without commitment as to whether this positioning is biological or social. It is the term used in the media and often on official forms. When your gender is asked for, what is meant is 'Are you a man or a woman?', with the occasional option of additional categories such as non-binary. And, to complicate matters further, the terms 'being a man' or 'being a woman' are generally used synonymously with 'being male' or 'being female', although, for some, these latter terms still carry something of their biological history.

Thirdly, the Gender Recognition Act in the UK (2004), and parallel legislation elsewhere, allows someone to change their initial assignment as man or woman, male or female, similarly without commitment to these categories being either social or biological.

What we are exploring, in this book, is the practice of differentiating people according to sexed categories, as men or women, or categories which reference this dominant binary. We could have used the terms *'sexed difference'* or *'sexual difference'* for this task. The latter, as we clarify in chapter 2, is associated with a particular psychoanalytically anchored theory and so was not suitable for us. We could, however, describe our enterprise as theorizing 'sexed difference', a term we regard as synonymous with gender. We are using 'gender' here, as is now widespread, to mean being positioned in relation to the categories 'man' or 'woman', a process of which we are attempting to make sense. Since the publication of Judith Butler's *Gender Trouble* in 1990 (discussed in chapter 6), work exploring this process has been referred to as 'gender theory'. That is the topic of this book.

Doing gender theory

To do gender theory we need to explore what is meant by the terms 'man' and 'woman' and other terms related to them, such as 'male' and 'female', or 'masculine' and 'feminine'. We also need to consider those which reference our foundational terms, such as 'gender fluid' or 'non-binary' (discussed in chapter 7). What informs the assignment of people to these categories? And what are the consequences of such assignments? Each of these tasks is inter-implicated with the other, as Beauvoir made clear in her seminal text *The Second Sex* ([1949]

2010). What we mean by the terms is linked to what informs their assignment to people and the personal and social consequences of such an assignment. 'But first, what is a woman?' Beauvoir asks (ibid.: 5). And she recognized – and we follow her – that this question is not answered by looking in a dictionary. To answer this question, we need to look at a range of factors: the biological diversity of bodies; what is made of those bodies in familial and wider social contexts; the economic and wider social structural consequences of sexed positionality and its implications for divisions of labour and power differentials; the (variable) cultural meanings, myths and imaginaries attached to sexed difference; the practices into which we are initiated in order to reproduce differences; the intersection of gendered categories with other aspects of social positionality; and the internalization of these external factors to produce the lived experience of gender – a gendered subjectivity which gives us a sense of ourselves as female, or male, or non-binary.

In this book we explore each of these factors. While aiming to provide an account of some of the key debates within gender theory currently, we are also defending a position. We argue that there is no single truth about what it is to be a 'man' or a 'woman', though this does not make the meanings of these terms arbitrary or subjective. The meanings are locally, culturally, socially and historically specific. They are mutually constituted alongside other categories of social identity. Their meaning is also being continually renegotiated. To argue this position is to argue against gender essentialism. We argue that there is no single authoritative set of conditions which determines sexed identity. Most, but not all, gender essentialist positions anchor sexed identification in biology (see chapter 1). Some anchor it in the structure of language (see chapter 2). Others anchor it in a subjective sense of self (see chapter 7). In rejecting essentialism, we are not ignoring biological differences or the importance of symbolic structures or subjective feelings but, rather, placing all of these in the context of a more complex story. This is the story which we are unfolding in this book.

Attention to the processes by which we become gendered, and the mechanisms and meanings within society whereby structures of gender inequality are maintained, requires attention to the lives of women and men. It also requires that we pay attention to the lives of people who cross such categories or fit uneasily within them. It necessitates seeing the ways in which gender and sexuality are interrelated with class, race, culture and bodily abilities and how they are implicated in colonial histories. All this needs to be done while retaining a feminist sensibility. This feminist sensibility we would characterize as both attending to the workings of power and privilege in the individual and social articulations of difference and putting such knowledge to work to achieve positive change.

Theoretical shifts

When we wrote *Theorizing Gender* at the end of the twentieth century, gender theory had been transformed by the work of Judith Butler (1990a, 1990b, 1993). The alignment of gender theory with queer theory, the performative account of gender, and the destabilization of the sex/gender distinction provided a new orientation to the question of sexed difference, as well as new directions for intervention in oppressive practices. We were dazzled, and remain so. But in the intervening years it has been possible to place Butler's work within a more multifaceted domain.

- We have been able to see the way Butler's work built on the groundbreaking *feminist phenomenology* of Simone de Beauvoir ([1949] 2010). We have included a careful interrogation of her work here, reflecting an increasing body of feminist scholarship in recent years (Card 2003; Deutscher 2008; Kruks 2012; Moi 2008; Sandford 2006). Such re-engagement with Beauvoir has been accompanied by a more general recognition of the importance of phenomenological resources for gender theory, with particular attention to the work of Merleau-Ponty (Young 2005; Heinämaa 2003; Alcoff 2006; Ahmed 2006; Salamon 2010; Gonzalez-Arnal et al. 2012; Dolezal 2015; Weiss 1999, 2015; Lennon 2018).
- Beauvoir also anticipated other aspects of feminist theory which have come to the fore since 2000. One is the emergence of what has been termed *the new materialism*, insisting that, although we have no unmediated access to the material, including the biological world, our accounts are answerable to it, and it plays an active role in the development of those accounts (Alaimo and Hekman 2008; Fausto-Sterling 2000). A key theorist here is Donna Haraway (1991, 1997, 2008, 2016), whose pioneering work we had acknowledged in our original book, and whose contribution has now been celebrated within the new materialist framework.

- There has also been a revival of interest in *historical materialism* (Coole and Frost 2010a; Jackson 2001; Walby 2011), another aspect of Beauvoir's account – an insistence on the way the economic and social world is structured by both capitalism and patriarchy. Such objective structures are both constituted by and constituting of gender difference. They work both locally and globally (Mohanty 2003; Parashar 2011).
- The work of post-colonial writers has highlighted the way capitalist and patriarchal structures both require and constitute the workings of colonialism (McClintock 1995; Spivak 1988; Mohanty 2003). The emergence of *decolonial feminism*, which has become increasingly prominent in the last decade, provides 'a way of understanding the oppression of women who have been subalternized through the combined processes of racialization, colonization, capitalist exploration, and heterosexualism' (Lugones 2010; see also Ortega and Alcoff 2009; Alcoff and Mendieta 2003; Ortega 2016).
- The work of decolonial feminists sits alongside that of writers giving an intersectional analysis of all aspects of social identity. Black feminist theory from the 1980s on (Crenshaw 1989, 1991; Collins 1990) insisted that we could not provide general accounts of gendered positionality and subjectivity, for they were mutually constituted with differences in race and class. Decolonial writers insist that such categories are constituted very differently for colonizers and the colonized (Lugones 2010). Such work became crystallized when Crenshaw (1991) coined the term *'intersectionality'*. What this work has made clear is that any account of gender must pay attention to its inter-articulation with race, class, ability, age, sexuality, religion, nationality and colonial legacy, as well as to the power differentials which are thereby marked.
- Another key development has been the increasing availability of both theory and memoir from writers who are sometimes grouped together under the umbrella term 'trans' (see chapter 7) (Bettcher and Garry 2009; McBee 2018; Namaste 2000; Stryker and Aizura 2013). This work has made clear how the diverse possibilities for living, which such accounts make evident, are central to gender theory.
- The developments in Butler's later work (2004a, 2004b, 2010) have also been indispensable, most particularly her attention to our embodied vulnerability to others and the material world and the

necessity of recognition by communities of others for ensuring a liveable life.

All of this work has informed the account which we offer here.

Gender essentialism

The widespread use of the term 'gender' to capture sexed difference has not been associated with any extensive rejection of gender essentialism. Indeed, there has been a resurgence of a very visible gender essentialism in everyday life. This is particularly marked in relation to children. Following the informative scan, prospective parents in the UK and the US now often throw pink- or blue-themed parties to announce the gender of their unborn baby. From birth, clothes and accessories are strongly differentiated in colour and style. Toys are divided into those appropriate for boys and those for girls. Behaviour is anxiously policed for signs of cross-gendering. Oddly, these factors seem to have increased as challenges mount to gendered inequalities both in the workplace and in the public world. It has increased and not decreased in the last decade. Now even Lego comes in differentiated colours and themes. Such moves have also been resisted, with some parents challenging retailers to modify their marketing practices. A curious example is found in discussions of education. Currently, in many places where both have equal access to education, girls outclass boys. This would seem to knock on the head previous arguments that the underachievement of girls was due to differences in their brains and to make clear it was a result of social and cultural factors. But such naturalistic arguments have only re-emerged in a different form. Boys, it is now claimed, have different brains to girls, and the teaching methods currently employed do not chime with them. (For a discussion of claims of differentiated brains, see chapter 1, and for the complexity of the educational data on which these claims are made, see chapters 3 and 5.) Such public reinforcement of supposed gendered differences in children comes (presumably non-accidentally) with a large rise in children claiming that their gender has been misassigned and seeking to change it (Hurst 2018).

The reinforcement of gender essentialism in everyday life runs alongside a sinister reinforcement taking place politically across the globe in which claims of gender essentialism – an insistence on natural or God-given differences between men and women that indicate appropriate social roles – are being harnessed to bolster right-wing populist claims and new nationalisms, often interwoven with influence from the religious right. These claims are linked to attacks particularly on the reproductive rights of women and are threatening to the legitimacy of LGBTQI+ communities. In recent years these movements have launched attacks on gender theory itself (Meret and Siim 2013; Kuhar and Paternotte 2017; von Redecker 2018; Kantola and Lombardo 2019). We turn to these developments below.

Gender essentialism has also returned within the feminist community, particularly but not exclusively in the UK, around the question of the rights of trans women. Interestingly, the debate is concerned primarily with the status of trans women rather than trans men. But some organizations made up of women suggest that WNT (women who are not trans) will suffer if the boundaries are drawn to include TW (trans women) as women (Murray 2017).[1] In this book we both draw the boundaries to include trans women and argue that this is an appropriate place to draw them. We refute the suggestion that this damages the interests of women with intersectional identities of other kinds (see discussions in chapters 5 and 7). We also return to these points further below.

The rise of right-wing populism

We, the authors of this text, are white, English-speaking, European, cis gender women (women whose claimed gender corresponds to the gender they were assigned at birth) working as academics in the UK. This locatedness is evident in the work that follows, though we endeavour to engage with voices from other perspectives. It is also evident in our viewing the times in which we are writing as particularly troubled for those seeking to promote gender equality. While resisting a simple progressive narrative of history, we acknowledge at the time of our writing a backlash against gained gender equality in many parts of the world, as well as the ongoing oppression and marginalization of women and sexual minorities in many others. We acknowledge that all times are troubled and troubling. However, we wish to point here to certain features of current concern which underscore our insistence that how we theorize gender is of immediate political importance.

A disturbing truth is that 53 per cent of white women in the United States voted for Donald Trump in the US elections held in 2016, despite widespread indication of his misogyny and his opposition to women's sexual and reproductive rights (Darweesh and Abdullah 2016; Ratliff et al. 2017; Valentino et al. 2018); 94 per cent of black women voted for Hillary Clinton. The more progressive gender agenda was thus supported in that election by black and Latino women. What this has helped clarify is that the possibilities of both a just anti-racist society and a society which promotes the rights of women and the LGBTQI+ community are interdependent. Gender rights intersect with rights of other marginalized peoples. Thus, being concerned with multiple axes of oppression globally is not an add-on for feminism. It is a condition of its survival. Trump's opposition to gender and sexual rights and their interconnections with his anti-immigration policies are typical of right-wing populism. 'The few gender issues that appear on the far-right agenda support traditional family and conservative gender roles, and unashamedly oppose women's sexual and reproductive rights and LGBT rights. ... Gender equality discourse is instrumentalised against immigration ... and feminist politics is framed as a dangerous "gender ideology"' (Kantola and Lombardo 2019: 3–4).

Judith Butler points also to the ways in which the language and politics of gender and sexual equality are manipulated to argue against immigration. In *Frames of War* she asserts that 'in recent years the positions associated with sexual progressive politics have been pitted *against* claims for new immigrant rights and new cultural exchanges in the US and Europe' (2010: 27). One narrative put forward is this: in the US and Europe there are progressive values that give equal rights to women, allow gay marriage and respect gender fluidity. But other cultures, particularly Muslim cultures, are represented as backward in this respect, and this is used to justify rejection of individuals and even military adventures in predominantly Muslim countries. In this narrative, many of the things for which feminists and LGBTQI+ activists have been fighting are appropriated to ensure that the rights and dignity of migrants and minorities are positioned as somehow in opposition to gender and sexuality rights. Paradoxically, such a position is taken while at the same time the very same gender rights are being undermined.

The interweaving of nationalism and right-wing populism manifest in Trump's United States is found in many other parts of the world. And the same pattern is repeated: chauvinistic nationalism is accompanied by attacks on gender rights (Alsop and Hockey 2001; Yilmaz 2012; Meret and Siim 2013). 'It's a vision of the world in which men are superior to women, inequality is the name of the game and tradition is what's being protected by these authoritarian rulers' (Scott 2018). Poland, Hungary and Brazil are striking examples, but there are strands throughout Europe and elsewhere (Meret and Siim 2013; Verloo 2018; Kantola and Lombardo 2019). Globally we see a resurgence of populist politics both on the left (the Podemos movement in Spain or Syriza in Greece, for example) and on the right (elections of Trump in the US and Bolsonaro in Brazil; or the emergence of the Finns Party in Finland or One Nation in Australia). Focusing specifically on the emergence of right-wing populist politics, Kantola and Lombardo point to the ways in which 'Feminist studies have shown how the discourse of radical right groups is visibly anti-feminist, anti-LGBT, conservative, nationalist, racist, xenophobic, Islamophobic and anti-democratic' (2019: 3).

There is an interweaving of such right-wing populism with religious fundamentalism, which informs the attack on gendered rights. In Poland, for example, the nationalist Law and Justice party, closely aligned with a conservative Catholic Church, was elected in 2015 and tried to impose a full ban on abortion, which was narrowly defeated. Attempts to restrict access to abortion are ongoing, and LGBTQI+ people in Poland continue to encounter discrimination. In Hungary, there are parallel developments in which church and state seek to roll back women's reproductive rights and the rights of sexual minorities to reinstate a traditional model of the family as a natural, God-given institution which is under attack (Peto 2016). Jair Bolsonaro became president of Brazil with a campaign that targeted the rights of women and was abusive to the LGBTQI+ community. His campaign was supported by conservative Pentecostal groups and was accompanied by alarming increases in violent deaths related to homophobia alongside racialized violence and increased violence against women. 'In his post-election-victory speech, Bolsonaro said his campaign had relied on the Bible, "the toolbox to fix men and women"' (Assis and Ogando 2018).

The authoritarian attack on gendered rights is found not only in states with unholy alliances with varieties of Christianity. Turkey, as part of its post-2016 coup, launched a crackdown on civil society, put LGBTQI+ defenders in prison, and fired rubber bullets at a

Pride march in Istanbul. Turkey's President Erdoğan consistently reinforces women's traditional role within the family and society, 'declaring that women are not equal to men ... and that biological differences meant women and men could not serve the same functions, adding that manual work was unsuitable for the "delicate nature" of women' (Agence France-Presse 2014). Here the resurgent nationalisms target Kurdish minorities as well as the migrants from Syria who are targets of the right across Europe. A recent AIDA report on Turkey suggests that 'the vulnerability of migrant women, especially of single women, to all types of sexual harassment and assault is high and invisible. This makes them a potential target of not only the local population ... which are generally very conservative, but also of male public officials who mostly rely on the impunity tradition of the Turkish state' (AIDA 2018).

These shifts to the right have sparked strong and inspiring opposition – for example, the 'Black Protests' in Poland against restrictions of women's reproductive rights and the gender justice movements in Brazil. The Women's March on Washington in January 2017, the day after Trump's inauguration, was attended by an estimated 4.5 million women and led to ongoing demonstrations in the US and other places, the mobilization of opposition to Trump, and a drive to get more women into US politics. It paid off when, in the midterm elections in November 2018, which were shaped by gender issues, a record number of women and minority representatives were elected to Congress. 'The 116th Congress [is] the most diverse in history, with 102 women, many more openly gay members, more blacks, more Latinos, the first two female Native Americans, a Somali immigrant and the first ever Palestinian American woman elected to the House' (Abramson 2019).

Gender theory under attack

Gender theory is complex, informed by philosophical, sociological, psychoanalytic, economic, art, literary and other theoretical insights. This book is no exception. We do our best to make the theory clear, spell out the complexity and explain what points are in contention. The theories we explore come from multiple sources, and their origins are ones which we try to acknowledge. Their importance has been made evident from collective attempts to grapple with difference and inequality. Gender theory is often criticized and required to demonstrate its relevance to activist struggles. Such struggles are trying to promote gender equality and diversity globally and to combat the harms which accrue in most, if not all, societies to women and gender non-conformist people, especially the harms of economic deprivation, sexual violence and lack of access to power. The plea from theorists has been, and from us still would be, that we have to *understand* how gender differences are produced and maintained if we are to counteract them. bell hooks says: 'I found a place of sanctuary in "theorizing," in making sense out of what was happening.' She is countering what she perceives as anti-intellectualism in some feminist circles by arguing that critical reflection is essential for practice. She acknowledges, however, that 'theory is not inherently healing, liberatory, or revolutionary. It fulfills this function only when we ask that it do so and direct our theorizing towards this end' (hooks 1991).

This link of theory and practice, a point of contention within feminism, has been seized on by opponents of gender equality worldwide. Within a larger attack on intellectual inquiry, gender theory, as a sphere of academic endeavour, has become demonized by religious leaders and alt-right political parties as corrupting of the social order and dangerous if taught in any form to children or young adults. In November 2017, while attending a conference in São Paulo, Brazil, which she had helped to organize, the philosopher and gender theorist Judith Butler was faced with a protest in which her effigy was burned as a witch and she was accused of destroying the family and encouraging paedophilia![2] It appears that far-right Christian groups organized the protests, and since then the country's far-right president, Jair Bolsonaro, has initiated measures promising to combat 'gender ideology'. Butler afterwards commented:

> the allegation is that I am the founder of 'the ideology of gender.' That ideology, which is called 'diabolical' by these opponents, is considered to be a threat to the family. There does not seem to be any evidence that those who mobilized on this occasion had any familiarity with my text *Gender Trouble*, published in late 1989. But they took that text to be promoting the idea that one can become any gender one wants, that there are not natural laws or natural differences, and that both the biblical and scientific basis for establishing the differences between the sexes would be, or already is, destroyed by the theory attributed to me. ...
>
> My sense is that the group who engaged [in] this frenzy of effigy burning, stalking and harassment want to defend 'Brazil' as a place

where LGBTQ people are not welcome, where the family remains heterosexual (so no gay marriage), where abortion is illegal and reproductive freedom does not exist. They want boys to be boys, and girls to be girls, and for there to be no complexity in questions such as these. The effort is antifeminist, antitrans, homophobic and nationalist, using social media to stage and disseminate their events. In this way, they resemble the forms of neo-fascism that we see emerging in different parts of the world. (Cited in Jasnik 2017)

As Butler signals, this attack was not an isolated event. Gender theory is being targeted in many other countries. Anti-feminist campaigns, demonizing so-called gender ideology, have been mobilized in various parts of the world, from Europe to the Americas to Australia (Corrêa 2017; Corrêa et al. 2018). Gender studies has been effectively banned from universities in Hungary, a member state of the European Union (Walker 2018). In Poland, another EU member state, from a

heretofore obscure foreign concept known only to specialists, gender [is] suddenly omnipresent in the tabloids, on Facebook and in the blogosphere. It [is] ... the focus of endless and heated debate ... in Poland's Roman Catholic parishes – consistently demonized in sermons as a threat to the family. Gender is presented as the heart of the 'Civilization of death', and as a source of perversion and degradation. Parents [are] warned that their children [are] in danger. (Graff 2014)

The role of the Catholic Church is important here. From as far back as the 1990s, when the United Nations introduced the term 'gender' in its documents, its use was attacked by some Catholic groups. However, in the last few years that attack has intensified. Pope Francis complains that 'indoctrination in gender theory' is going around the world, undermining the natural and God-given division between the sexes and suggesting that sexual behaviour is not governed by objective moral norms (Glatz 2015).

What is clear in all these attacks is that gender theory is opposed because it is viewed as *denying gender essentialism*, suggesting instead that the divisions between the sexes, and the distinct characteristics and social positions assigned to each, are socially malleable. Gender theory, it is claimed, involves rejecting the naturalness of heterosexuality, the primacy of the heterosexual family and the fixity of gendered identity. In fact, gender theory is a broad area of study which includes many theorists who would endorse some versions of gender essentialism. In this book, however, while discussing alternative strands of theory, we proudly hold up our hands to opposing just the kind of gender essentialism that such populist movements seek to enforce. Their engagement makes clear that these apparently theoretical debates have highly political consequences.

The boundaries of the category 'woman'

Feminists of all kinds are opposed to the populist movements which are seeking to reverse and halt advances made in women's access to increased social power and reproductive rights. But fault lines have opened within feminism itself, which also have their source in a return to gender essentialism in some quarters. Current legal and much everyday practice in the UK, and many other parts of the world, recognizes the possibility of people changing the sex/gendered category assigned to them at birth. The fault lines within (particularly UK) feminism concern the rights of trans women (trans men do not seem to occasion the same concern) and the claim made by some feminists that these rights conflict with the rights of women whose intersectional identities (see chapter 5) are of a different kind. For us it is important for feminists to support the position of trans women and men in the face of the global backlash against the rights of all kinds of women and LGBTQI+ people as a consequence of the populist movements described above, which reject difference and oppose minority and migrant groups of all kinds (see also Hines 2006 and 2019 for further critique). This is not a time, we suggest, when feminists should feel comfortable about returning to essentialism about sexed difference. To do so is to have some alarming bedfellows.

The current discussions are sometimes conducted in terms of who is and who is not a *real* woman or man (Murray 2017). These discussions often revisit those aired within second-wave feminism concerning whether any people who were born with/retain/retain traces of what we currently think of as male bodily morphology can appropriately be thought of as women. (We should, of course, expect that, whatever the salient considerations are here, they should also allow us to consider the question of whether any of those who were born with/retain/retain traces of what we currently think of as, female bodily morphology are appropriately considered men.) Many of those resistant to the acceptance of trans women as women are reverting to conceptions of sexed identity as fixed by biological roles in reproduction or bodily morphology. But this move relies on a discredited biologism, which feminist biologists (see for example Fausto-Sterling 1993, 2000) have themselves made problematic, and which we discuss and reject in chapter 1. But not all gender essentialists place the essential identifying features in biology. Others see these as anchored in shared experiences, including shared experiences throughout life of being oppressed as a woman. Some would suggest that we cannot capture the distinctive form of oppression directed against women as women if we allow into the category women those who have spent part of their lives considered by others to be men.[3]

The possibility of telling a *single* story about the nature and basis of women's oppression, however, dissolves with the recognition that discrimination works not homogeneously but in an intersectional way (Koyama 2006). It matters to the nature of the oppression we suffer what the other mutually constituting categories in play might be. As discussed further in chapter 5, for instance, the oppressions which black women face are informed by the intersections of being black and female (an intersection which is further complicated by interconnections of class, sexuality, dis-ability, age, and so on). For all of us, our experiences and our identities are intersectional, particular and diverse. Trans women may share certain oppressions by virtue of being trans but also share other forms of discrimination with women who are not trans. 'You don't need to have ovaries to have sometimes felt scared walking in the dark, and those who were assigned a female gender at birth are not the only ones with #MeToo stories to tell' (Hinsliff 2018a). The most cursory attention to trans narratives and hate crime statistics will dispel any sense that to grow up with gender identity misplacement is to grow up privileged (Whittle and Turner 2009). '"It is held against me that 'you were raised with male privilege', but actually I was beaten up all the time for being effeminate,"' says Clara Barker, a trans scientist at the University of Oxford .... "Because I was trans I was severely depressed, I was bullied in my workplace, so it's like, 'What privilege is that?'"' (Hinsliff 2018b).

The claim that being female consists in some specifiable set of shared experiences, including experiences of oppression, has been found wanting by critical race theorists, disability theorists and decolonial feminists (hooks 1984; Collins 1990; Garland-Thomson 1997; Lugones 2010), who point out that there are no universal sets of experiences that all women share and no single model of oppression.

These considerations make clear that, while there will often be discriminatory practices concerning some women being women, which do need to be addressed, they will not necessarily include all women. Period poverty, abortion, issues of pregnancy and childbearing, treatment of the menopause and issues to do with ageing will be some of these issues, as will, for example, medical issues concerning the health and well-being of trans women. Keeping women safe from physical harm, sexual assault and murder is key across the board.

We would argue that there are no general conflicts of interest between cis women and trans women as collective groupings. Practices of exclusion, abuse, violence and discrimination are endemic to both, and we need to make common cause to protect and enhance the lives of all through dialogue and coalition-building. But there are some striking features about the debate. One is the lack of insight which some feminist women show about the lives and experiences of those who may, in many different ways, be gender non-conformist. With this lack of insight comes a tightening of the boundaries around what is required to be a *proper* woman, a privileging of some experiences (Phipps 2016), and a reinforcement of the binary man/woman. But it is the grip of this binary which is the source of violence and dislocation suffered by many groups, including those for whom neither side of the binary currently offers a comfortable resting place. And there is the urgent issue of the distress of gender non-conforming children. Children can find the pressures to conform so tough that they are earlier and earlier seeking escape from their assigned sexed identity to explore what currently seems the only other one on offer. Such children need society to *let them be*, to position themselves on the gender spectrum where they will. This will not be achievable while the position of their adult counterparts remains policed.

The structure of this book

This book offers a set of key theoretical resources which we regard as necessary if we are to grasp what is involved in falling under the categories 'man' or 'woman' or related categories. It offers theories which try to make sense of the process of becoming gendered in terms of both social position and lived experience. We show our hand, of course, in talking of becoming gendered as a process rather than as a matter which is simply settled when we are born. We deal these theories out like a pack of cards in separate chapters, at the same time as signalling the way in which, for us, they are interwoven.

We start by paying attention to what Beauvoir calls *the data of biology*, looking at the work of feminist biologists and contemporary new materialist feminists to evaluate the role which the biological body plays in determining our gendered classifications and the consequent psychological and behavioural patterns that attach to them. We reject a naturalizing account which regards biology as determining a binary division into sexed kinds and a consequent set of social divisions. Nonetheless the biological body is part of the story here, and we follow new materialist feminists in assigning importance to it.

We then turn our attention in chapter 2 to *the psyche*, specifically the development of sets of sexed psychological identifications, as a consequence of what is made of bodily difference and the significance attached to it, in both intimate familial and more public, cultural settings. The theorists we look at here are the founding fathers of psychoanalysis, Freud and Lacan, and some of the feminist sexual difference theorists who interrogate, challenge and make use of their work. Using critical race theorists, we also compare how this work is made use of in theorizing sexed difference and in theorizing raced difference. We highlight the important concept of the imaginary, which has its origin in this psychoanalytic work. Again, we resist an account which sees a necessary binary sexual division within individual psychic development and public symbolic structures. But the theories we consider provide crucial resources for making sense of the processes of developing a gendered sense of self – a sense of self which results from what is made of bodily difference privately and, interconnectedly, within the public imaginary.

The third chapter turns from the domain of the biological and the psyche to the domain of economic and social structures. Drawing on Marx's historical materialism, Marxist feminists and socialist feminists interrogating the interweaving of capitalism and patriarchy, we show how gendered positionality structures the possibilities for, and outcomes of, engagement in the social world. These points are illustrated by data concerning the differential position of men and women in contemporary societies. What happens to us, as women and men, is conditioned by the material and economic structures of the historical and geographical locations in which we are placed. These are very variable. But gender affects the ways each of them is organized. Part of what it is to be gendered is to be positioned in particular ways in these economic and social structures, as well as in the linguistic structures and social imaginaries discussed in the previous chapter. There is no universal account of these structures. Patriarchal consequences are achieved in multiple ways, even when we confine ourselves to exploring the interweaving of class and gender. But we also note, drawing from black feminist thought and theorists of disability, that the workings of these structures cannot be articulated by restricting ourselves to class and gender. Moreover, post-colonial and decolonial feminists have long stressed the ways in which capitalism and patriarchy require the history of colonial exploitation and its contemporary legacy. We return to this discussion in chapter 5.

In chapter 4 we turn to the ground-breaking work of Simone de Beauvoir. In her 1949 text *The Second Sex*, Beauvoir weaves together the different strands of theory we have so far introduced. We foreground her work both for the key theoretical resources she provides, particularly from phenomenology, and for the exemplary way in which she makes clear how multiple factors are entangled in the account we offer of becoming gendered. She recognizes that we are assigned sexed positionality most commonly on the basis of biological features. But the consequences of such assignment depend on the (variable) *meaning and significance* attached to these categories, including what Beauvoir calls the social *myths*, what we would call the imaginaries, attached to men and women. It also depends heavily on the economic and legal structures within which we are placed. But Beauvoir adds another element to the discussion of *becoming woman*. She links the above factors, what she terms the objective conditions, to an account of gendered subjectivity, by attending to the lived experiences of women (and occasionally men) at different stages of their lives. These experiences are a consequence not only of being positioned within certain external structures but also of a process of internalizing the meaning and norms attached to this sexed positionality. Moreover, such internalization also contributes to the maintenance and reproduction of the objective inequalities.

In chapter 5 we turn our attention to what is regarded as one of the key cornerstones of contemporary gender theory, namely the discussion of intersectionality. As signalled at the end of chapter 3, the work of second-wave and earlier black feminist theorists identified that the consequences of our gendered positionality varied according to our raced, cultural, national and other social positionalities. Other writers also made evident differences concerning sexuality and bodily abilities. We therefore need to consider how these different categories relate to each other. The discussion here looks at the intersection in terms of the objective structuring of the social world but also, following the lead of Beauvoir, in relation to the lived subjectivity of individuals within that world and the kind of intersectional identifications which constitute our sense of self. This discussion of intersectionality is also informed by the contributions of decolonial writers interrogating the application of Western gendered terms within the colonial encounter. The outcome of these discussions is a rejection of any universal accounts of the contents of gendered categories.

Next, in chapter 6, we turn to the work of Judith Butler. The publication of Butler's *Gender Trouble* in 1990 and the articulation of her performative theory of gender changed the face of gender theory. It offered the most radical challenge thus far to gender essentialism in any form. Butler gave an account of the production of individual gendered identities, the social meanings of gender, and differing material outcomes in terms of performative acts. These acts were in accordance with socially given, gendered scripts, whose meanings the acts both reflected and helped constitute. Butler importantly recognized the interweaving of norms of gender and norms of sexuality, so that the gender binary itself was a requirement of a heterosexual model of sexuality and the family. But the meanings of our gendered categories and categories of sexuality, she stressed, are intersectional, unstable and shifting. Crucially, the meanings and the existence of the gender and sexual binaries themselves can be destabilized in unpredictable ways by the workings of performativity itself. We attempt to take on board the key insights of Butler's account while also stressing the constraints of our bodies and of economic and social structures, which were given scant attention in her earlier work. In addition, central to our account here is the attention she gives, in later work, to our *vulnerability to others*, and to social practices, in making sense of ourselves. She stresses the need each of us has for recognition by others if we are to make sense of ourselves, and if we are to be able to live a life alongside them.

The key role of our gendered categories in making sense of ourselves, and negotiating a public space in which we can live alongside others, is the focus of our final chapter. Here our primary resources are trans theorists who engage with the lives of those who are in different ways gender non-conformist, some of whom may change their original gendered assignment. The variety of meaning and contextual specificity attached to our gendered terms, particularly as they intersect with categories of sexuality, is marked here. It reinforces our central claim that there are no sets of necessary and sufficient conditions determining what is required to be a woman or man. But there is something else which becomes clear here and which is central to our approach. There is nothing arbitrary or whimsical about the categories in terms of which we make sense of ourselves or others. Moreover, the appropriateness of any categorization is not simply a matter of subjective feelings (though these are important). Our gendered terms are public categories whose shifting usage has *to make sense to a community of users* as tools to negotiate liveable patterns of intersubjective relations, in both intimate and public spheres.

We hope the approach to gender articulated in this book will widen the communities in which shifting conceptions of gender, and the increasing fluidity of the boundaries, can find recognition.

1 The Data of Biology

We ... often behave and talk as if the sexes are categorically different: men like *this*, women like *that*. ... In toy stores sex-segregated product aisles ... assume that a child's biological sex is a good guide to what kinds of toys will interest them. ... When we think of men and women in this complementary way it is intuitive to look for a single powerful cause that creates the divide between the sexes. ... Wouldn't it make sense if *testosterone* ... makes men like *this*, while its minimal presence in females helps to make women like *that*? ... This is Testosterone Rex: that familiar, pervasive and powerful story of sex and society. Weaving together interlinked claims about evolution, brains, hormones and behavior, it offers a neat and compelling account ... [But] Testosterone Rex is wrong, wrong, and wrong again. (Fine 2017: 17–22)

The idea of the male brain and the female brain suggests that each is a characteristically homogenous thing and that whoever has got a male brain, say, will have the same kind of aptitudes, preferences and personalities as everyone else with that 'type' of brain. We now know that is not the case. We are at the point where we need to say, 'Forget the male and female brain; it's a distraction, it's inaccurate.' ... It is now a scientific given ... that the brain is moulded from birth onwards and continues to be moulded through to the 'cognitive cliff' in old age when our grey cells start disappearing. So out goes the old 'biology is destiny' argument. (Gina Rippon, quoted in Fox 2019)

Sexed/gendered difference

In contemporary discussions of sexed differences, there is a renewed search for a determining factor which both divides us clearly into men and women and fixes the distinguishing features of each category. In favour again are sex hormones, particularly amounts of testosterone

(Fine 2017). The other favourite contender is the brain (Rippon 2019). In many theories, the quantity of testosterone is thought to determine the development of the brain. With Fine and Rippon, we hope to challenge the assumptions informing such claims.

The concern of this book is to explain how we end up as sexed human beings, with self- and other-assigned categorizations as men or women, male or female (or trans men or women, or intersex, or non-binary), with which we may be happy or unhappy, but which, either way, is one of the defining features of both our subjectivity and our social positionality. As we noted in the introduction, this area of investigation is now termed 'gender theory', and the term 'gender' has come, in everyday usage, to signal such sexed positionality. Under discussion is the status of our categories of sexed difference – categories that may be marked by use of the terms 'male' or 'female' or 'man' and 'woman'. There is a complexity here considering what terminology to use. 'Male' and 'female' are employed throughout the animal and, to some extent, plant kingdoms and so have more claim to be categories whose identifying criteria are fixed by biological science, criteria which may vary for different scientific purposes. But in everyday practice, for humans, we do not make a distinction between, for example, being female and being a woman. Here we are concerned with these categories as used in everyday interactions to characterize ourselves and others we encounter. What we are exploring is the (most common) binary division of people into male and female, a categorization which becomes fundamental to people's sense of their identity, frames the way they are seen by others, and carries with it associated expectations of patterns of behaviour and social positionality. The division into male and female bodies, men and women, is linked in a complicated way to a division into *masculine* and *feminine* people – where masculinity is a set of psychological and behavioural traits that are considered particularly appropriate to those classified as male, and feminine traits appropriate to those classified as female. The link between being male and masculinity and being female and femininity is a normative one. It is what is supposed to happen but is often deviated from. And, indeed, there is never an absolute coincidence. In investigating how we end up as men and women, or as non-binary, we are therefore investigating a phenomenon that has bodily, psychological, behavioural and social dimensions. It also has mythical or imaginary ones. For we are surrounded by stories and images which convey meanings about what it is to be a woman or man which interact with the other strands of individuation. In this first chapter, we will be exploring the contribution made by what Beauvoir (see chapter 4) calls *the data of biology*.

In the introduction we introduced the notion of *gender essentialism*, the suggestion that there is some fixed set of conditions which determine whether we are male or female, men or women. Those who adopt gender essentialist positions most commonly anchor them in biology. It is assumed that biology will provide us with the answer to the questions of what determines whether a person is male or female, man or woman, or maybe some combination of both. In this book we resist the claim that biology is determining in this way. But to resist this claim is not to make our biological bodies irrelevant to the complex story of how we end up gendered. They are part of the picture but not the whole of it. Moreover, our biological bodies are themselves infinitely complex, open and changing, susceptible to multiple understandings, and interwoven with our wider material and social environments in ways that render it impossible to isolate the contributions they make from other aspects of our becomings (Rippon 2019).

Sexed categories as natural kinds

Sex difference research has been a continually thriving area for at least the last two hundred years (Cameron 2007; Fine 2012). There are two fundamental assumptions underlying this work which will be scrutinized separately here. First is the assumption that the binary division of bodies into male and female is part of the natural order of the world. Within this assumption, facts about our biology provide an explanatory grounding for our sexed categories in a way that makes a division into male and female a recognition of objective facts of nature, which, in some sense, demand attention. Objective here means having a unifying factor that is independent of our practices of classification. There are differing accounts of what the most basic biological determinants of this binary division are, and research into the biology of sexed difference explores the roles played by, for example, visible morphology, brains, hormones and chromosomes. But such exploration takes place within an assumption that the sexed kinds 'male' and 'female' are biological kinds, reflecting a naturally occurring grouping of properties that have important causal effects, particularly within the biology of reproduction – for example, 'the ability to make a distinctive contribution to reproduction – i.e. [for females] to gestate, give birth to and breast-feed babies' (Stone 2007: 44). We will return to evaluate these claims below.

Psychological and behavioural sex differences and their biological anchorage

The second key assumption of much scientific work on sex differences is that the assumed division into male and female bodies is accompanied by other differences, associated psychological and behavioural dispositions, which have consequent effects on social positionality. There is, of course, disagreement as to what range of responses are supposed to be conditioned by sex differences in this way. Recurring themes concern greater aggression and competitiveness in men and greater nurturing qualities in women, greater spatial and abstract reasoning abilities in men and greater linguistic skills in women. The differences picked out are supposed both to causally explain and, sometimes, to justify the differing social positions that men and women typically occupy. 'People with the female brain make the most wonderful counselors, primary school teachers, nurses, carers, therapists ... People with the male brain make the most wonderful scientists, engineers ... musicians, architects ... toolmakers' (Baron-Cohen 2003: 11). The defence of sex differences of this kind is given causal anchorage in the hormones and chromosomes that contribute to distinct bodily characteristics and/or evolutionary theory and/or in claimed physical differences in male and female brains. An example of this kind of thinking was found in discussions following the crash of Lehman Brothers, and consequently of the global financial sector, in 2008. There was speculation that the high-risk strategies and large-scale financial speculation which led to this crash would not have been pursued if the financial traders had not been predominantly men. And here the reference was not to learnt patterns of gendered behaviour but to the link between the supposed male hormone testosterone and risk-taking. 'There is a very simple reason why most financial traders are youngish men. The nature of trading incorporates all the features for which young males are biologically adapted. ... All the actions of testosterone are echoed by the qualities of a successful trader' (Herbert 2015: 116–18, cited in Fine 2017: 151).

It is research into sex differences of this second kind which feminist writers were initially most concerned to contest. That is, they have been concerned to contest that psychological and behavioural differences are anchored primarily in biological ones. In the debates surrounding such research into psychological and behavioural sex differences there are two steps which need to be evaluated. First is the claim that there are empirically significant differences between the psychological characteristics and behavioural dispositions of those people classified as male or female, men or women. Second is the claim that these psychological and behavioural differences are to be explained by biological features, by hormones, genetic variations anchored in chromosomes, and/or differences in male and female brains – biological traits whose presence is frequently explained by evolutionary selection. As Deborah Cameron noted in 2007, from the 1990s a 'steady trickle of books' about the sex differences of men and women 'began to develop into a raging torrent'; from scientific papers which appear to suggest cognitive or behavioural differences, to popular science books and self-help books designed to aid communication across the presumed gap between men (who are from Mars), and women (who are from Venus), to coin an ubiquitous current usage' (2007: 2).

It is not possible here to give a comprehensive review of the research into psychological and behavioural sex differences, and there are some really excellent texts which provide a critical review of this work, from biologists, psychologists and historians of science (see, for example, Bleier 1984; Fausto-Sterling 1992, 2000; Fine 2012, 2017; Cameron 2007; Jordan-Young 2010). It is, however, worth looking at examples of currently active research to give a sense of the kinds of difficulties surrounding it. If biological explanations are to be offered for psychological and behavioural differences between men and women, then these differences must themselves be established. Clearly, if we look around us, wherever we are, there are a large number of psychological and behavioural differences between those classified as men and those classified as women. But if these are to be biologically based then they must not be differences that vary historically or cross-culturally. Moreover, once we add that restriction, then the characteristics for which we might seek biological explanations become much fewer and highly contested.

The biological explanations offered for the supposed differences currently utilize two, often interwoven, strands of theory. One is evolutionary psychology. The second is research into differences between male and female brains.

Evolutionary psychology

Evolutionary psychology is a development from sociobiology, which assumes that behavioural differences between men and women of multiple kinds are adaptive for survival and have been selected in a process of evolution. The work of sociobiologists suggested that our genes programme our behaviour. Genetic similarities, which had been taken to explain physical similarities among relatives and to explain the recurrence of certain illnesses in families, are viewed in a much more problematic way to be the basis of complex behavioural traits such as 'shyness, alcoholism or criminality' (Fausto-Sterling 1992: 62) and, crucially for our purposes, behavioural differences between men and women. Sociobiology assumed sexual differences have evolved through natural selection to the maximal advantages of both sexes. It is important to be clear exactly what this programme requires – namely, that patterns of behaviour, supposedly empirically observed now, are of adaptive value.

> Ideally, to show that a behaviour is an evolutionary adaptation, researchers must demonstrate that (1) the behaviour is heritable, (2) there is or was behavioural variability among individuals in a population, and (3) that differential reproduction, caused by the presence of the behaviour in question, led to an increase in the frequency of individuals tending to exhibit that behaviour in a population. Since researchers cannot go back in time to directly observe the evolution of current behaviours, they most often rely on indirect evidence. (Fehr 2011)

This has the consequence that hypotheses are invented for the *supposed adaptive advantage* of currently observed patterns of behaviour at some supposed earlier time in our evolutionary history. As many biologists, feminist and otherwise, have pointed out, this amounts to little more than the invention of *Just So* stories.

> For example, Thornhill and Palmer in their book, *A Natural History of Rape* (2000), argue that rape is either a by-product of male adaptations to desire multiple sexual partners, or an evolutionary adaptation itself. In the adaptation view, rape is a facultative reproductive strategy, meaning that rape is the result of natural selection favouring men who commit rape when its evolutionary benefits in terms of producing offspring outweigh its evolutionary costs. (Ibid.)

There has been significant criticism of such stories (Travis 2003). For example, Elisabeth Lloyd (2003) highlights not only the complete lack of evidence that rape is of adaptive value but also the assumption that rape has a unitary meaning across historical times and cultures.

At the more general level, there is scepticism that complex social behaviour could simply be programmed in. This is especially the case since the patterns of behaviour that would maximize the chances of genes surviving are highly contextual. They depend on the environment in which the organism is placed, and in the case of human societies there is simply no continuity of environment. Moreover, it has been argued that such pictures misunderstand the way in which genes work: 'a proper understanding of brain development suggests that while genetic information plays a key role in the unfolding of many details of the brain's structure, extensive development of nervous connections occurs after birth, influenced profoundly by individual experience' (Fausto-Sterling 1992: 77); 'complex traits arise not simply (from genetic information) but also from the intrusion from the external environment and chance variations in development' (ibid.: 88). We will return to this point. But what seems clear is that it is just not possible simply to read off complex patterns of behaviour from genetic modifications.

In the developments which evolutionary psychologists have made to sociobiological theories, psychological mechanisms are added into the picture. Human behaviours are not directly selected but, rather, are the product of psychological mechanisms that were selected. These mechanisms are 'hardwired' into the brain. This, if anything, has simply widened the range of behaviour for which evolutionary explanations are offered. Behaviours which did not exist in prehistoric times can now be explained as the outcome of a mechanism that *was* selected at that earlier point. So, we find bizarre examples. In the 2007 *Journal of Social Psychology* Peter Jonason argues: 'Researchers have found that men and women pursue sex-appropriate strategies to attract mates. On the basis of intrasexual competition, men should be more likely to enact behaviours to look larger, whereas women should be more likely to enact behaviours to look smaller.' (We might ask why, but he does not.) This, he claims, explains why, on undertaking exercise regimes, 'male participants focus their energy on gaining muscle mass and enhancing their upper body definition, whereas female participants focused their energy on losing weight with emphasis on their lower body' (Jonason 2007: 12). Here the *Just So* element of the suggestion seems evident. As Deborah Cameron remarks regarding many of the claims of this sort: 'the only evidence for historic sex differences is the modern sex differences it is meant to explain' (Cameron 2007: 112).

Such evolutionary stories, stories attempting to ground social behaviour in mechanisms of adaptive development, are supposedly reinforced by animal studies showing that male/female differences are found in non-human societies in ways that supposedly parallel those found in human ones. One study (Alexander and Hines 2002) that has gained much attention was one where toys which we might think of as 'male' and 'female' (trucks, cooking pans, dolls, stuffed animals) were given to vervet monkeys, and, it was argued, differences between preferences of human boys and girls were also found in the preferences of the male and female monkeys. This, it was suggested, indicated that these preferences were anchored in brain mechanisms which were shared across species. This study was repeated six years later with rhesus monkeys, with some similar and some different results. In Fine's summary: 'male and female monkeys alike enjoy playing with both stuffed toys and mobile objects, but in males the cuddly dolls appealed a little less' (Fine 2012: 125). What are we to make of these studies? They are methodologically problematic in terms of the numbers involved, the possibility of apparently significant variation being a consequence of the set-up of the study and the absence of sufficient attention to other important variables. But, even leaving these on one side, it is quite unclear what conclusions can be drawn because we have no idea what the objects meant to the monkeys. The apparent preference of female vervets for cooking pans, for example, takes place in a context in which they cannot have a meaning anything like that which they have for female children. Moreover, primatology shows that the behaviour of monkeys diverges between male and female as they get older, particularly in relation to behaviour towards infants, but also that much of this behaviour is learnt. It is something they are initiated into by older monkeys. Also it is variable: 'a male macaque monkey in Takasakiyama, Japan, becomes an involved carer while his counterpart in Katuyama perfects paternal indifference' (ibid.: 127). It is this broader picture which the studies cited seem to ignore. More generally, there has been debate about the ways in which animal groups are looked at through the structuring lens of human society and the supposed discoveries then used to justify as natural the very social order from which they began. Moreover, animal studies have thrown up much more fluid variations of sexual difference and sexuality than are recognized by those who appeal to them to justify normative patterns in human societies (Roughgarden 2004). There is a great diversity in forms in nature: 'in species ranging from fruit flies to lizards and primates she [Roughgarden] finds behaviours that include multiple sexes, sexual switching between male and female, same-sex sexual play and much else besides' (Rose 2004).

Male and female brains

The second dominant strand of research into the biological basis of supposed cognitive and behavioural differences between men and women centres around the notion of 'male' and 'female' brains. Such research can overlap with that of evolutionary psychology, given the latter's emphasis on the mechanisms by which behavioural dispositions are hardwired into us. But not all of those who argue for sexually differentiated brains do so on the basis that such differences are adaptive. The hunt to discover sex differences in the brains of men and women (and between white men and those of supposed 'other races') began early in the nineteenth century, when such supposed differences were linked to psychological characteristics such as intelligence, maturity, rationality, sensuality, childlike natures, and so on. Most of these claims died a death earlier last century (Harding 1993). There has, however, been a recent revival in the claim that there is a difference between 'male' and 'female' brains. They are commonly linked to theories about the effect on brain formation of the exposure to differing amounts of testosterone in the womb (Fine 2017). Central here has been the work of Simon Baron-Cohen. In *The Essential Difference* he argues that male brains are suited to systematization and female brains to empathy and understanding others, popularized, as Cameron (2007: 104) points out, as 'men's brains are built for action and women's for talking.' Higher amounts of testosterone are supposed to produce brains less suited to communication and emotional sensitivity and more suited to maths and logic. Studies from brain-damaged people suggest that (for right-handed people) the left side of the brain is utilized for verbal activities and the right for spatial skills and non-verbal processing. The claim is that male and female brains differ because testosterone results in a 'more cramped left hemisphere', the hemisphere associated with linguistic competence, which in women is supposed to be greater (ibid.: 103). This leaves a larger right hemisphere for systematizing. This, it is claimed, has been found in rats and some birds. There are many problems with even this one strand of the theory. Firstly, even in rats the link between the hormone, changes in the brain and then behaviour are difficult to chart. Secondly, the mapping from rats to humans is not established. Thirdly, a recent 'neuro-imaging study of twenty four newborns ... found no evidence of a relatively smaller hemisphere in males' (Fine 2012: 106). Rebecca Jordan-Young (2010), who has spent the last thirteen years examining the studies on brain differences, suggests that many of the conclusions are riddled with inconsistencies – 'a hodge-podge of tiny samples, inadequate controls, conflicting data and extravagant conclusions' (Rose and Rose 2011). More recently, Gina Rippon has suggested that

> Several things went wrong in the early days of sex differences and brain imaging research. With respect to sex differences, there was a frustrating backward focus on historical beliefs in stereotypes ... Studies were designed based on the go-to list of the 'robust' differences between females and males, generated over the centuries, or the data were interpreted in terms of stereotypical female/male characteristics ... One major breakthrough in recent years has been the realization that, even in adulthood, our brains are continually being changed, not just by the education we receive, but also by the jobs we do, the hobbies we have, the sports we play. ... If, for example, being male means that you have much greater experience of constructing things or manipulating complex 3D representations (such as playing with Lego), it is very likely that this will be shown in your brain. Brains reflect the lives they have lived, not just the sex of their owners. ... With input from exciting breakthroughs in neuroscience, the neat, binary distinctiveness of these labels is being challenged – we are coming to realize that nature is inextricably entangled with nurture. What used to be thought fixed and inevitable is being shown to be plastic and flexible; the powerful biology-changing effects of our physical and our social worlds are being revealed. (Rippon 2019)

Rippon's work on brain differences echoes approaches adopted by many contemporary biologists. Ruth Bleier encourages us 'to view biology as potential, as capacity ... Biology itself ... develops in interaction with and response to ... our environment' (1984: 52). The *plasticity of the brain* means not only that it is reorganized in response to stimuli but also that the same function can be taken over by different parts of it. Anne Fausto-Sterling points out that 'organisms – human and otherwise – are active processes ... material anatomic connections in the brain respond to external influences ... environment and body co-produce behavior and ... it is inappropriate to try to make one component prior to the other' (2000: 241). The picture which such biologists are offering us is not one in which biology is irrelevant to how we behave but one in which it is itself open to modification and development. It is not a picture in which pre-given male and female patterns of response are hardwired into brains in a way that was selectively adaptive in our prehistory.

The sex/gender distinction

In the 1980s, the failures which theorists detected in attempts to explain psychological and behavioural sex differences in terms of hardwired biological differences led to the making of one of the most influential distinctions in feminist gender theory – namely, that between sex and gender. For most working with this distinction (for example, Oakley 1985) *sex* differences – the division into male and female bodies – were seen as biological differences, which it was the domain of the biological sciences to investigate and define. *Gender* was the term used for the behavioural and psychological traits associated with these different bodies. Gender, here conceived of as *masculinity* and *femininity*, something like *styles* of behaviour and psychological response normatively associated with male and female bodies, was thought of as socially constructed and, consequently, as bearing no necessary relation to biological embodiment. As we have noted above, over recent years the meaning of the term *gender* has changed. It has shifted from denoting masculinity and femininity, styles of behaviour, to denoting being male or female, categories of sexed difference, without commitment as to whether this difference is biological or social.

The sex/gender distinction became one of the most fundamental assumptions in feminist gender theory from the 1970s on.[1] It was fuelled by the recognition of the very different ways in which people with male or female bodies can display masculinity or femininity. Cross-cultural studies showed how norms varied across cultures (Herdt 1994; Mead 1949a, 1949b), as well as the diversity and difference in the norms of gendered behaviour within a culture. For example, the masculinity displayed by a vice-chancellor skilfully eroding democratic constraints on university governance is a very different phenomenon from that shown in a boxing ring. And both of these now overlap with patterns of behaviour displayed by female bodies, for we now have female executives and female boxers. Moreover, as the American anti-slavery and women's suffrage campaigner Sojourner Truth made clear more than a hundred years ago at the Women's Convention in Akron, Ohio, the norms of femininity for women vary profoundly with class and colour:

> That man over there says that women need to be helped into carriages, and lifted over ditches, and to have the best place everywhere. Nobody ever helps me into carriages, or over mud-puddles, or gives me any best place! And ain't I a woman? Look at me! Look at my arm! I have ploughed and planted, and gathered into barns, and no man could head me! And ain't I a woman? I could work as much and eat as much as a man – when I could get it – and bear the lash as well! And ain't I a woman? I have borne thirteen children, and seen most all sold off to slavery, and when I cried out with my mother's grief, none but Jesus heard me! And ain't I a woman? (Truth 1851)

From the earliest feminist campaigns in the West, there has been a recognition of the very different material conditions, and consequent gender norms, experienced by middle- and upper-class women and by the working classes. The higher class women were supposed to display gentility, not to be exposed to physical or mental exertion, to cultivate prettiness in their persons and their houses, and to display high codes of chastity and propriety. Working-class women were required above all to be strong, to carry the burden of work inside and outside the house. They were less constrained by the demands of chastity and propriety (McClintock 1995).

There are, therefore, widely variant norms of gendered behaviour across classes, cultures and geographical locatedness. This variation was seen as indicative of a distinction between sex (thought of as biological) and gender (in the sense of behavioural norms). It also supports the view that, in understanding the construction of gender (in that sense), we are understanding a social process and not a biological one. Masculinity and femininity are categories the content of which is socially variable. Both the scope of the categories (i.e. to whom they apply) and their content (i.e. what is required to be masculine or feminine) are therefore susceptible to modification and change. They are able to float free of attachment to specific bodily form, despite being *normatively* attached to bodily form in different ways in different socio-historical contexts.

Nonetheless, this highly significant point does not necessarily support the distinction between sex and gender which feminist theorists of the 1980s suggested. The problem with the view is not the part which stresses the way gendered patterns of behaviour are socially mediated but the opposition that it sets up between gender and sex. There is an assumption within these theories that the *sexed* binary is simply a given, a consequence of biology. Many writers problematize the sex/gender distinction, not because they think gendered behaviours have a biological base, in the way discussed above, but because our understanding of the biological division into male and female is itself culturally influenced (Butler 1990a; Gatens 1996).

How many sexes are there?

Much late twentieth-century work in the philosophy of science (Haraway 1991; Martin 1987; Harding 1992, 1993, 1998; Laqueur 1990) has drawn our attention to the ways in which our scientific theories, models and metaphors are influenced by the cultural framework in which we are placed. It is recognized that there is no unmediated access to the world. The concepts and frameworks of interpretations in terms of which we organize our observations mediate all our encounters. There are no raw facts, as it is often said. They all come to us cooked in some way. Consequently, what scientists see in the results of their experiments is influenced by the framework of interpretation which they bring to them. And this reflection has been borne out by research into the history of sex difference research. The biological theories which give an account of sex differences are the products of particular historical and culturally specific moments of production. Such a recognition has allowed biological accounts of sex differences to be revisited with an eye as to where cultural assumptions have influenced them. Of key importance in this regard has been the assumption that there are *simply two sexes*, male and female, a model which has come increasingly under challenge in recent work.

For thousands of years male and female bodies were considered to be fundamentally similar (Martin 1987). Women were thought to have the same genitals as men, only hidden inside the body. In the eighteenth century, however, there was increasing emphasis on bodily differences between the sexes. The concentration on genital sexual difference and secondary sex characteristics such as breasts and facial hair became expanded so that more and more parts of the body were seen as sexualized. By the late nineteenth century male and female bodies were viewed as opposites, and the female body became a central focus of medical attention. First the uterus and then the ovaries were regarded as the seat of femininity. Early in the twentieth century the essence of femaleness and maleness came to be located not in bodily parts but in chemical substances: sex hormones. Nelly Oudshoorn (1994) excavated the history of the theory whereby the essence of sex differences was seen as being fixed by hormones. As work progressed, the original assumption that each sex was governed by its own hormones gave way to the recognition that 'male' and 'female' hormones are present in both sexes. Here was a possibility for dualistic notions of male and female to be abandoned and a variety of sexed positionalities to be introduced. Given the cultural context, however, traditional classifications prevailed, yielding a theoretical framework within which the hormones work in distinct ways to produce two discrete categories. Where it is not possible to assign a body to one of these categories, then something is seen to have gone wrong and as requiring medical intervention to rectify.

Hormones are, of course, only one way of marking sexed difference. Alice Stone suggests:

> A human being is biologically male if they have XY chromosomes, testes, 'male' internal and external genitalia, relatively high proportions of androgens, and 'male' secondary sex characteristics. A human being is biologically female if they have XX chromosomes, ovaries, 'female' internal and external genitalia, relatively high proportions of oestrogen and progesterone, and 'female' secondary sex characteristics .... 'male' and 'female' here ... being used as a shorthand ... and could be replaced by a list of the relevant genital parts ... and characteristics. (2007: 34)

Linda Alcoff suggests that 'women and men are differentiated by virtue of their different relationship of possibility to biological reproduction, with biological reproduction referring to conceiving, giving birth, and breast-feeding, involving one's body' (Alcoff 2012).

What has become clear, however, is that the several distinct biological markers of maleness and femaleness – visible morphology, hormones and chromosomes – are not always found together. The biologist Anne Fausto-Sterling (2000) has drawn attention to the fact that bodies which possess the usual male (XY) or female (XX) chromosomal make-up can have a variety of external genitalia and secondary sex characteristics. Her work identifies at least five possible classificatory types suggested by different patterns of biological clustering.[2] Were we interested in classifying in relation to fitness for reproduction, this wider range of categories would seem to serve this purpose more accurately. Some clusterings facilitate reproduction and some do not. There will be bodies fit for reproduction who contribute to the process in one way and bodies who are fit for reproduction and contribute to it in another way. Then there will be bodies that are not fit for reproduction and do not fit into either of these categories. There will, moreover, be added complications. The contributions to reproduction, which Alcoff associates with the female body, can come apart. The body that can gestate might not be able to suckle. The body that produces eggs might not gestate. Moreover, with developing technology, there will be a shift in which bodies can make contributions of differing kinds to reproduction. What does seem clear is that a classification in terms of possession of properties causally relevant to reproduction does not map neatly onto our everyday binary classification into male and female. Of course, many male and female bodies can make no contribution to reproduction.

Fausto-Sterling (1993) points out that the existence of bodies we now classify as intersex, because their visible morphology involves what are classified as both male and female characteristics, has always been known: hermaphrodites often featured in stories of human origins. She draws attention to the range of bodies which are included within this category. Bodies which possess the usual male (XY) or female (XX) chromosomal make-up can have a variety of external genitalia and secondary sex characteristics: 'the varieties are so diverse ... that no classificatory scheme could do more than suggest the variety of sexual anatomy encountered in clinical practice' (1993: 22). Nor is the phenomenon as rare as we might suppose. Some have suggested that it may constitute as many as 4 per cent of all births. Many of these 'unruly' bodies are now treated by surgical intervention and by hormones at birth, or sometimes at puberty, and assigned to one of our prevailing sexual categories. Marianne Van den Wijngaard scrutinized the basis of the decisions made concerning which category the children were to be assigned to:

> genetic sex appears to be an important criterion. For women it is decisive. Doctors usually 'make' a little girl when a child has two X chromosomes.

When the child is a boy in genetic respects ..., however, the size of the penis is decisive. If the penis is of a certain minimal size [to enable a normal sexual life in the male role], the team decides to help the child become a boy. If not a vagina is created and the child is 'made' into a girl. (1997: 86–7)

In the making of the girl, the creation of a penetrable vagina is considered central, and the 'deviant clitoris' looking like a penis can be either removed or shortened, often with scant respect for its consequences for the sexual pleasure of the 'being made' girl. Such practices are now being robustly challenged by activist groups of those whose bodies have been regarded as unruly in this way. There are campaigns to prevent surgical/hormonal intervention at an early age and a request that children are allowed to develop and have a view on whether they are happy with their bodies as they are or wish for medical intervention to bring them closer to one side of the biological binary norm.[3] Such activism is suggesting ways in which we might raise children in a culture that recognizes interwoven sexed/gendered variation (Fausto-Sterling 2000: 4).

What is indicated by the treatment of children classified as having intersexed bodies is *not* that the biological classification into two sexes is that which nature dictates. It reflects instead a cultural need to reinforce and defend a clear classification into male and female and a modification of bodies which appear to cross the divide.

The case of sport

An assumed biological binary not only informs the treatment of intersexed bodies but also forces a spurious assumption of homogeneity within the categories of male and female themselves. As we have seen, the different markers of biological sex – genes (chromosomes), hormones, genitals, reproductive function, secondary sexual characteristics – do not always line up neatly together in the same way, even in cases where the label of intersex is not attributed. The difficulties here have become very public in relation to sport. Given that, currently, in many sports, the best men and the best women perform to different levels, professional sports have, in most cases, been divided into men and women's competitions.[4] This has been crucial in getting the contribution of women to sport better recognized – a funding and media battle that is, however, still ongoing. But it faces difficulties over the complexity of the biological data and their failure to yield a determinate account of maleness and femaleness.

At the time of the Cold War, sex tests were introduced for female athletes, initially consisting in asking them to undress. The test was visible body morphology. This moved to testing by hormones and then by chromosomes. But there have been anomalies. Someone who later gave birth was excluded from the women's competition. In 1985 the Spanish hurdler María José Martínez Patiño, to all appearances female, was excluded for having one X and one Y chromosome. In 2009 a storm broke out over Caster Semenya, a South African athlete who won the 800 metres women's final at the world championships and was asked to take a test to prove she is a woman. To her horror, and with gross intrusion into private medical facts, the suggestion that she might not really be female was then broadcast around the world.[5] There is no suspicion of cheating here. Semenya has been identified and brought up as a girl, and there is no suggestion that she has been taking additional hormones. The results of any tests she has taken have not been made publicly known, but she is now allowed to compete in certain women's races only if she takes testosterone inhibiting drugs. Semenya's challenge to this ruling was rejected in May 2019. There has, however, been a successful challenge by the Indian professional sprinter Dutee Chand to regulations excluding female athletes with naturally occurring high levels of testosterone (the hyperandrogenism rule). Chand was excluded for four years, told she 'was not a girl', and suffered mental upset and public humiliation before the rule was modified for some events in 2018 (Sen 2018). Both cases are ongoing as we write.

The difficulty here is the viewing of the hormone testosterone as essentially a male hormone, with the assumption that higher levels make someone more male than female. But from the nineteenth century it has been known that this is a flawed picture. Hormones are not sex exclusive. What is being found in these athletes is a naturally occurring variation in bodies that are in other respects recognized as female, just as the length of Usain Bolt's legs and those of some basketball players is a naturally occurring variation. Katrina Karkazis raises the question 'And what of testosterone and athleticism?' and concludes that the answer is far from simple. Although giving testosterone can increase muscle mass and power, it does not seem to build a better athlete. 'Labelling women "biological males" draws a dubious connection between sex, testosterone, and athleticism that relies on long-discarded ideas that men and women can have a "true sex", that testosterone is a "male sex hormone", and that testosterone is the key to superior athleticism. None of these are true, and it's long overdue that people stop saying they are' (Karkazis 2019).

The sports federations have become embroiled in controversy by treating binary sex difference as a biological matter to be fixed by experts, when there are so many diverse ways in which the distinct biological markers of sexual difference can be combined together. Vanessa Heggie points out:

> there has never been scientific (or philosophical, or sociological) consensus that there are simply two human sexes, that they are easily (and objectively) distinguished, and that there is no overlap between the two groups. Nor have [scientists] agreed that all of us are 'really' one sex or the other even if bits of our bodies or our identities don't entirely match that sex. You can examine someone's genitals, their blood, their genes, their taste in movies, the length of their hair, and make a judgement, but none of these constitute a universal or objective test for sex, let alone for gender.
>
> When groups, whether in sport or elsewhere, turn to scientific definitions to try to exclude some people from the category of 'woman', it is worth remembering this fact: scientists have never agreed on which kind of sex really matters to our identities, or to our right to call ourselves men, or women, or neither, or both. (Heggie 2015)

Trans bodies and biology

The link between biology and sexed identity has been rendered even more complex with the increased visibility of trans bodies – that is, bodies initially assigned to the categories male or female that come to resist that position by invoking the other side of the binary or claiming a position as non-binary. Although trans people sometimes articulate their subjectivity in terms of having a male brain in a female body, or vice versa, there is little biological evidence to support such a claim, particularly in the light of neurobiological research rejecting a division into male and female brains. Nor, thus far, is there any indication of there being biological markers which signal transitioning choices. But this does not make biology irrelevant. In ways which we will explore more fully in chapter 7, the body is of pivotal importance to trans identity. Its visible morphology and characteristics, such as breasts, facial hair and muscular structure, are used as markers of sexed identity, which enable interpersonal recognition within social space. Consequently, many trans people modify their bodies through surgery and the taking of hormones. Testosterone, for example, whose determining power we have been resisting thus far in this chapter, is a widespread aid to trans people who are seeking a more masculine appearance in order to enable recognition, by others and themselves, of their sexed identity. The consequence is to make even more complex the relation between biology and sexed identity. For there are men with many of the biological features of many other men, in terms for example of bodily morphology, hormone levels, facial hair and musculature, who nonetheless have retained ovaries, have wombs and give birth. This undermines Alcoff's suggestion (see above) that we can anchor sexed identity in possible roles in reproduction.

Nature/culture and the new materialism[6]

The distinction between sex and gender mirrored a supposed distinction between nature and culture. Sex was nature. Gender was culture. The arguments in the previous sections challenge that distinction from the perspective that culture influences the way in which we interpret the biological data. Nothing is simply given. But that does not mean that the natural world, what we think of as the data of biology, has no role to play in our practices of assigning and claiming sexed difference. Arguments, now identified under the term 'new materialism', also challenge a picture of 'culture' as something that can float free of, and be unconstrained by, nature. The distinction between nature and culture (sex/gender) is challenged not only by the recognition that culture mediates what we count as nature but also by a recognition that nature has *some* explanatory role in relation to culture. The material itself has agency. We must not, argues Colebrook, 'conflate the *being* of a thing with the mode in which it is known' (Colebrook 2000: 78; original emphasis). What is termed the *new materialism* stresses that, although culture 'structures how we apprehend the ontological, it doesn't constitute it' (Alaimo and Hekman 2008: 98). Instead culture itself is viewed as anchored in and interwoven with nature. Nature is something which itself is an agent in the formation of culture. In relation to accounts that are offered of sex and gender, such a focus is linked to biological accounts of the body. Surely, it might be thought, there are facts about my body which bear *some relation to* my identity as male or female or intersex or transsex? Aren't there some biological features which suggest/ ground the cultural distinctions we adopt?

The new materialism, then, identifies a project of bringing 'the materiality of the human body and the natural world into the forefront of feminist theory and practice' (Alaimo and Hekman 2008: 1). The narrative surrounding this project has sometimes been articulated like this. Feminists have been suspicious of biological accounts of the body because they associated them with a form of determinism that suggested the inevitability not only of a binary sex difference but also of the psychological features, social roles and bodily styles which are taken to accompany it. In the flight away from biology, however, there is a danger of ignoring the materiality of our bodily life and viewing our everyday sexed categories as exclusively the result of our cultural classificatory practices. But this is problematic, for, it is suggested, it makes our categorization of the world float free of constraint. Moreover, it appears to rule out engaging with the scientific/biological in any positive way. Instead we are limited to critique. Therefore we need to return to biology to explore our bodily materiality and its intersections with our classification into sexed kinds.[7] In the words of Gill Jagger (2015), summarizing this new materialist work:

> Uniting the various strands in the new materialism ... is a broad aim to give the materiality of matter a more active role. This includes redressing the 'biophobia' that would seem to characterize much contemporary feminist body theory ... It also involves rethinking the nature/culture dichotomy to recognize that it is not just that nature and/or matter are products of culture but that culture is also in some sense a product of nature. Indeed, nature is that without which culture wouldn't exist at all.

Elizabeth Grosz suggests there is a certain absurdity 'in objecting to the notion of nature, or biology itself, if this is (even in part) what we are and will always be. If we *are* our biologies, then we need a complex and subtle account of that biology ... How does biology – the structure and organisation of living systems – facilitate and make possible cultural existence and social change?' (2008: 24). Grosz makes these remarks in the context of a paper exploring the work of Darwin, encouraging us not to be afraid of Darwinian ideas, for these ideas are not necessarily determinist and can provide a grounding for understanding the open-ended process of our becoming whatever we might be. Grosz here is stressing the points made by feminist biologists which we have highlighted above, namely the openness of biological processes, their interaction with environmental factors, and the plasticity of our brains in response to them. Nonetheless, she draws some problematic conclusions which are not endorsed by the biologists we have so far considered. In embracing natural selection she appears to give it a foundational explanatory role so that 'language, culture, intelligence, reason, imagination, memory – terms commonly claimed as defining characteristics of the human and the cultural – are all equally effects of the same rigorous criteria of natural selection' (2008: 44). Moreover, within this process, a binary sexual difference is required, as, 'one of the ontological characteristics of life itself' (ibid.). And this sexual differentiation, and the sexual selection with which, for Grosz, it is interwoven, is then invoked to ground racial and other forms of bodily differences.[8]

However, Grosz's work seems to run counter to that of the feminist biologists we discussed in the previous section. It is one thing to argue that we cannot ignore the contribution which nature itself makes to the terms in which we make sense of it. It is quite another to take a particular interpretation of our biology to be authoritative in the way Grosz has done. To allow for the possibility of constraints is not necessarily to assign to a particular biological account a privileged position in articulating the nature of those constraints. The very openness of biological processes which she herself has stressed, and which is insisted on by biologists such as Anne Fausto-Sterling, seems in conflict with a model which insists that a particular way of systematizing that biology is fixed and unchangeable. Riki Lane argues that 'mobilizing a reading of biology as open-ended and creative supports a perspective that sees sex and gender diversity as a continuum, rather than a dichotomy – put simply, "nature" throws up all this diversity and society needs to accept it' (2009: 137). Lane, as a trans theorist, is confronting what is seen as an anti-biologism within some gender theory and exploring the complex interpellation of biological and cultural factors in the aetiology of trans subjectivity, but without treating Grosz's biological account as authoritative.

Entanglements

New materialists stress that there is something independent of our conceptualizations which sets constraints on what can be said about it. While respecting that claim, we also recognize that we cannot disentangle the bit which is *given* from our ways of thinking about it. What needs addressing, according to Karen Barad (2007), is 'the entanglement of matter and meaning', the inter-implication of the discursive and the material in which no priority is given to either side. Barad explores this entanglement with particular reference to the work of the physicist Niels Bohr. Viewing matter as an active 'agent' ensures that matter and meaning are mutually articulated. Importantly, however, although the empirical world of matter takes an active part, this does not involve according it either some sort of immediate givenness or a straightforwardly determining role.

In her approach, Barad is following in the footsteps of Donna Haraway, who in 1985 had published her 'Cyborg manifesto' (reprinted in Haraway 1991). Haraway's project is to overcome the binary between nature and culture, replacing the two terms with *nature/culture*, in which different elements cannot be disentangled. She was also concerned to draw attention to the complex factors which go into constituting what is to count as nature for us. Most crucially, she was concerned to undermine the supposed naturalness of certain binaries, insisting on a breaching of boundaries between human and animal and between animal and machine. Thus came her invocation of the *cyborg*: a creature 'simultaneously animal and machine' populating a world 'ambiguously natural and crafted' (1991: 149). In pointing to the cyborg as the figure which captures our 'bodily reality', Haraway is resisting any appeal to a pure nature which is supposed to constitute our bodily being. There is no clear boundary between what is natural and what is constructed. In Haraway's picture, however, the body, along with the rest of the natural world, has what she calls 'a trickster quality that resists categories and projects of all kinds' (1997: 128). Nature is viewed as an agent, actively contributing to the indivisible *nature/culture* with which we are faced. 'We must find another relationship to nature besides reification, possession, appropriation and nostalgia' (Haraway 2008: 158). This other relation is to view nature as 'a partner in the potent conversation' (ibid.) in which we attempt to constitute it. What is so notable about Haraway's work is the careful respect shown to the concreteness of bodily existence and to the biological narratives, alongside narratives of historical and cultural kinds.

The *nature/cultures* with which Haraway concerns herself resist disentanglement into biological grounding and derived formations. Rather, they work in an interdependent way. Reflecting in a lecture on the 'enzymes of the electro transport system ... biological catalysts in energy-producing cells', she concludes: 'Machine, organism and human embodiment all were articulated – brought into particular co-constitutive relations – in complex ways which [were] ... historically specific' (2008: 162–3). The agency of the human, manifest in the articulation, narrative and visualizing of the process, required the agency (as Haraway calls it, in a use of the term 'agency' without a suggestion of intention) of the organism, and that of the machine, in 'past and present ... socio-technical histories' (ibid.: 163). This is to recognize that our account of what we take to be nature emerges from a complex interaction of scientific investigations, cultural metaphors and the networks of technology which condition theory. Haraway's attention to the availability of technology as influencing our theorizing is of particular interest when we are thinking about sexed differences. For it is in part the development of surgical technologies, enabling bodily changes, that facilitated, for example, the sexed categories of trans man or trans woman. Donna Haraway's writings are centrally important in establishing not only the way culture mediates our understanding of nature but also the impossibility of maintaining any dualism of 'nature' and 'culture'. The two are irrevocably intertwined. It therefore seems mistaken to treat biology as if it had disentangled the natural and the cultural and presented us with nature disentangled. Biology itself is just one form of the entanglement.

In refusing biological determinism in relation to the formation of sexed identities, then, we do not have to deny that our biological bodies have a role to play. Certain very general facts of nature can give a kind of intelligibility to our having the concepts that we do, without determining them. The historical and current need[9] for both sperm and egg for human and much animal reproduction, and their origin in bodily organs typically found in bodies with distinct visible morphologies, is suggestive of how we might have fixed on a binary sexed classificatory practice. This is the framework to which Alcoff is drawing our attention. But further research and diverse cultural practices have shown these biological features to be less than determining. The complexity of the entanglements between biology, cultural practices, and technological developments, which Haraway highlights, has allowed for changes in the way in which reproduction is possible – via IVF, for example, and sperm donation – and, thereby, to diversity in the familial and kinship structures within which children are raised. Historical, cultural and socio-economic factors have always resulted in very diverse sets of relations within which children are raised, but recent developments have the consequence that these structures do not require one parent sexed male and one parent sexed female. And with these changes the conditions prompting a sexual binary may themselves be undermined.

The entanglements to which Haraway draws our attention, and which we are highlighting within the context of a project addressing sexed difference, are not simply entanglements of matter and meaning. The biological body is placed in entanglements with the bodies of other humans in varieties of kinship and other social relations. And we are in relation to animals, with the matter of the planet as a whole and all its inhabitants, which Haraway (2016) also calls kinship relations. We are entangled in economic systems, as well as within systems of meanings and the workings of the imaginary. Some of these we will address in the rest of this book.

2 Gendered Psyches: Psychoanalysis and Sexual Difference

We ascribe a castration complex to women as well. And for good reasons, though its content cannot be the same as with boys. In the latter the castration complex arises after they have learnt from the sight of the female genitals that the organ which they value so highly need not necessarily accompany the body. At this the boy ... falls under the influence of fear of castration, which will be the most powerful motive force in his subsequent development. The castration complex of girls is also started by the sight of the genitals of the other sex. They at once notice the difference and, it must be admitted, its significance too. They feel seriously wronged, often declare that they want to 'have something like it too', and fall a victim to 'envy for the penis', which will leave ineradicable traces on their development and the formation of their character and which will not be surmounted in even the most favourable cases without a severe expenditure of physical energy.

You may take it as an instance of male injustice if I assert that envy and jealousy play an even greater part in the mental life of women than of men. It is not that I think these characteristics are absent in men or that I think they have no other roots in women than envy for the penis; but I am inclined to attribute their greater amount in women to this latter influence. (Freud 1933; repr. in Minsky 1996: 225–6)

Psychoanalysis

In this chapter we will be looking at the accounts offered by some psychoanalytic thinkers of the development of gendered subjectivity. We are here turning our attention to our gendered sense of self and the factors which contribute to its establishment. We are using psychoanalysis, despite the deeply patriarchal views of its founding fathers, to harvest theoretical resources that can cast light on this process. Of particular importance for us is Freud's recognition that our ego, our sense of ourselves, is a *bodily ego*, and that the awareness of this body (and the bodies of others and our world) is *affective* – that is, emotional and sensory. What matters to our sense of our bodily selves is not simply anatomical characteristics but how we feel about them, which bits are important to our sense of self and which bits invisible. Freud also alerts us to the fact that our subjectivity is moulded by our early encounters with significant carers and our shifting identifications with them. Lacan switches our attention to the role played both by the Imaginary (our affective engagement with images) and the Symbolic (language and other public structures of meaning) in the process of becoming subjects. But he presents us with a determined patriarchal framework of public meanings within which we must necessarily place ourselves. Along with Irigaray and other feminist writers influenced by psychoanalysis, we modify Lacan's account to foreground an interwoven imaginary and symbolic which provides the texture not only of our lived experiences as gendered subjects but also of other aspects of our embodied identities. This is a texture which creative intervention can modify and disrupt to provide less oppressive possibilities for living.

What we will call into question, however, is the suggestion from many psychoanalytically inclined writers that the emergence of a subject, aware of itself as such, is simultaneously and necessarily the emergence of a subject identifying in terms of sexual difference, a difference the nature of which is pre-given in the social and symbolic order. The gender essentialism which we are thereby rejecting is more pronounced in Lacan and feminist theorists who make use of his work than it is in Freud. He was more hesitant. He recognizes that we are supposed (in some sense) to end up as proper men or women, with all aspects of the other repressed. However, he also recognizes that this is a difficult and complex process which is rarely fully achieved.

Why Freud?

The quotation at the start of this chapter includes some of the best-known and most infamous remarks of the founder of psychoanalysis, Sigmund Freud. He made them as he explored what, for him, was the problem of how a woman emerges from a child with a bisexual disposition. They are the remarks which have led many feminists to dismiss Freud, and often psychoanalysis in general, as simply another system of patriarchal thought (Beauvoir [1949] 2010; Firestone 1970; Millett 1970). The idea of 'penis envy' has become a cultural joke. Nonetheless, for many other writers, psychoanalytic thinking has been viewed as essential for making sense of exactly what Freud identifies here: how do we *become* girls and boys, women and men, from young children whose dispositions in terms of activity, aggressiveness, pleasure in our bodies, strength of attachments, etc., are not differentiated in terms of sex? Freud does not think the answer to his question is a biological one. He accepts that there are anatomical differences between the sexes, but, as we discussed in the previous chapter, he also accepts that the binary here is not as absolute as we might think. Science suggests, he claims: 'an individual is not a man or a woman but always both – merely a certain amount more the one than the other. ... the proportion in which masculine and feminine are mixed in an individual is subject to quite considerable fluctuations' (Freud 1933; repr. in Minsky 1996: 215). So if biology is not sufficient to explain our taking on of sexed difference, then we must look for other explanations of how our psychic identities and dispositions become those of men and women.

Before looking directly at Freud's account of the development of sexed identifications, it is important to understand the theoretical accounts he offered of the structure of the mind. For Freud, the self was not unified and transparent to itself. Our selfhood is commonly taken to consist primarily of consciousness – that is, the part of ourselves available for reflective scrutiny. In contrast, psychoanalysis takes a more complex view, dividing the conscious self from the *unconscious or hidden* aspects of ourselves (Freud 1986: 127–91). Freud suggests that we are never in a position to know the whole 'truth' about ourselves or the world of culture we produce. He argues that this is because of the existence of a largely unknowable, unconscious dimension in us all, which creates a split in who we are. The unconscious is the realm of emotion and desire, *affect*, and of the unconscious *phantasies* which capture such affect. It is governed not by 'the reality principle' in play in the evaluation of factual beliefs but by emotion and desire, pleasure and pain (Minsky 1996: 81). The unconscious, for Freud, is formed by the mechanism of *repression*, whereby unacceptable desires and feelings are repressed and thus become unavailable to consciousness. Nonetheless, such affects break through and disrupt the order which our conscious states are attempting to find in the world, producing *the affective feel* which a situation has for us. So the fear or anxiety we may perceive on approaching a situation (a return to an old school for example), for which we can find no rational source, may have its origin in disturbing experiences we have banished to the unconscious.

In his later writing Freud introduced another set of categories in his attempt to make sense of the divisions within the self: *the ego, the id* and *the superego* (Freud 1923). The ego is often viewed as a person's explicit sense of self. It strives towards a coherent identity via the repression of unacceptable chaotic and pleasure-seeking desires into the realm of the unconscious. The ego is governed by the 'reality principle', needing to accommodate the self to rational demands. *The id* is the instinctual pole of self. It is the domain of affect. Its contents are partly, but not wholly, unconscious. The rules and norms of (social) reality are manifest in *the superego*, our conscience. The ego is never fully stable and always threatened with disruption from unconscious desires and phantasies.

The bodily ego

The formation of the ego, for Freud, is linked to the resolution of the Oedipus complex, the recognition of sexual difference, and the repression of unacceptable desires (all of which we return to below). It has, however, a key aspect which will be of central importance to understanding subjectivity. As Freud explains, 'the ego is first and foremost a *bodily* ego' (1923: 26; emphasis added). This means that our sense of self is a sense of a body and involves an awareness of that body as having a certain shape or form. Crucially, however, the shape or form we experience our body as having is not dictated simply by anatomy. For Freud, the contours of the body emerge for us, as part of ourselves, by means of being experienced affectively. Which parts of our body are integral to our sense of our self depends on the feelings they produce and the role they play in mediating our interactions with the world. Certain aspects of the body have a salience, and other anatomical parts do not (the insides of the body, unless painful; perhaps the back of the knees). Some parts are more significant than others, linked to experiences of pleasure and pain, or to the possibility of effective agency (the hands for example), or to relations with others (the face); and these determine the overall shape or form which the body is experienced as having.[1] In a discussion of toothache Freud (1914) characterizes the way in which the aching tooth is experienced as the dominant aspect of the body: 'Concentrated is his soul ... in his molar's aching hole.' Later, in *The Ego and the Id*, he points out that 'pain seems to play a part in the process ... the way in which we gain new knowledge of our organs during painful illness is perhaps a model of the way by which, in general, we arrive at the idea of our own body' (1923: 25–6).

Freud (and also later psychoanalysts) stresses that this sense of bodily shape and form, the *bodily ego*, is also influenced by the affective interactions we have with others. Schilder points out: 'The touches of others, the interest others take in the different parts of the body, will be of enormous importance in the development of the postural schema [as he calls it] of the body' (Schilder 1950: 126). The interest which others take in different bits of our body, the bits which get named and pointed out as well as the bits which are never mentioned, all contribute to our sense of our bodily contours and the significance which is invested in them. This is clearly key to our awareness of sexual difference. For in many cases the penis is noticed, celebrated and valorized, while the presence of the clitoris and labia is rarely mentioned, discovered only from sensations.

Schilder points out the *multiplicity* of experienced bodily forms: 'It is one of the inherent characteristics of our psychic life that we continually change our images [of our bodily self]; we multiply them and make them appear different ... We let [the body] shrink playfully ... or we transform it into giants' (1950: 126). We will return to this below, but here we might note that, although we can *phantasize* about having different bodies, our sense of the body which constitutes ourselves is constrained by a materiality, even while that materiality does not dictate its own significance and is open to the kind of multiple possibilities which Schilder mentions. In one context and stage of life, our lactating breasts may be key, in another the strength and power of our legs, in another the painful effects of a crumbling spine; in many contexts, the colour of our skin. However, where the link to such materiality is lost, or severely distorted (as in some cases of anorexia), then we have lost the link to reality which for Freud is the mark of the ego. At this point we enter into a form of psychosis.

Our sense of *other* selves/other egos is also a sense of them as bodily and linked to the shape we take those bodies to have. The significant bodily parts are those taken by ourselves and others to signify a position in intersubjective relations (for example, sexed bodily morphology, such as breasts, penis, labia, facial hair; raced bodily morphology, such as skin colour, hair types, facial features; normalizing features, such as body weight, skin texture, numbers and function of limbs). When we now talk of body image, we mean those aspects of our body which we experience as significant, as marking us out as what we are. Which aspects play this role can be variable. Our affective relationship to them can also be variable, from pride and pleasure to shame and disgust.

Freud and sexual difference

Freud focuses on how our sense of self emerges from what we make of our earliest bodily experiences and, crucially, the passionate emotional entanglements which arise within our particular families. In giving an account of what we make affectively of our body as a consequence of our familial interactions, Freud makes central use of the Greek myth of Oedipus (Freud 1933; repr. in Minsky 1996). For him, the Oedipal crisis occurs when the child is between three and five years old. This is the moment when we emerge from our entanglements with the body of the mother into fully fledged human beings. The Oedipal crisis allows us to make the transition from our merged, narcissistic identity with the mother into separate beings. It makes possible our separation from the mother as our first love and our entry into culture and the world beyond her body. For Freud, this process of individuation happens at the same point as, and by means of, the discovery of sexual difference. In becoming a distinct 'I' or ego, I become sexed. I become aware not just of myself as separate but of myself as a boy or a girl. Freud dramatizes the child's first awareness of sexual difference in terms of the visual perception of the presence or absence of the penis on the bodies of those around it. The moment of discovery of bodily difference is based on the presence or absence of the penis. Here Freud is dramatizing, as a visual encounter at a moment, a process of differentiation which takes place over time. But by dramatizing it *as* a moment, he brings into focus something like a shock of recognition of similarity or difference. We become formed by processes of identification and disidentification. The child must identify with the father figure to become a boy and with the mother figure to become a girl.

The boy

The way in which this Oedipal moment plays out is different for the boy and the girl. In the context of his guilt in relation to his father, who is perceived as a rival for his mother, and his supposed perception of the mother's or girl's lack of a penis, the boy falls prey to the terrifying idea that girls are different because they have been castrated and that therefore he may fall victim to the same fate. This, he phantasizes, is likely to be at the hands of his father as a result of his ambitions to steal away his mother. It is important to understand that, for Freud, the small boy's fear of castration is experienced symbolically and not only as the threat of being physically mutilated. To avoid potential annihilation, the small boy, Freud argues, is finally persuaded by his castration anxiety to give up his mother and reconcile himself to the deferment of his phantasies about her until he is an adult and can find a woman of his own as a substitute. From this moment on, he makes an alternative identification with his father – that is, someone with a body like his own. It is at this crucial and emotionally fraught time, Freud argues, that the unconscious is formed out of the repression of the boy's love for and identification with the mother. The formation of the unconscious allows the pain of this loss to be concealed from consciousness, but it results in a divided subject. For many boys, in the context of their lingering castration phantasy, 'femininity' is viewed as a position of loss and castration and therefore one of inferiority, even though in their earliest identification with the mother they were a part of this 'femininity'.

The girl

Things go differently for the girl. In his lecture 'Femininity' (1933), Freud describes how, at the beginning of her Oedipal crisis, the girl, also in love with the mother, discovers sexual difference and perceives herself as lacking in relation to the boy's penis (and, retrospectively, understands the cultural inferiority this implies). She angrily rejects her mother for not giving her a penis, which she (the mother) also lacks but nonetheless desires in someone else. The girl, like the little boy, rejects 'femininity' as a desirable state to be in. The fact that the mother is always female, and that her assumed heterosexual desire is for a body which is different from, rather than like, her own, provokes the rejection of 'femininity' in the unconscious of the little girl as well as the boy. According to Freud, it is penis envy which achieves what he thought was impossible to accomplish without it – the girl's crossing over from her love for her mother, as the primary object of her affections, to her heterosexual desire for her father, and eventually other men. Freud rejects biological explanations for this change of heart, suggesting that there is very little reason why the girl, sexually self-sufficient with her clitoris, should ever be drawn towards her father, except, initially, as the one evidently favoured by her mother, and therefore perhaps the most promising source of access to a penis through an identification with him. Eventually, when this unrealistic project fails, Freud argues that the girl abandons this temporary identification with her father and falls in love with him and later those like him. Now she phantasizes having a baby with him instead of her mother, while at the same time making a secondary identification with her mother. This, for Freud, achieves a successful outcome for the girl's Oedipal crisis. This is an oversimplified summary, but it is difficult, even as we try to articulate it, not to be struck by the *contingency* of the moves which Freud makes here. Indeed, he was never fully happy with the account he offered. To become a girl/woman, for him, is tied into achieving heterosexual desire. He is trying to explain what strikes him as difficult – why a girl should shift from both loving and identifying with her mother to rejecting her.

Sexual difference: in summary

Contrary to what is often thought to be Freud's emphasis on biological drives, his central concepts of the unconscious and bisexuality may be seen as freeing sexuality and sexed identity from a dependence on biology. (However, he never entirely rules out what he calls 'constitutional' factors, meaning the biological body.) It is not bodily difference per se that is key but what the child makes of these differences in the context of emotional entanglements with family members, within a social order that makes the presence or absence of a penis the most salient feature of a body.

Becoming sexed, for Freud, was not a biological process but a psychic one. Moreover, despite what he viewed as the inevitability of such a process, if we are to avoid psychic breakdown, it is never entirely successful. Since most children identify with both parents, subjectively, the pure categories of sexed identity and sexuality rarely exist. Even when they appear to be pure it is only because unacceptable dimensions of sexual difference have been firmly repressed into the unconscious. The overriding impact of Freud's theory is that the pure, binary identities of 'masculinity' and 'femininity', heterosexuality and homosexuality, historically purveyed by culture, are largely unrealized because children of both sexes are both bisexed and bisexual. They fall in love with and identify with both parents and, to differing extents depending on family dynamics, subsequently express or repress those desires and identifications as adults in culture.

Reflections

What are we to make of this use of the Oedipal myth to tell a story about how we end up with our sense of ourselves as male or female? There are some key things to notice about the account. In his description of the onset of the Oedipus complex, Freud incorporates three processes in the evolution of an individualized subjectivity. One is the development of a sense of ourselves as separate from our primary carers. Second is the recognition of sexual difference, that human beings are divided into male and female and that we ourselves fall into one of these categories. Third is the development of heterosexual desire. In his account, all of these processes are interdependent and take place within a picture of a nuclear family unit in which the key players are the mother and father, with the mother envisaged as the primary carer and the father as an authority figure. To become aware of ourselves as a discrete human being is to become aware of ourselves as male or female. This gives us our sense of our bodily identity by means of certain features of that body becoming salient, most particularly the presence or absence of a penis. Successful gendering then requires the achievement of heterosexual desire, which requires coming through the complicated psychic struggles of the Oedipus complex. In the accounts Freud offers, male and female homosexuality are a consequence of our Oedipal conflicts not being fully resolved, and thereby a failure fully to achieve our identities as male or female.[2] Nonetheless, given the difficulty of the processes he describes, traces of such desire remain present in most of us.

We might wonder, however, whether the processes which Freud picks out as required for the development of a sense of self are tied together in the way he suggests. Maybe to become a self is not the same thing as becoming a sexed self. And it is now clearly evident that this latter process is not necessarily that of becoming a heterosexual self. Freud's categories of 'masculine' and 'feminine' seem to centre obsessively on the father and the penis, and the concept of penis envy has been one of the most criticized elements of his account.[3] Why should the child initially assume that everyone, including the mother, has a penis, and why should this bit of the anatomy provoke envy? (Beauvoir 2010; Firestone 1970; Millett 1970). Irigaray (1985a) has pointed out that Freud sees the girl as a defective 'little man'. It is, of course, not clear how literally we are to take the scenes he dramatically invokes, in which the child recognizes that they themselves and/or the mother lack a penis. There are many examples of children unaware of the anatomical features of their parents until quite a late age without this impacting on their sense of themselves as female or male. Juliet Mitchell (1974) suggests that penis envy is a laughable idea only if we interpret it literally and fail to understand that it refers *symbolically* to the child's unconscious envy of the power that the penis, here standing for men and masculinity, has over the mother.

The preoccupation with the penis is symptomatic of a central difficulty, for us, with Freud's theory, and indeed psychoanalytic theory in general – that is, that it gives too foundational a role to sexual difference in the formation of subjectivity. For Freud, our sense of ourselves requires a sense of ourselves as male or female. The boy does not judge himself to be like the mother because, for example, he shares with her his black skin or his love of running. Rather, his body is judged as like the father, in having a penis. This is what confers a sense of his identity. Within a psychoanalytic perspective, our sexual identity constitutes us as subjects in a way that our race/ethnicity, class and (dis)abilities do not. This has the consequence of suggesting that the sexed binary is a necessary part of human subjectivity. In this way, Freud is also a gender essentialist, though of a different kind from the biological essentialists discussed in the last chapter. For him, there is no way of avoiding our sexed identities, even though to adopt them comes at great psychic cost and the repression of multiple aspects of ourselves.

Given these problems, why are we still paying attention to Freud? Why is he taking up so much room in a book like this? What is most relevant, for us, is his analysis of sexed identity as tied up with what we make of bodily difference as a consequence of emotional factors deriving from our history of intimate and familial relationships within a specific cultural framework (in his case, upper-class Vienna at the beginning of the twentieth century). These relations are most significant in childhood but remain in play throughout our lives. They remain influential in the often unconscious phantasies which inform our reactions to situations, even when they are not available to reflective consciousness. They inform the identifications and desires which are central to our sense of self. Moreover, this self is never fixed and finished. It consists of multiple strands. It never coincides with a socially normative ideal. Freud directly addresses how we become constituted as sexed subjects, a process in which we attach considerable significance to bodily difference, but always recognizes the instability of this process. Anatomy is relevant here, but it is not determining. Juliet Mitchell points out that 'psychoanalysis is not a recommendation for a patriarchal society, but an analysis of one' (Mitchell 1974: xiii). Freud's account, she suggests, characterizes what we make of bodily difference in a society marked by male dominance, a dominance which permeates family relations and structures our affective responses to our bodies and those of others. And, largely across the world, we still live in societies marked in this way. What Freud could not imagine, and what is only just beginning to be imagined, is an alternative.

Lacan's three orders

In the accounts of the emergence of subjectivity, which we derive from Lacan, a shift has been made from the drama of intimate family relations to the domain of social structures. Lacan's theory makes use of three overarching categories or 'orders': the Real, the Imaginary and the Symbolic (Lacan 1978; Laplanche and Pontalis 1985). *The Real* in Lacan is the primordial chaos, the ineffable, that which is given its structure by the human power to name. It remains inaccessible and cannot be experienced as such. *The Imaginary*[4] is the domain of passionate attachments, manifest in our relation to images. *The Symbolic* is the domain of coherent and rational meanings. It is that by which we think about the world and become conscious subjects.

For Lacan, our route to becoming subjects goes through two stages. He agrees, with Freud, that the baby at first is immersed in the body of the mother (or mother substitute), its body a locus of pleasurable (and painful) sensations. At this point there is no sense of self. Our progression from this, at about eighteen months, involves the Imaginary, our identification with an image. This Lacan terms the mirror phase. A baby first sees itself in a mirror and becomes fixated with that image. Gradually and jubilantly the child comes to view the image in the mirror as an image of itself. For Lacan, the baby's relation to the mirror, and its identification with the image it finds there, is not cognitive but affective (Lacan 2005: 75–82). It is joyful or jubilant, sometimes aggressive and angry, in relation to the image which the mirror reflects back. This is the moment when the baby, seeing its image in the mirror (or in the mother's mirroring look, reflecting back to the baby an image of itself), experiences itself as something separate and distinct, with edges, something with an apparently separate, integrated identity. There is the formation of an Imaginary 'I' or ego via *identification* with the image in the mirror. In the same way that Freud dramatized the moment of recognition of the absence or presence of a penis, Lacan is providing a dramatic representation of a process which takes time, and which for some children involves a mirror and for others not. What is key is an identification with something outside them, in virtue of an affective charge, which leads to a sense of self as a whole, separate and integrated entity.

It is useful to point out that, as a stage of development, the emergence of a sense of a unified bodily self is not, for Lacan, tied to a sense of sexual difference. He places no restrictions on the images which can form the basis for our identifications here. In this discussion he makes comparisons with the animal world, in which young animals, for example, can become fixed on animals of other species and follow them around, clearly thinking they are part of their tribe (Lacan 2005: 75). This is because, for him, the apparently unified ego, anchored in this Imaginary, is an *illusion*. The object with which the subject struggles to identify is external, and the subject's identification with it is a *misrecognition*. *The other*, in the form of the image in the mirror, or of others, is woven into this ego or sense of self, but mistakenly. Nonetheless, the domain of the Imaginary, as the domain of *identifying* ourselves, others and the world at large *in terms of images which carry affective charge*, is pervasive throughout our lives, manifest in the emotional investments we make with people and objects or things (such as fictions, films, consumer goods, holidays and pop stars).

For Lacan, however, we must free ourselves from these illusory emotional identifications and become *subjects*, through language – the realm of the Symbolic. We become subjects via *subjection* to the Symbolic order, which is formed by language. According to Lacan, our psychic processes are formed from these structures. We become human by inserting ourselves into an already existing Symbolic order: 'in man and through man *it* speaks ... his nature is woven by effects in which is to be found the structure of language' (2005: 575). We come into existence as subjects through identifying ourselves with the meanings of language which pre-exist us and which will continue to define the world after we are gone. Language tells us what we are. We may have been happily identifying with our mirror image, or with a cat, but on learning language this illusion is corrected. Crucially, for Lacan, language tells us both that we are a boy or a girl and what being a boy or a girl amounts to.

Lacan and sexual difference

In a refiguration of Freud's concepts, Lacan, then, transforms the bodily, sexual world of the Oedipal crisis into the cultural world of language. For Lacan, sexed identities exist in the intersubjectivity of language – the realm of the Symbolic. What distinguishes Imaginary identities and our subjectivity in language is that the first is rooted in the private world, whereas the second is anchored in the public domain of culture. But it is into this public culture and language that we need to insert ourselves, and be inserted by others, if we are to be conscious, autonomous, rational subjects.

Within the Symbolic, the penis is transformed into the *phallus*. 'The phallus is a signifier' (Lacan 2005: 581), a *sign* which carries meaning. The phallus is the first sign of (sexual) difference. It is the privileged term. The phallic position is the position signifying power and dominance. It also signifies rationality and autonomy. We are positioned as male or female by our relation to it. The phallus is also viewed by Lacan as the most fundamental signifier. Following our grasp of phallic significance, we gradually come to grasp all meanings in language as based on difference, exclusion and absence. For Lacan, the foundational terms here are those of sexual difference, which provide the model for the rest. In this Symbolic realm we cannot become a subject without becoming a sexed subject. To become a subject at all requires us to place ourselves and be placed in relation to the phallus. As with Freud, the stories for the boy and the girl differ. Boys enter culture positioned as those who are the inheritors of the phallus, those to whom it rightfully belongs. This is what makes them boys/men. The link between the penis and the phallus has not been entirely removed here. It is presumably the presence of a penis which leads some children to be positioned and position themselves within language as boys. But it is significant, and a point to which we will return later, that the link is not a necessary one. There is nothing *anatomical* which dictates who is to be assigned the phallic position within culture. According to Lacan, to enter/be entered into culture as a girl or a woman is to be identified with an absence or lack, as that which does not have the phallus and therefore stands in a problematic relation to rationality and autonomy. Women, therefore, although they must use language, are positioned within it only in terms of what they lack.

Lacan thus paints a gloomy picture of a patriarchal system in which we are all imprisoned. Those who are positioned as inheritors of the phallus (and are thereby men) are offered cultural power. Women, on the other hand, seem to be irretrievably locked in absence and lack within language, caught up in what Lacan calls a female 'masquerade' which simply supports and confirms male power. However, even the position of men is precarious. Because of the disjunction between the Real and the Symbolic, and therefore the lack of identity between the penis and the phallus, even masculine identity remains phantasized (that is, idealized). Men recognize that they are supposed to inherit the phallus but that this position is itself an unrealizable ideal.

Symbolic essentialism

There are important advantages in Lacan's repositioning of Freud's theory within a symbolic and linguistic framework. This reworking of Freud has been particularly influential in what has been termed the 'turn to language' within contemporary theories of the self (Weedon 1987).[5] The role which language and the symbolic play in the formation of subjectivity offers a means of integrating the public world of culture with the world of the individual psyche. The role of language and the symbolic in forming the individual shifts the psychoanalytic story from its anchorage within a particular kind of nuclear family and also appears to remove its necessary moorings in anatomical features. It is the symbolic phallus, not the anatomical penis, which is given centre stage. The actual father becomes the symbolic father. The stress is on public meanings attached to sexed categories, and is reflected in both the structure of language and the stories, myths, laws and practices which language enables. We no longer need to assume a particular nuclear family structure or dramatic moments of recognition of bodily difference to explain how we end up sexed subjects. We are told we are girls or boys. We are also told what it is to be a boy or girl, and we make ourselves accordingly. Lacan's insights here are comparable to the account which Beauvoir offers of the internalization of public meanings of 'woman' and their sedimentation in bodily practices (see chapter 4). Lacan's position is also dazzlingly utilized and turned against itself in Butler's account of gender performativity (discussed in chapter 6).

Nonetheless, Lacan's picture of the nature of the Symbolic realm and its determining role in producing subjectivity is deeply problematic. Sexual difference is no longer biologically based but has become a precondition of the linguistic and cultural realm. 'Language came into being through sexual difference' (Butler 2004b: 208). This implies that we have to accept a binary sexual difference if we are to be able to speak at all. Butler wonders: 'What does it mean for such an order to be symbolic ... If it is symbolic is it changeable?' (ibid.: 212). For Butler, as we shall see in chapter 6, the answer is 'yes'. For Lacan, the answer seems to be in the negative. The symbolic order precedes us. It is that into which we have to be inserted if we are to become thinking selves. Lacan always argues that we have no choice about identifying ourselves with the conscious meanings of culture, because it is only through our entry into the constraining, pre-existing meanings of language that we can become coping human subjects at all. He therefore paints a picture of a totalizing and suffocating patriarchal culture, founded on sexual difference, from which we can escape only at the risk of our subjectivity dissolving into madness.

For Lacan, *all* identity, meaning and culture is constructed in relation to the phallus. This is the privileged term. But why should all meaning circle around this single term? Irigaray, in particular, to whom we return below,[6] argues that Lacan's theory displays a blind refusal to recognize that women are anything other than defective men (Irigaray 1985a; Minsky 1996: 290). Lacan says that he is not trying to *justify* the rule of the phallus in culture but, rather, attempting to unravel how its power is derived. But, at the same time, he argues that we cannot do without it. So we are stuck in a patriarchal system of meanings which we have to accept if we are to become subjects at all. The inevitability of sexed difference, which for biological essentialists is given with the biological body, is for Lacan a consequence of the structure of the Symbolic. But it is inevitable nonetheless.

Moreover, in recognizing the importance of the public structure of the symbolic, which Lacan forces us to do, there is a danger that we lose sight of Freud's account of the complex psychic processes involved in the emergence of sexed subjectivities. On Lacan's picture, not only is sexual difference determined, but we are determined in relation to it once we have positioned ourselves within language. Biddy Martin (1994), while accepting the role of the symbolic in the formation of the psyche, argues that our inner life cannot be reduced simply to inserting ourselves, or being inserted by others, into linguistic categories. There is also, she insisted, a movement in the other direction, outwards from the psyche. This lack of reducibility of the psyche to the symbolic, she suggests, is a result of the temporal nature of subjectivity. We encounter situations carrying our history with us. This makes a difference, as Butler later makes clear (see chapter 6), to the way in which categories 'land' for us. There are very different manners in which individuals position themselves in relation to the linguistic categories of sexed difference. And, importantly, some of these positionings are *resistant*. These differences will be the result of particular familial and other emotional and desiring engagements which particular bodies have undergone, together with the intersection of categories of sexed difference with other categories of difference, to which Lacan pays no attention (see below, and the discussion of intersectionality in chapter 5). Maria Lugones (2010) points out that these linguistic categories are not only patriarchal but colonial, and the ways they are taken up in decolonial settings are resistant ones.

The importance of the Imaginary

We have to remember, however, that Lacan did not only offer us a picture of linguistic essentialism. He also made use of the concept of the Imaginary – the domain of our affective relations to images, prompting identifications, desires and pleasures which refuse to obey the logic of the Symbolic realm. This domain of the Imaginary continues to inform, condition and disrupt our attempted orderly rational selves throughout our lives. For Lacan, of course, the Imaginary domain was problematic, as it offers us *misrecognitions* of ourselves. He argued therefore that the Imaginary dimension of experience needs to be made subject to the Symbolic order, the structure of language and signs, which releases desire from the grip of the Imaginary and into the intersubjective social world, where claims can be assessed in rational ways.

Other writers, however, have taken the concept of the imaginary (hereafter with a lower case 'i' to distinguish it from Lacan's use) and engaged with it differently. The first move, contra Lacan, was to refuse a clear-cut division between the imaginary and the symbolic. Instead, it is claimed, the symbolic has embedded in it an imaginary order, and the imaginary is informed by symbolic structures (Irigaray 1985a, 1985b; Castoriadis 1994; Gatens 1996; Lennon 2015). Our initiation into culture, via language, images and symbols, is not only an initiation into ways of ordering the world into categories; it is an initiation into ways of feeling and responding to it. Categories, images and symbols carry affect. They have an imaginary dimension. As Castoriadis expresses it, language is not only a *code*, 'a quasi-univocal instrument of making/doing, reckoning and elementary reasoning. The code aspect of language (the cat is on the mat) is ... inextricably entangled with its poietic aspect carrying the imaginary significations' (Castoriadis 1994: 150). Our recognition that what is on the mat is a cat carries with it a socially acquired affective reaction to cats, a reaction which may be quite different in different cultures, which have variable imaginaries attached to cats (for example, for the British they are cuddly, but for the ancient Egyptians they were gods – our example, not his!). Castoriadis further remarks: 'Psychoanalysis obliges us to see that the human being is not [just an animal possessing reason] ... but essentially an imagining being ... representation, affect, desire are mixed together ... it is impossible to separate them' (1997: 351–3). For writers endorsing such an approach, experiences of ourselves, our bodies, other people, other bodies, and the lived environment through which we move – all have an imaginary dimension. The perceived world is encountered by means of shapes/forms/images, which not only organize it cognitively but suggest appropriate ways of responding to it affectively. It is by means of such a dimension that a sense of ourselves and a sense of our world takes shape for us at all (here there are echoes of Freud's account of the bodily ego). Consequently, although we can criticize false and damaging imaginaries (of which more below), we cannot draw a sharp distinction between the imaginary and the symbolic. All knowledge, it is suggested, bears the marks of the affective imaginary, as well as the supposedly rationalizing symbolic.

The concept of the imaginary is therefore central to understanding the way in which sexed identities become produced and reproduced. Sexed identities, along with other categories of social difference, are not simply codes for arranging bodies with different characteristics. They carry imaginaries which propel us (often unreflectively) into *ways of feeling* about those bodies. Thus, Irigaray (1985a) claims, Lacan was not pointing out linguistic rules which position men as powerful and women as lack but, rather, highlighting a dominant imaginary of them as such. The imaginaries attached to materially different kinds of bodies can be variable. They can, in cases of oppression, be debilitating. Internalized by the self, they can produce devastating effects. Fanon describes how, on his arrival in France, he discovers the imaginary attached to his blackness: '"Dirty nigger!" ... I was deafened by cannibalism, intellectual deficiency, fetishism, racial defects, slaveships, and above all, above all else, "Sho good Banana"' (Fanon 2001: 185–6). Anne McClintock (1995: 42–3) describes a prevalent imaginary that attached to the working class in the nineteenth century, portrayed as 'childlike, irrational, regressive ... the Irish, Jews, feminists, gays and lesbians, prostitutes, criminals, alcoholics, and the insane – who were collectively figured as racial deviants, atavistic throwbacks to a primitive moment in human prehistory', associated with 'biological images of disease and contagion', and consequently viewed as social outcasts refusing integration into society. There are echoes here of contemporary imaginaries of 'benefit scroungers' placed in opposition to 'hardworking families' and imaginaries of migrating communities as criminal, potential terrorists.

Castoriadis noted that the imagination has a logic of its own and has a resilience which can result in its persistence even when challenged by claims of truth or falsity. We cannot, therefore, modify damaging representations of, for example, women, simply by claiming they are false (women too can reason or carry heavy weights), for the way women are imagined, and the response of men (and women) to female bodies, will not necessarily be changed. Moira Gatens gives a good illustration of this point in her discussion of the attitudes of judges and jurors in rape trials. Judges and jurors are subject to training which instructs them that neither a woman's sexual history nor her trustworthiness can be gauged from her appearance (Gatens 1996: 136–41). Nonetheless, their responses to witnesses as trustworthy or provocative can remain unchanged, governed by an imaginary response in line with dominant social associations. This point is expressed by Gatens in the following way: 'masculinity and femininity as forms of sex-appropriate behaviours are manifestations of an historically based, culturally shared phantasy' (ibid.: 130). To change these responses is difficult. They often lie below the level of reflective engagements. To shift imaginaries requires creating alternatives which must be capable of making sense to participants, in what Castoriadis would characterize as both codifying and affective ways.

Luce Irigaray and the feminist imaginary

Irigaray's early work (1985a, 1985b) follows Lacan in seeing sexual difference as foundational to language and culture (of which more below). She focuses on the differences between male and female subject positions interconnectedly in both symbolic and imaginary forms, and she recognizes, through her acceptance of the psychoanalytic framework, that cultural, symbolic and imaginary associations are constitutive of the formation of subjectivity. Subjects are initiated into the significance of bodily difference in the process of coming to be subjects at all. Irigaray departs from Lacan, however, in challenging the *inevitability* of such symbolic and imaginary structures and their resistance to change. Though locating much of her writing in conversation with psychoanalysis, she employs a concept of the imaginary which differs from both Freud and Lacan. The imaginary, for her, is not always an unconscious structure, nor can it be disentangled from the symbolic. Irigaray's notion has similarities with that of Castoriadis in its interweaving of the cognitive and affective and the conscious and the unconscious. She suggests that the imaginary framing of our modes of being in the world is sometimes not evident but is latent in the public symbolic, in myth, in works of art and literature. Also in her writings she aims to make this latent imaginary explicit en route to a reimagining, particularly of the feminine. She makes a distinction between male and female imaginaries. The dominant imaginaries, for her, are masculine; they are anchored in typically male experiences of the world. Because of the pervasiveness of this male imaginary, women often experience themselves and the world in terms of it. Irigaray criticizes dominant cultural imaginaries for being *phallogocentric*, for presenting women as the 'other' to the rational man of Western thought, as the lack which forms the necessary and negative opposite to the plenitude of masculinity, matched with imaginary associations in which female bodies are experienced as chaotic, formless and threatening. For her, 'the feminine finds itself defined as lack, deficiency ... She functions as a hole, in the elaboration of imaginary and symbolic processes' (Whitford 1991: 66–7). Irigaray reads Freud closely to uncover *his* unconscious fantasies and fears of the other sex. What the canonical texts of both Freud and Lacan reveal, she claims, when read against the grain, is how notions of pathological femininity, penis envy or castration anxiety emerge in Western thought as an expression of deeply entrenched patriarchal fears of sexual difference, fears in fact of femininity.[7]

As we noted above, changing imaginary salience is not subject simply to will or argument. As the imaginary remains the domain of affect, its modification requires the devising of alternative images which can be affectively engaging. Margaret Whitford comments: 'There is no simple manageable way to leap to the outside of phallogocentrism, nor any possible way to situate oneself there, that would result from the simple fact of being a woman. ... She [Irigaray] deliberately attempts to speak as a woman, from a nonexistent place, which has to be created or invented as she goes along' (Whitford 1991: 124–5). It is in this context that she employs one of her most famous metaphors. If we look at women's bodies through the flat mirror of the male gaze and consequent masculine theorizing, the distinctiveness of their sex can be viewed only as a hole, as an absence. If, however, we look at female bodies with the speculum (the curved mirror which can be used by women for self-examination) we detect the specificity of their sexuality and the plenitude of their sexual organs (Irigaray 1985a, 1985b). Damaging imaginaries can be countered only with alternative imaginaries (here the imaginary of the hole replaced with that of plenitude). We do not reach this alternative by simply invoking the reality of women's bodies outside of imaginary formation. Nonetheless, the creative reworking of the category is anchored in our corporeal anchorage in a world.

The inevitability of sexual difference?

Irigaray argues that the 'human race is divided into *two genres* ... What is important ... is defining the values of belonging to a sex-specific genre' (Whitford 1992: 32). What sexual difference theorists – Irigaray (1985a, 1985b), Rosi Braidotti (1994, 1998) and Elizabeth Grosz (1994) – share with the psychoanalytic framework, to which they are both indebted and critique, is a belief in the inescapable nature of sexual difference, its foundational role in language and culture. For these theorists: 'we must maintain the framework of sexual difference because it brings to the fore the continuing cultural and political reality of patriarchal domination ... [a] framework [that] persists at a symbolic level' (Butler 2004b: 210). They thus accept the Lacanian claims about the foundational role sexual difference plays in relation to culture and language, while insisting that the content of the sexed categories is open to change. 'What is at stake in the debate ... is the positive project of turning difference into a strength, of affirming its positivity' (Braidotti 1994: 187). Elizabeth Grosz insists on 'the irreducible specificity of women's bodies, the bodies of all women, independent of class, race and history' (Grosz 1994: 207), a difference that is 'originary and constitutive' (ibid.: 209).

We need to be clear about the kind of essentialism that is in play here. The early work of Irigaray has been criticized on the basis that it requires an essentialist conception of 'woman'. Such accusations have been fuelled by the suggestion that Irigaray was invoking biological essentialism in the accounts she gives of the female body. For some readers she appears to be evoking a female body, as it is, without the overlay of patriarchal ordering, a pre-discursive pre-Oedipal body. This then forms the basis of our reimagined 'woman'. But the accusation of biological essentialism at this point does seem to be a misreading. Irigaray here is making an intervention explicitly at the level of the imaginary and symbolic. She does not suggest we could have unmediated access to a female body. Rather, her project is a utopian one (Whitford 1991). She is attempting to facilitate women experiencing their bodies in a positive way. She is clear, however, that the body she is describing is one experienced through the imaginary. In the words of Rosi Braidotti: 'The process is forward looking, not nostalgic. It does not aim at recovering a lost origin' (Braidotti and Butler 1994: 43). At this point, 'sexual difference feminism [w]as a project of reimagining and revaluing the concepts of femaleness and multiplicity which govern our culture' (Stone 2006: 122). The essentialism concerned the inevitability of sexual difference itself, and this came from a shared assumption with Lacan – namely, that it was foundational to language and culture.

In Irigaray's later work (1993, 1994), however, there is a shift from a purely Lacanian concern with the Symbolic and Imaginary to a consideration of 'nature' and a suggestion that nature provides us with an originary binary difference: male and female bodies display different 'rhythms', which manifest themselves in our perceptions and experiences (Stone 2006: 1–44). Here Irigaray's position, in becoming further removed from the Lacanian one that informed her earlier work, shares elements with that of the new materialism we discussed in chapter 1 and moves problematically close to essentialism. For Lacan, as we noted above, the Real becomes unavailable to us once we enter into the world of images and language. For Irigaray, however, nature, which for her is the material world as a whole, and us insofar as we are part of it, is something which we experience and encounter even though these encounters are mediated through culture. In relation to sexual difference she then claims that women and men have *naturally* different characters and rhythms of existence, which explains but does not determine the manifestation of sexual difference within culture. This sexual difference is open to change and critical revision, even while we retain a basic dualism of kinds of human beings.

A key question in the context of this diversity is why the division into two sexes is supposed unavoidable. Irigaray also suggests that such a division carries with it *necessarily* different modes of perceiving and experiencing for men and women. But it is also very unclear why these should be characterized as a result of nature rather than as what we have made of nature. In this account there appears to be the problematic assumption, which we highlighted in chapter 1, that we can somehow disentangle nature and culture and identify what contributions are made from each side. Moreover, as we noted earlier in this chapter, Freud, while stressing the bodily nature of the ego, did not think that its exclusive sexed binaries could be explained by biological factors. Instead it took a rocky psychic process to achieve them.

Colonizing gestures

The threat of essentialism links to other criticisms that have been made of sexual difference theories. Such theories, it is claimed, cannot both acknowledge the deep differences between women and privilege sexual difference over other kinds of difference, such as race. This is a criticism which can be raised against the theory in both its forms, whether it anchors essential sexual difference in the imaginary and symbolic realms or within the nature which is supposed to underlie them.

In this context, attempts to specify and redesignate 'woman' and 'femininity' within the imaginary and symbolic have been accused of ahistoricity and false universalism. In the hands of Irigaray and those of other sexual difference theorists, the assumption is often made that all women are subject to the same oppressive imaginary and symbolic structures. But such a 'globalizing reach' is problematic. Judith Butler claims that 'the failure to acknowledge the specific cultural operations of gender oppression [is] itself a kind of epistemological imperialism ... colonizing under the sign of the same those differences that might otherwise call that totalizing concept into question' (1990a: 18). The charge of universalism here is part and parcel of the charge of universalism directed against psychoanalytic thought in general. The analysis of the symbolic and imaginary structures which inform psychoanalytic theory is not necessarily an account of the imaginaries of 'woman' globally, or even across different positions within a society. Their dominance may make them appropriate targets of critique, but we should also recognize the existence historically, cross-culturally and within contemporary culture of other discourses in which, for example, women are not conceived of primarily in terms of lack. We should, that is, not assume that our experience is entirely mediated by a symbolic and imaginary of the kind described by Lacan and, following him, Irigaray. We can 'embrace Irigaray's brilliant critical readings of specific androcentric texts while demurring from her global hypothesis about their collective input' (Fraser and Bartky 1992: 10).

Gayatri Spivak agrees that the critiques of the symbolic and imaginary orders, central to the writings of sexual difference theorists, make sense in the context of very particular strands of philosophical thought. She sees the dangers of Western feminist thought reinventing itself as the universal woman: 'I see no way to avoid insisting that there has to be a simultaneous other focus: not merely who am I? but who is the other woman? How am I naming her? How does she name me? Is this part of the problematic I discuss?' (Spivak 1987: 155). Spivak is insisting that the critical techniques which feminists have applied to male definitions of woman should be applied with equal ruthlessness to feminist redefinitions – to make evident which women are being privileged by such accounts, and who is being excluded as not quite womanly enough: the 'other' or outside against which those with power position themselves. There can be no single account. The different contents will reflect women's different positions, the fact that, as Nancy Fraser puts it, 'We position ourselves as "women," to be sure, but also as workers, as parents, as lesbians, as producers and consumers of culture, as people of color, and as inhabitants of a threatening biosphere' (Fraser and Bartky 1992: 30). Once these other dimensions of identity are allowed in, they seem to call into question whether sexed identity necessarily remains the primary site of both identification and resistance. (We return to this point with the discussion of intersectionality in chapter 5.)

Psychoanalysis: race and disability

In assessing the importance of psychoanalytic categories to theorizing the development of subjectivity, it is therefore important to see if they can be put to use with regard to other aspects of identity, in addition to that of sexed difference. There is a small but important body of work applying the concepts and categories of classical psychoanalysis to discussions of race *and* to discussions of differently abled bodies (Fanon 1968; Bergner 2005; Inahara 2009). In this work it is recognized that sexual difference constitutes the subject, but so too do other kinds of difference. Gwen Bergner argues that 'an account of racism that ignores subjectivity is only half the story ... race ... is instituted in the subject on the level of the unconscious' (Bergner 2005: xxiii).

One important strand of work utilizes the Lacanian framework but suggests that the phallic position within culture is not attached simply to masculinity. The distinction between the phallus, as a symbolic position of power, and the penis, which we noted earlier, means that the phallic position can be appropriated for other features. Arguably it is attached to *whiteness* and *able bodiedness* (and, we might suggest, high class position). White people and the able bodied enter into the symbolic as the proper inheritors of privilege and power, with those categorized as non-white or non-able bodied excluded. As Bergner points out, 'the symbolic order organizes a regime of racial difference that founds subjectivity ... Like the phallus whiteness signifies desire; the absence of whiteness signifies subjective lack' (2005: xxvi). In the imaginaries interwoven with the symbolic, these differently raced bodies and differently abled bodies carry different affective saliences, which often work below the threshold of conscious awareness and are therefore particularly difficult to dislodge. The lack which in psychoanalytic theory is attributed to women is therefore attributed more widely. We have quoted above Fanon's discovery of the imaginary attaching to black skin in a European colonial state. Rosemarie Garland-Thomson discusses the 'cultural fiosema that haunt' the social imaginary attaching to the disabled body (1997: 288) in which the disabled body is reflected back as 'grotesque spectacle' (ibid.: 285). The way in which sexual difference theorists have tried to rework imaginaries of 'woman' has also been the focus of attention for critical race theorists and theorists of (dis)abilities. bell hooks attempts to link the diversity of contemporary black experience in America back to historical roots in that Southern black rural world. For hooks, this is not an act of 'passive nostalgia ... but a recognition that there were "habits of being ... which we can re-enact", to provide ways of re-imagining black bodies in livable ways' (1990: 35). Nancy Mairs reimagines the disabled body with her claim 'as a cripple, I swagger' (Mairs 1986: 90). Cheryl Marie Wade 'insists on a harmony between her disability and her womanly sexuality in a poem characterizing herself as "The Woman with Juice"' (Garland-Thomson 1997: 285). All of this work recognizes that we are initiated into an integrated symbolic and imaginary which produces and reproduces social power relations. But these writers do not regard the meanings we inherit as fixed and stable. Instead, our categories and the imaginaries they carry are open to resignification and creative renewal, posing alternative and multiple imaginaries which can make both cognitive and affective sense to the different groups of people who share a social space (Lennon 2015).

It is not only the Lacanian framework which can be invoked in addressing multiple aspects of our identity. The Freudian heritage in psychoanalytic theory highlights how the emotional salience of our bodily contours derives from the history of encounters in which that body has participated. Bergner points out that socialization from familial, kinship and other immediate encounters with others is not exclusively to do with sexed subjects. Moreover, she highlights parallels between Freud's primal scenes, dramatizing the recognition of sexual difference, and scenes from narratives describing moments of recognition of racial difference. In his account of the trauma of watching his aunt being whipped by her master, Frederick Douglass ([1885] 1982) pinpoints this moment as that when his subjectivity was instantiated as that of a slave. In both Freud's and Douglass's accounts, early memories are reinterpreted to dramatize initiation into hierarchies of difference. There are other examples of such scenes. Audre Lorde gives the following account of an encounter on a subway:

> The AA subway train to Harlem. I clutch my mother's sleeve, her arms full of shopping bags, Christmas heavy. The wet smell of winter clothes, the trains lurching. My mother spots an almost seat, pushes my little snowsuited body down. On one side of me a man reading a paper. On the other, a woman in a fur hat staring at me. Her mouth twitches as she stares and then her gaze drops down, pulling mine with it. Her leather-gloved hand plucks at the line where my new blue snowpants and her sleek fur coat meet. She jerks her coat close to her. I look. I do not see whatever terrible thing she is seeing on the seat between us – probably a roach. But she has communicated her horror to me. It must be something very bad from the way she's looking, so I pull my snowsuit closer to me away from it, too. When I look up the woman is still staring at me, her nose holes and eyes huge. And suddenly I realize there is nothing crawling up the seat between us; it is me she doesn't want her coat to touch. (Lorde 1984: 147–8; see also Ahmed 2000: 38)

What this suggests is the possibility of using resources from Freud's work without duplicating some of its most problematic aspects. 'The Oedipus complex thus signals not the specific story of a boy's erotic demand for his mother and sexual rivalry with his father, but a child's general internalization and projection of desire, authority, aggressivity, and identification ... the Oedipus complex varies across cultures according to kinship patterns, but nonetheless [is an important resource for articulating] the mechanism of subject formation' (Bergner 2005: 25).

Conclusions

The possibility of using the work of both Freud and Lacan for other aspects of subjectivity, in addition to sexed difference, highlights the key resources that the psychoanalytic framework can offer, despite the problems which we have highlighted here. Freud's theory is valuable both because of its stress on unconscious elements of the self and for making clear that identities are linked to what we make of our bodies in the light of emotionally charged identifications within the family (or wider structures of kinship or significant others). Sexed and sexual identities derive from living in relationships with people. Lacan's focus on the dynamics of subject formation, by means of the symbolic and the imaginary, shows the importance to subject formation of initiation into public structures of meaning (texts rather than people).

In discussing these theories, we have highlighted the dangers of falling into gender essentialism. Psychoanalytic theorists of sexed difference regard such difference as a fundamental and unavoidable aspect of the self. For Freud, such a claim emerges from the psychic processes of becoming subject. For Lacan, the essentialism derives from the structures of language. Irigaray shifts from this Lacanian position to anchoring an essential difference in nature. Once other dimensions of subjectivity are recognized, however, it is less clear that binary sex difference should always retain foundational priority. These other aspects of identity are recognized as contingent and historically explicable, but not inevitable. Could this also be the case for sexual difference? Judith Butler suggests psychoanalytic writers may have done 'nothing more than abstracted the social meaning of sexual difference and exalted it as a symbolic and, hence, pre-social structure' (2004b: 212). We will return to her discussion in chapter 6.

The other kind of gender essentialism evident in psychoanalytic writings concerns not the necessity of binary sexed categories but their content: the meanings and imaginary association which mark 'man' and 'woman'. To avoid falsely universalizing claims, which can easily reinforce other dimensions of social power, we must note the variableness of such content and the possibilities of remaking it in multiple ways. We argue throughout this book that the codifying and imaginary content of our sexed categories is always local and provisional and interwoven with multiple aspects of subjectivity.

3 Historical Materialism

> The mode of production of material life conditions the general process of social, political and intellectual life. It is not the consciousness of men [*sic*] that determines their existence, but their social existence that determines their consciousness. (Marx [1859] 2013)

In this chapter, we move from looking at gender as a feature of subjectivity to considering it as structuring the material, social and economic worlds we inhabit. In Beauvoir's terms (as discussed in chapter 4), we are looking at the objective features of our social world rather than at the subjective features of our psyche. In Marx's framework, it is the material conditions of life that shape human action and social relations – and, indeed, as the above quote indicates, consciousness itself. By material conditions, Marx means the objective features of the world in which we are placed, the state of the land, the weather, what resources the land offers us, the technologies we have. But he also means the objective structures of society which condition the distribution of resources socially – that is, the economic structures and the organization of work and the production of things. To understand the world around us and the positions we fill in society, we must look to the objective material conditions in which we are located and the social relations they produce. While Marx offers a particular *analysis* of these objective conditions which focuses primarily on the capitalist mode of production, he also offers a *method* to explore social relations, one that sees the material reality of society as structuring its organization and development. Within this framework all social relations are historically contingent and dynamic rather than necessary or static features of the world. When applied to gender, historical materialism is 'a method of analyzing relations between men and women as social rather than natural'

(Jackson 2001: 284), a method with political intentions, which is 'interested [not only] in explaining the world but also in transforming it' (Hennessy and Ingraham 1997: 4). Marx propagated a historical materialist method 'to show that things which seem natural and unassailable ... are actually social, historical constructions which are amenable to social change' (Coole and Frost 2010b: 26). This method informs a range of analyses beyond Marxist ones which are anchored primarily in capitalist modes of production and focus on class. It is this broader application of historical materialist method, in relation to gender, to which we pay attention in this chapter.

Gendered societies

If we look to the world around us, we can see that gender is a key feature of social organization (Bradley 2012; Clisby and Holdsworth 2014; Connell and Pearse 2015; Robinson and Richardson 2015). Taking the UK as an example,[1] in the workforce we can see that men and women still tend to be concentrated in different areas of work; men are more likely to fill high-level decision-making jobs and, across the workforce, to earn on average more; women are more likely than men to take on the bulk of childcare and to adapt their work (for example, by moving to part-time work or lower skilled jobs) when they have children.[2] Girls on average achieve higher grades in their GCSEs and enter university in higher numbers than men (Department for Education and Skills 2007), but male graduates still earn on average 20 per cent more than female graduates. Gendered pay differentials persist across the workforce, with women earning on average just 80 pence for every pound earned by men; 98 per cent of childcare workers are female, and four out of five jobs in science, technology, engineering and maths (STEM) are held by men.[3] In the UK over 80 per cent of FTSE 100 directors are male. In 2016, there were in fact more CEOs named David in FTSE 100 companies than there were women.[4]

We can see therefore that, by looking at the workplace through a gender lens, we observe not only gendered *patterns* in the way work is organized but also *inequalities in the distribution of power and resources* between men and women. Not only in the economy but also in politics and in the judiciary, men outnumber women in positions of power. In the 2017 UK elections, a record number of female MPs were returned to the House of Commons, but still women made up only 32 per cent of MPs.[5] That same year, just 22 per cent of High Court judges were female.[6]

Health trajectories are also gendered. While women in the UK are more likely to be diagnosed with a mental health problem, and more likely to self-harm, men are much more likely to commit suicide; 75 per cent of recorded suicides in 2015 were male.[7] Suicide is the biggest killer of men aged twenty to forty-nine in the UK. The risk to women of heart disease is often underestimated (Maas and Appelman 2010), yet women in the UK are three times more likely than men to die after a heart attack. On average, women live longer than men, yet they are more likely to live in poverty in their old age.

Figures on violence indicate that in the UK, as elsewhere in the world, men are more likely to be the perpetrators of violent crime, with over 90 per cent of homicides committed by men. Men are also more likely to be the victims of recorded violent crime, although women are considerably more likely to be the victims of rape, sexual assault and domestic violence.[8] Intimate partner violence is gendered: 44 per cent of female homicide victims in the UK were killed by a current or former partner (usually male) compared to just 6 per cent of male victims.[9]

These patterns of gendered divisions are echoed across the world. Globally, women, particularly older women, are more vulnerable to poverty. With just a few exceptions, the old-age at-risk-of-poverty rate of women significantly exceeds that of men in most countries.[10] Box 3.1 picks out some key findings from recent UN data. Such patterns of gendered inequality persist globally in all spheres of society. In politics, at the end of 2018 just 24 per cent of all national parliamentarians worldwide were female. Women are underrepresented in the national political bodies of all countries (with the exception in 2018 of Rwanda, Cuba and Bolivia), although some variation in this is evident across regions. Around 40 per cent of parliamentarians were women in Nordic countries compared to just 17 per cent in the Pacific region, for example.[11]

Box 3.1

Globally, over 2.7 billion women are legally restricted from having the same choice of jobs as men. Of 189 economies assessed in

2018, 104 economies still have laws preventing women from working in specific jobs, 59 economies have no laws on sexual harassment in the workplace, and in 18 economies, husbands can legally prevent their wives from working.

Labour force participation rate for women aged 25–54 is 63 per cent compared to 94 per cent for men.

Women are more likely to be unemployed than men. In 2017, global unemployment rates for men and women stood at 5.5 per cent and 6.2 per cent respectively. This is projected to remain relatively unchanged going into 2018 and through 2021.

Women are over-represented in informal and vulnerable employment. Women are more than twice as likely [as] men to be contributing family workers.

Globally, women are paid less than men. The gender wage gap is estimated to be 23 per cent. This means that women earn 77 per cent of what men earn, though these figures understate the real extent of gender pay gaps, particularly in developing countries where informal self-employment is prevalent. Women also face the motherhood wage penalty, which increases as the number of children a woman has increases.

Women bear disproportionate responsibility for unpaid care and domestic work. Women tend to spend around 2.5 times more time on unpaid care and domestic work than men [...] It is estimated that if women's unpaid work were assigned a monetary value, it would constitute between 10 per cent and 39 per cent of GDP.

Women are still less likely to have access to social protection. Gender inequalities in employment and job quality result in gender gaps in access to social protection acquired through employment, such as pensions, unemployment benefits or maternity protection. Globally, an estimated nearly 40 per cent of women in wage employment do not have access to social protection.

Women are less likely to be entrepreneurs and face more disadvantages starting businesses: In 40% of economies, women's early stage entrepreneurial activity is half or less than half of that of men's. Women are constrained from achieving the highest leadership positions: Only 5% of Fortune 500 CEOs are

> women. Violence and harassment in the world of work affects women regardless of age, location, income or social status. The economic costs – a reflection of the human and social costs – to the global economy of discriminatory social institutions and violence against women [are] estimated to be approximately USD 12 trillion annually.
>
> *Source*: www.unwomen.org/en/what-we-do/economic-empowerment/facts-and-figures.

While girls are outperforming boys at school in many developed countries (Van Houtte 2004), if we take a global view we see a more complex pattern emerging. Overall, girls are more likely than boys never to gain access to education. If girls do enter school they are less likely than boys to progress to secondary level: 31 million girls worldwide are not in school. 'Of the 774 million illiterate adults 2/3 are women. The share of illiterate women has not changed for the past 20 years.'[12]

Globally, we can see that violence against women is endemic across the world, and common patterns of violence are identifiable. The UN estimates that '35 per cent of women worldwide have experienced either physical and/or sexual intimate partner violence or sexual violence by a non-partner at some point in their lives', with some countries putting the figure as high as 70 per cent.[13] Eighty per cent of people trafficked across the world are female,[14] and trafficked girls and women are particularly vulnerable to sexual violence (Madill and Alsop 2019). Research indicates that such violence has significant repercussions: 'Women who have been physically or sexually abused by their partner at some point in their life are twice as likely to have an abortion, twice as likely to suffer from depression, and in some regions are 1.5 times more likely to acquire HIV compared with women who have not experienced [partner violence].'[15]

The above data give a glimpse into the pervasiveness of gender in the structuring of the social world. We can see that being born male or female has significant consequences in terms of our life chances.[16] In this chapter, we examine the ways in which a historically materialist, theoretical perspective can be employed as a resource to help us understand how and why gender is socially significant. Whereas thus far we have been concerned with theoretical perspectives that locate sexed difference as an outcome of biology or as a feature of the psyche, this chapter is concerned with the objective material conditions and social structures that result in individuals following gendered social paths, locally, nationally and internationally.

From Marxism to Marxist feminism

Some key aspects of Marx's theory are relevant to understanding how materialist analyses of gender have developed. For Marxists, the key locus of inequality is class. As Marx and Engels ([1848] 2017) famously remarked at the beginning of the *Communist Manifesto*: 'the history of all hitherto societies is the history of class struggle.' Within capitalism, the antagonism between the two main social classes, the proletariat (the working class) and the bourgeoisie (the owners of the means of production), is the major driver of change. Class inequality is inherent to relations of production as the accumulation of profit is derived from the bourgeoisie's exploitation of the proletariat's labour. Only via class struggle, the overthrow of capitalism and a move towards a communist 'classless' economy, in which the worker is no longer alienated from his or her labour, can equality be achieved.

In Marxism, there is a distinction made between the base and the superstructure. The base constitutes the materials and relations needed to produce society. The superstructure is constituted by a range of institutions, ideas and cultural practices which work to maintain the base and thus preserve class relations (in capitalism, those relations are based on the exploitation of the proletariat by the bourgeoisie). The superstructure includes what Marx called *ideology*, sets of ideas in terms of which people attempt to make sense of their position in the world. Under capitalism, such ideas are distorted and mystifying and serve to justify the status quo. Ideology for Marx promotes the interest of those who are economically dominant. Ideology is reproduced in the media, in arts and culture, in education, and in everyday conversations and practices.

Marx is often accused of economic determinism – the claim that ideology and other features of the superstructure stem directly from the economic mode of production. However, a more nuanced reading sees this as a more dialectical relation, so that the realm of ideas influences the economic base and social organization, as well as the other way around (see, for example, Hennessy 1993, 2000). In either reading, the superstructure, within a capitalist system, acts to legitimize and often naturalize class and other social divisions. We learn via education, legal practices and the mainstream media, for example, that the way society is organized is the way that it should be.

A key criticism of Marx's work has been the lack of attention to gender, that there is an assumption in his account that, with the overthrow of capitalism and the elimination of class groups, men and women will be equal. Of his contemporaries, Engels did seek to address the so-called Woman Question in *The Origin of the Family, Private Property and the State*:

> According to the materialist conception, the determining factor in history is, in the last resort, the production and reproduction of immediate life. But this itself is of a twofold character. On the one hand, the production of the means of subsistence, of food, clothing and shelter and the tools requisite thereto; on the other, the production of human beings themselves, the propagation of the species. The social institutions under which men of a definite historical epoch and a definite country live are determined by both kinds of production: by the stage of development of labour, on the one hand, and of the family, on the other. (Engels [1884] 1972: 71–2)

Here, Engels defined women's oppression as 'rooted in the emergence of capitalist relations of production, the rise of private property, the economic isolation of the family and monogamous marriage, which secured the inheritance of private property' (Alsop 2000: 21). Their liberation would be secured via a class revolution which brought women fully into the sphere of production. He remarks, for example, that, 'With the transfer of the means of production into common ownership, the single family ceases to be the economic unit of society. Private housekeeping is transformed into a social industry. The care and education of the children becomes a public affair' (Engels 1972: 138).

In his adaptation of Marxist analysis, Lenin saw the communal organization of domestic labour and women's increased waged labour as integral to women's equality (Lenin 1966). But, as with Engels, the vision to move domestic work from the home into the public sphere failed adequately to challenge established divisions of labour between men and women. Domestic work in the public sphere would still be performed overwhelmingly by women.

Soviet theorists, such as Alexandra Kollontai, tried to broaden debates on equality beyond the narrow focus on production to include issues related to personal and intimate relations (Kollontai [1909] 1977, [1921] 1977; Lokaneeta 2001; Roelofs 2018). Kollontai extended Marxist writings on the 'Woman Question' not only by developing the analysis of women, the family and domestic labour[17] but also by turning attention to the realm of the emotional, psychological and ideological (Kollontai 1977; Field 1982; Ebert 1999; Lokaneeta 2001). Kollontai did not see the Soviet transformation of relations of production as being able to create gender equality unless attention was also given to transforming matters of love, sexuality, marriage and the family alongside the process of economic restructuring (Ebert 1999). Kollontai was critical of the

> idea that proletarian sexual morality is no more than 'superstructure,' and that there is no place for any change in this sphere until the economic base of society has been changed. As if the ideology of a certain class is formed only when the breakdown in the socio-economic relationships, guaranteeing the dominance of that class, has been completed! All the experience of history teaches us that a social group works out its ideology, and consequently its sexual morality, in the process of its struggle with hostile social forces. (Kollontai [1921] 1977: 249)

Pre-empting the work of second-wave feminists, Kollontai saw the personal as political (Field 1982). Family and marriage, she argued, were historical categories, the product of particular economic and social conditions which have emotional and psychological consequences (Ebert 1999). In Kollontai's vision of the future, sexual relations would be founded on comradeship and egalitarian values, with women as free as men to engage in relationships, liberated from the sexual double standards of capitalist society and economic dependence on men. For her, socialist relations of production which are no longer geared towards the accumulation of profit for capitalists had the potential to enable the emergence of a new communist sexual morality.

Kollontai's pioneering work on the 'Woman Question', and her radical vision of love, sexuality and marriage, made her unpopular with the Soviet leadership and ran contrary to dominant, patriarchal ideas of sexuality and the family. She was discredited – in effect exiled as a Soviet ambassador – and her ideas, work and contribution to Russian revolutionary history 'erased from the cultural memory' (Ebert 1999).

We can see, in the 'actual living socialism' within the Soviet bloc, that changes to class relations produced via the reorganization of the mode of production did not lead to a radical reorganization of family and interpersonal relations, as political attention remained focused overwhelmingly on women's participation in the labour market as the means to emancipation, without any parallel attention to reconfiguring the realm of personal relations. Gendered divisions of labour persisted in the domestic sphere despite women's work outside of it, and traditional patterns of family life and intimate partner relations prevailed (Einhorn 1993; Alsop 2000).

Second-wave Marxist feminism

Within the second wave of feminism, Marxist feminists sought to combat the gender blindness of classical Marxism by integrating a gendered perspective into the analysis of capitalism, in particular through more detailed attention to the interrelationship between domestic and waged labour and to the organization of reproduction. Within the emerging 'domestic labour debate', a key concern of many Marxist feminists was for Marxist analyses to better theorize the contribution of women's reproductive labour to capitalist accumulation. Here, it was argued, firstly, that capitalism relied on the unpaid work of women within the family to reproduce the workforce (both on a daily and a generational basis) and, secondly, that a Marxist analysis of capitalist production should take account of unpaid as well as waged work in the production of surplus value. To acknowledge the importance of such reproductive work, it was variously argued that either housework should be socialized – i.e. removed from the private sphere into the public sphere – or that wages for housework should be introduced (Dalla Costa and James 1972; see Tong 1989 for further examples). Angela Davis advocated the radical transformation of the organization of domestic labour. She argued for its socialization, noting that 'A substantial portion of the housewife's domestic tasks can actually be incorporated into the industrial economy. In other words, housework need no longer be considered necessarily and unalterably private in character' (1982: 223).

Marxist feminists further refined Marxist analyses to demonstrate the particular uses of female labour to capital. Beechey (1979), for instance, argues that it is women's role within the reproductive sphere that marks out married women (in particular) as a cheap and expendable pool of labour that can be drawn on in times of high employment demand but easily discarded in economic downturns. While there was much debate as to the applicability of applying the reserve army of labour thesis to all women workers, given the gendered segregation of jobs in the labour force, Bruegel (who herself drew attention to the limitations of the model) noted that 'Such a theory clearly has important implications: it places the specificity of female labour within a general Marxist model of capital accumulation and so provides some material basis for the differentiation of male and female wage labour, and it also shows up the similarities between the situation of women as wage labourers and that of other groups of workers such as immigrants' (Bruegel 1979: 12).

Patriarchy

Feminist theories which engage with Marx's work fall broadly into two camps: those that seek to deploy and adapt both his historical materialist method and analysis of capitalism, such as the analyses described above; and those that adopt his historical materialist method but propose a different analysis. For many feminists engaging with Marxism, what remained inadequately explained and theorized, even in Marxist feminist revisions of Marxism, was the basis of social differences between men and women, for such differences pre-date and post-date capitalist modes of organization and therefore seem to show independent organizational structures interacting with capitalism. To avoid recourse purely to capitalism as originating and sustaining women and men's differential social positions, many feminists adopted the concept of patriarchy to characterize additional objective material and social structures which condition gendered social differences.

Historical materialism and patriarchy

Patriarchy in broadest terms refers to the systematic organization of male power over women, and it has been theorized in various ways by feminists to demonstrate the systemic, specifically gendered, oppression of women in society. The concept of patriarchy is a tool to highlight the subordination of women, not as a by-product of capitalism but as a direct result of institutionally embedded structures and practices which privilege men and which extend beyond purely economic analyses of gendered inequality. For example, it was argued that analyses with a narrow focus on the economic bases of gendered inequalities fail to account sufficiently for the prevalence of male violence. As the data at the beginning of this chapter indicate, men continue to be the main perpetrators of violent crime. Within early second-wave feminism, Susan Brownmiller's (1975) *Against Our Will*, for example, foregrounded male sexual violence as a means of subjugating women. As Jackson (1997) points out, Brownmiller's text is theoretically inconsistent, falling at times into essentialism to explain the ubiquity of rape by men, while at other times drawing on materialist methods to show the ways in which rape is socially produced as rape. These inconsistencies aside, Brownmiller's book was ground-breaking, as it not only challenged prevailing notions of rape by conceiving it primarily as a social and political act but also broadened analyses of gender inequality to incorporate the issue of male rape, thus defining sexual violence as a key axis of patriarchal power (Jackson 1997).

Within feminist thought, the concept of patriarchy has been used in different ways. It is neither 'a single nor simple concept' but is instead attributed 'a wide variety of different meanings' (Beechey 1979). There is, however, one key distinction. In some (radical) feminist theory, patriarchy was represented as a universal feature, as a 'trans-historical and trans-cultural phenomenon' (Acker 1989: 235). It pointed to a universal structure, originating in a male nature, which is inherently violent and domineering (Daly 1978). It is thus used to provide an account of the origin of women's oppression and its continuation. Employed in this way, it is universalizing, homogenizing and essentializing of women's (and men's) experiences. This usage does not fit with a historical materialist method. Heidi Hartmann (1979), in her analysis of the relationship between Marxism and feminism, argues that, while Marxist approaches had tended to be 'sex blind', feminist accounts of patriarchy can pay insufficient attention to both history and materialism.

For other theorists, those we are concerned with here, patriarchy is used to describe objective material and social structures, the existence of which conditions the differential paths which men's and women's lives take in society. In these accounts, men's power is not defined simply as a consequence of individual acts of sexism or as rooted in biological or psychological sexed differences; rather, it is seen as structural and systemic, reproduced through a range of social institutions. The nature of these structures differs historically and cross-culturally, and different theorists stress different aspects of them. Juliet Mitchell, for example, argues for a historical materialist method, though her analysis conceptualizes patriarchy primarily in ideological terms, operating 'primarily in the psychic realm' (1974: 9), and pays less attention to other features such as labour and economic rewards. Shulamith Firestone (1970) defines patriarchy as having 'a materialist base' (Hartmann 1979: 9), extending Marxist methodology to the realm of reproduction. For Firestone, 'sex-based hierarchical relationships' should have analytical primacy, as, for her, all other forms of social hierarchy are conditioned by the sexual hierarchy (Howie 2010). In Firestone's account, 'the key to sexed inequality was women's biological capacity to carry and nurse children' (Cannon 2016: 230). However, women could be liberated from their biology through the development of reproductive technology, which would in turn 'make sexual distinctions socially irrelevant in all aspects' (ibid.: 231). While her vision of equality is rooted in the social transformation of the material conditions of society through the use of reproductive technology, Firestone's account has been critiqued for focusing too narrowly on reproduction at the expense of other material conditions and for being biological reductionist, seeing women's biology as something to be transcended.

In her essay *The Main Enemy* (1977), Christine Delphy uses a Marxist materialist method to put forward a model of capitalist society in which there exist two distinct modes of production: first, an industrial mode which is the arena of capitalist exploitation and, second, a family, domestic mode of production where women provide domestic services and where childbearing occurs. It is this second mode of production that Delphy explores as the site of patriarchal exploitation. She argues that, by virtue of marriage, women share a common class position. Since the majority of women marry, she suggests, all women are likely or destined to participate in these family relations of production. As a group that is subjected to these relations of production and to the ideologies which reinforce and perpetuate gender inequalities, women therefore constitute a class (Barrett and McIntosh 1979). Essentially her argument is that the 'appropriation and exploitation of their labour within marriage constitutes the oppression common to all women' (Delphy 1977: 16). Thus, women are oppressed and exploited by the two systems of patriarchy and capitalism. The attractiveness of Delphy's hypothesis lay in her attempt to construct a theoretical analysis from which to address the material basis for the oppression of women rather than an attempt to integrate women into an already existing theoretical model. The organization of reproduction therefore is not just a feature of capitalism. Thus the focus of Delphy's work is similar to that of Marxist feminists, but without an adherence to Marx's analysis of capitalism.

In her analysis, Delphy theorizes patriarchy in relation to the domestic mode of production (in relation to reproduction) and defines exploitation in the industrial mode of production in terms of capitalist exploitation. While she acknowledges that there are interactions between the domestic and the industrial mode, she has been critiqued for imposing a domestic/public split on to patriarchal/capitalist exploitation – i.e. women are exploited primarily by patriarchy in the domestic sphere and by capital in the industrial sphere. As a result, her account does not allow for analysis of the ways in which patriarchy operates within the industrial sphere either independently from or in conjunction with capitalist exploitation (Walby 1990).

Dual-systems theories and their critique

In an attempt to fuse Marxist and feminist analyses, Heidi Hartmann (1979) develops a materialist analysis of patriarchy which outlines the ways in which patriarchy and capitalism interact with each other, an approach often labelled as dual-systems theory. For dual-systems theorists there are two analytically identifiable structures – capitalism and patriarchy – and the position of women and men in society is fixed by their intersection and fusion. For Hartmann, the 'material base upon which patriarchy rests lies most fundamentally in men's control over women's labour power. Men maintain this control by excluding women from access to some essential productive resources ... and by restricting women's sexuality' (1979: 11). In contrast to Delphy, Hartmann sees patriarchy as pervasive in all areas of society: 'The material base of patriarchy, then, does not rest solely on childrearing in the family, but on all structures that enable men to control women's labour' (ibid.: 12). Both patriarchy and capitalism in her account are flexible structures that interact with each other in a process of 'adaptation' and 'mutual accommodation'. She suggests that 'in capitalist societies a healthy and strong partnership exists between patriarchy and capital.' Nonetheless, Hartmann argues, historical analysis demonstrates tensions between patriarchy and capitalism in early formations of capitalist relations, particularly through male workers' strong resistance to female waged labour. In Britain, trade unions, themselves patriarchal institutions dominated by the male working class, sought to exclude women from certain jobs, to keep male wages higher and to preserve men's control over women's labour within the home through the ideology of the family wage (which argued that male workers should earn enough to provide materially for wives and children, as this is what men are supposed to do). Capitalism accommodated patriarchal interests, in this instance, as women's domestic labour served a key reproductive function, and support for male workers here fostered a divided and ultimately weaker workforce.

Dual-systems theorists such as Hartmann see it as necessary to analytically separate patriarchy (men's control over women's labour) and capitalism (the exploitation of wage labour by capital), even though in actuality practices overlap. In response to dual-systems theories, Young argues against constructing patriarchy as a separate structure in addition to capitalism and argues instead for a single-systems approach in which class and gender oppression are 'analyzed as facets of a single socioeconomic system'. She advances a historically materialist analysis of women's position in capitalist society in which she argues that 'we need a theory of relations of production and the social relations which derive from and reinforce those relations which takes gender relations and the situation of women as *core* elements' (Young 1981: 50). Here, a gender division of labour rather than patriarchy is posited as the central category of analysis. Acker similarly problematizes the use of patriarchy as a separate analytical conceptual category, suggesting instead that 'shifting our focus to the question of how gender is implicated in all social processes will lead to better answers about how the subordination of women is continually reproduced as well as better answers to a range of sociological questions' (1989: 239). By separating out gender or patriarchy from other social processes, Acker argues, we miss the ways in which gender, class and race are always *mutually constituted* (Acker 2006a).

Black socialist feminists were critical in highlighting the implicit racism of accounts that focused exclusively on the intersections of class and gender oppression without paying attention to the ways in which capitalist and patriarchal (and other oppressive) structures were also interwoven with structures of racism to shape differently the experiences of black women and men under capitalism (see Anzaldúa 1987; Carby 1989; Davis 1982; hooks 1981, 1984; Lorde 1984; Collins 1990; Mirza 1997). As Crenshaw (1989: 139) argues, in her case for an *intersectional* approach, the particular experiences of black women have been 'theoretically erased'. We return to the issue of intersectionality in chapter 5.

From patriarchy to gender regimes: Walby and Connell

Walby on gender

Sylvia Walby, in response to Heidi Hartmann's theory, argued in her early work for the retention of the concept of patriarchy but theorized the multiple and varied ways in which patriarchy manifests. In *Theorizing Patriarchy* (1990), she identifies six key structures that determine patriarchal relations. According to her analysis, different articulations of patriarchal relations within the six structures – paid work, housework, sexuality, culture, violence and the state – produce different forms of patriarchy. Here she differs from Young in that she does see the analytical value of retaining patriarchy as a concept. Her account expands Hartmann's analysis by moving from a focus on the intersection of capitalism and patriarchy – and thus a preoccupation with the economic realm – to the exploration of the multiple sites of patriarchy to include aspects such as violence, sexuality and culture. In so doing, she seeks to provide a framework in which variations in gender relations over time and between different social and cultural contexts can be accommodated and explained.

In her later works, Walby drops the term 'patriarchy' in favour of 'gender regime', which she says refers to 'the same underlying concept', whereas using the term 'patriarchy' had a 'tendency ... to be misinterpreted' (2011: 104). It had become associated 'incorrectly' with its ahistoric, essentialist usages and, as a result, had become a problematic term. A gender regime, in Walby's account, is defined as a 'set of inter-connected gender relations and gendered institutions that become a system' (ibid.), and within a gender regime she identifies four institutional domains: the economy, the polity, violence and civic society. In her new framework, paid and unpaid work are included under the economy; polity encompasses the state but also institutional religions; violence remains as an institutional domain; but sexuality and culture, as well as media and knowledge institutions, are identified as part of civic society.

Nonetheless, in common with her previous work, Walby offers a structural account of gender and sees the interactions within and between the different institutional domains as constitutive of different gender regimes. In terms of gender regimes as a whole, she identifies two main types: domestic and public. In a domestic gender regime, practices operate usually to exclude women from public life – for example, women are generally excluded from paid work outside the home. In a public gender regime, women are not excluded from public life but gender inequalities are perpetuated instead through processes of segregation. For example, women can take up positions in paid work outside the home but usually do different jobs. These types of gender regime do not exist necessarily in pure forms; in some societies elements of domestic patriarchy can co-exist with public patriarchy, for instance. Walby further identifies different types of public gender regime. Most notably, she draws a distinction between neo-liberal and social democratic forms, in which the former 'is marked by lesser regulation of finance and employment than the social democratic variety, and by lesser provision of state welfare' (2011: 113). Each gender regime further differs 'according to the way in which it intersects with other regimes of inequality' (ibid.: 105) – for example, capitalist or racist systems of inequality. Here, Walby stays in line with dual- or multiple-systems theory by seeing such systems of inequality as interlocking but analytically separable.

Walby aims to develop a structural account of the ways in which gender is materially produced that retains the concept of gender but also accommodates the diversity of gendered experience and changes in gender relations (and changes to the gender structures) over time in line with historical materialist method. She argues that structural analyses, while often critiqued as too static and rigid, do not have to be so (see Pollert 1996 for critique): 'this is not a necessary feature of such accounts. I hold that political action is crucial to changes and the maintenance of gendered structures ... The significance of politics for the analysis of gender relations is not to be underestimated' (Walby 1997: 6). Here, structure and agency are defined as mutually constitutive, with agency conceptualized primarily in terms of collective rather than individual action. For example, the feminist movement is seen as a key driver of change in terms of reforming gendered structures. In this sense, Walby's account of agency has overlaps with Marxist models, which emphasize collective action and struggle as instigators of social change.

Critics of Walby's earlier work suggested that she had paid insufficient attention to the discursive production of gender (Pilcher 1999) – that is, to the domain of *meaning*. As we shall explore in later chapters, both phenomenological and post-structuralist accounts give a central role to the meanings that are attached to being male and female in the production of differential structural relations between men and women. Walby pays more attention to discourse within her later works, but her account remains anchored within the Marxist account of ideology. Discourse is seen in the main as *an effect* of material conditions rather than as a precursor. Any attention to discourse, Walby argues, should be mindful of the 'power relations under which representations are constructed and deployed' (1990: 99). On the changing discourses of femininity, for example, she stresses that 'These changes have followed rather than led the material changes in gender relations' (ibid.: 108). In line with historical materialist tradition, understanding the ways in which we think about and construct ourselves and the world is seen as rooted in the objective conditions in which we exist. For McDowell, a further weakness of Walby's account is that she does not explain women's *attachment* to men or to gender regimes or the pleasures they can gain from gender relations, even if some of those are oppressive (1999: 20). We return to this below and in chapter 4.

Connell on gender

In the light of these criticisms, it is useful to turn to the work of Connell on gender to explore an alternative structural account. Connell, like Walby, argues that a certain amount of theoretical abstraction is useful to help us understand the different positions that men and women occupy and the ways in which these differences generally favour men. The model she constructs, she argues, is 'a tool for use, not a fixed philosophical scheme. So, it is a practical question how useful it is, and how far in time and space it applies' (Connell and Pearse 2015: 75). Like Walby, Connell regards it as important to 'treat gender as a structure in its own right. We should not collapse gender into other categories ... But we must also remember that gender relations always work in context, always interact with other dynamics in social life. And from these interactions come many of the forces for change' (ibid.: 86).

In her later work, Connell proposes a structural account which foregrounds four overlapping dimensions (or structures): power, production, emotional relations (cathexis) and symbolism.[18] These all form part of a wider gender order (which is the equivalent of Walby's 'gender regime'). The term 'gender regime' in Connell's account is used instead to refer to the patterns of gender relations within any given institution (similar to structures or institutional domains in Walby's framework). In terms of the four overlapping dimensions, power is interpreted broadly to encompass the multiple ways and locations in which gendered power is exerted – in relation, for example, to sexual violence, the power of the state and attendant bureaucracies – and is defined as operating at both macro- and micro-, local and global levels, and in both discursive and material forms. Production relates also to consumption and accumulation and the ways in which men and women are differently located within these processes. The sexual division of labour is key here, not only in the home and paid work but also in related areas such as education, where occupational trajectories are instituted and reproduced.

Connell places the dimension of symbolism as one of the four key structural features alongside power and production. This suggests that, unlike Walby, she sees the dimension of meaning not simply as a product of other material objective features but as operating as an objective structure of its own. But, while for analytical purposes the dimensions are separated out, in practice Connell acknowledges they are always interwoven. For example: 'Though a division of labour is a different thing from a symbolic representation, no division of labour could long be sustained without symbolic categories' (2009: 85). Popular discourses tell us, for example, that women constitute a different kind of worker, that they are better at certain kinds of tasks, that they should prioritize home and children over workplace ambition – all justifications and screens for wage differentiation within the workforce.

The fourth dimension, 'emotional relations', does, however, seem to be of a different kind. Connell acknowledges the significance of emotional attachments to gender and sexual identities in shaping and reinforcing gendered structures. Attachments within the family, within romantic love and sexual relationships, in terms of emotional labour within the workplace and household are recognized as a key dimension of gender (and can explain in turn an individual's emotional attachment and resistance to gendered practices and identities). But here Connell seems to have shifted from paying attention to the historically variable objective material and social structures with which this chapter has been concerned to pay attention to dimensions of *subjectivity and the psyche* with which these objective features interact. This is an important move and suggests the need for consideration of the interaction of such historically materialist accounts with the psychoanalytic ones discussed in the previous chapter. Thereby, the imaginaries attached to gendered difference, as discussed in chapter 2, are justifying and enabling the reproduction of objective structural inequalities.

There is another distinctive aspect to Connell's approach. She is concerned with materiality in two ways: firstly, objective and institutional materiality and, secondly, *the materiality of the body*. Although Marx accepted the materiality of the body as put to work in our transformation of nature into social structures, he paid it little attention. Historically materialist versions of patriarchy also pay the material body scant attention. But, in ways that parallel the new materialism we discussed in chapter 1, Connell is concerned with how embodiment is entwined with historical and social materiality: 'Bodies have a reality that cannot be reduced; they are drawn into history without ceasing to be bodies. They do not turn into signs or positions in discourse (though discourses constantly refer to them). Their materiality continues to matter' (Connell and Pearse 2015: 48).

For Connell, gender is always dynamic and historically produced. Change within gender orders occurs as a result of external and internal tendencies. External tendencies include the development of mass communication, processes of urbanization, the proliferation of new technologies, and the mechanisms of capitalist production that in turn are both gendered and impact on gendered structures and practices. Internal tendencies for change are varied, and Connell points in particular to three key factors which are potentially disruptive of the gender order. She recognizes, firstly, that gender categories are unstable, and that the discursive meanings of gender are open to change. Secondly, she argues that structures 'develop *crisis tendencies*, that is, internal contradictions that undermine current patterns, and force change in the structure itself' (Connell and Pearse 2015: 87). For example, within production there is a contradiction between the need for women in the workforce and women's inferior place in terms of pay and prospects, which leads in certain instances to challenges to gender regimes (for instance, the enshrinement in law of equal pay and opportunities; the introduction of gender audits in firms). Finally, Connell pays particular attention to colonialism as an internal tendency for change. The post-colonial world order has a continuing and dynamic impact on both the metropole and the peripheries, which lends itself to the fracturing of both the gender order and the way in which capitalism is organized. 'The continued existence of empire, the dynamism of the global metropole, the replacement of direct colonial power with post-colonial direct power, the new structures of dominance in neoliberal globalization – all continue to seize and restructure the societies of the world periphery' (2009: 92). Connell thus draws attention to globally connected inequalities which are key to any historically materialist account.

Historical materialism and globally connected inequalities

Historically materialist accounts of both gender and class seek to link individual and collective experiences at the local level to global systems and structures. Coole and Frost describe how a material approach draws attention to the circuitous links between our everyday, immediate experiences and globally operating practices of commerce and politics; 'familiar practices', they argue, 'are effects of distant power relations that they also help to reproduce' (2010b: 36). Such materialist analyses within gender theory (for example, Hennessy 2000) all highlight the materially situated, global interconnections of women's lives. The material conditions of gender are informed at the macro-level within the process of global capital accumulation. Hennessy and Ingraham argue, in their defence of materialist feminism:

> Women's cheap labor (guaranteed through racist and patriarchal structures) is fundamental to the accumulation of surplus value – the basis for capitalist profit-making and expansion. A feminism that aims to improve the lives of all women and at the same time recognizes their differential relation to one another cannot ignore the material reality of capitalism's class system in women's lives. Class objectively links all women, binding the professional to her housekeeper, the boutique shopper to the sweatshop seamstress, the battered wife in Beverly Hills to the murdered sex worker in Bangkok. (1997: 3)

For materialist writers (see also Ebert 1996), political transformation will be achieved by making visible such connections between local experiences and broader social structures, connections, for example, between the bunches of flowers with which many women and men throughout the world nurture their relationships and the life of the Colombian woman producing them. 'Many contradictions', Hennessy suggests, 'are not seen or experienced as local instances of a global social system because the ways of knowing that are most available do not allow them to be understood this way' (2000: 6).

The collapse of the Rana Plaza factory in Dhaka, Bangladesh, in 2013 hit the world's headlines for leading to the death of 1,132 workers and injuring more than 2,500. The fatalities and injuries brought to the fore the abysmal and hazardous work conditions endured by those employed within the factory. Around 80 per cent of the workforce had been young and female, all low paid. Cracks in the building had been visible before its collapse. Workers had voiced concerns but had been ignored by management. Such were the structural deficiencies in the building, it took just 90 seconds to crumble. What further scandalized the world was that, in the wake of the disaster, it became apparent that the workforce was producing garments for well-known Western brands. The environmental and economic exploitation of the young women was part of the production of popular fashion items to be consumed in the Western world.

Despite initial shock and outrage in the West at the fatalities, the cycle continues, with young women in the developing world continuing to labour in appalling conditions for meagre pay to produce fashion items to be sold in the developed world. The demand in higher income countries for 'fast fashion' – cheap, throwaway fashion goods – is thus enabled by the exploitation of women's labour elsewhere. As the example of Rana Plaza illustrates, attention to what Hennessy calls the 'global social logic' is vital to understand the interconnectedness of systems of exploitation across the world. She argues that 'a global social logic makes ... sense of the ways capitalist imperialism binds the very different patriarchal oppression of "first" and "third" world women in exploitative relations of consumption and production' (1993: 31).

If we take the further example of the global care industry, we can see a pattern of women migrating from emerging economies to provide care in advanced economies and sending remittances home to their own families (Yeates 2004; Cuban 2013). 'All of these women are linked together as if in a chain in order to fill a "care deficit" in advanced economies. Working women (and even those who aren't in paid employment) become dependent on migrant women for care, with the latter's children bearing the brunt of this relationship' (Cuban 2013).

The insistence on looking at a 'global social logic' is foregrounded in the writing of many post-colonial and decolonial feminist writers (Spivak 1987; Mies 1998; Mohanty 1986, 2003, 2013; Lugones 2003, 2007, 2010; Seneviratne 2018). Alexander and Mohanty point out, for example, that the international division of labour is central to the production of people, including the production of people as gendered subjects, in different ways in different parts of the world (1997: 5). Therefore, we need historical materialist approaches to explain and make clear not only structures of gendered difference but structures of inequalities *within* our gendered categories. The ways in which race, gender and class, and other axes of social division are mutually constituted are explored further in our chapter on intersectionality.

Conclusions

In this chapter, we have been exploring historically materialist analyses of gendered life paths which point to objective material conditions and structural features of social organization as key causal features in maintaining differential positions between men and women. We have pointed to the ways in which international capital and the structures of patriarchy work together to govern both our classed and our gendered positionality. However, it is clear that these structures are interwoven with other structural hierarchies, such as raced positionality, (dis)ability and age. They are also structures which condition the workings of colonialism, in the analysis of which 'historical materialism [is taken] as a basic framework and a definition of material reality in both its local and micro-, as well as global, systemic dimensions' (Mohanty 2003: 501). By taking a historically materialist approach to these hierarchies of social position, the writers we have discussed are insisting that objective features concerning the distribution of resources, the organization of productive and reproductive work, the make-up of political hierarchies and the judiciary, the governance of policing, and the control of the domains of ideology are playing a key causal role. But these objective features are historically and culturally variable and susceptible to change via collective agency.

There are variations in terms of the different components of which social hierarchies are organized and in the goals for their dismantling. Class, as a consequence of capitalist organization, requires the dismantling of capitalism in order for it to disappear as a dimension of difference. For other social hierarchies, the goal is not necessarily the eradication of difference but, rather, the eradication of social hierarchy based on that difference. There are disagreements between theorists concerning how successfully this can be achieved within capitalism. There is anti-discrimination legislation in liberal and neo-liberal states. For example, in the UK, legal action can be taken against discrimination on the basis of a number of factors, including gender, ethnicity, age, religious belief and sexual orientation – but not class. Walby and her colleagues (2012) note how class is not a justiciable inequality in jurisdictions: its inclusion (in discrimination legislation) would be a challenge to the underlying logic of capitalism. Walby does see better gender scenarios as possible in different types of capitalist system. In contrasting social democratic and neo-liberal gender regimes, she argues that, in the former, there is the possibility of greater gender equity, for example through the social organization of childcare. However, given that capitalism is an economic system premised on inequality through the exploitation of labour, the extent to which gender equality can be achieved within capitalism remains contested by many materialist feminists (for example, Hennessy 2000). Walby et al. argue that gender, sexual, racial and other equalities are only possible when class inequalities are eradicated, and this is unachievable within capitalism.

The criticisms which have been made of materialist feminism have suggested that the reproduction of hierarchical social differentials requires attention not just to the objective material factors but also to the *domain of meaning* – the meanings of, for example, what it is to be male and female, which are manifest within public discourses. Discourses are anything which can carry meaning. Language, images, stories, scientific narratives and cultural products are all discourses. But discourses are also things we do. Social practices such as gender segregation in the workplace, beauty pageants, giving away the bride in marriage, and dressing boys in blue and girls in pink also carry meaning.

Attention to meaning within feminist theory led to a move away from analyses of the *material* conditions of gender to the analysis of language and culture – a shift Barrett (1992) describes as from 'things' to 'words'. The 'post-structural turn' in academic social theory has led to detailed attention to the workings of language and other aspects of discourse in relation to gender (see discussion in following chapters). The domain of meaning does, of course, feature in some materialist writings. As we saw above, for Walby, it is treated in parallel to the Marxist consideration of ideology, and seen to be both a consequence of and a mode of reinforcing the power relations which are set up by the materialist structures. But, it has been argued, things are much messier than such a picture would suggest. Many conflicting and contradictory ways of understanding the world are current at any one time, and the causal influences are not simply from the materialist structures to the domain of ideas but also work in the other direction. Connell recognized the domain of meaning as a more autonomous regime but did not pay the kind of detailed attention to its workings that we find in phenomenological and post-structuralist writings.

It has also been argued that materialist analyses, in stressing objective material conditions and structural inequalities, ignore the ways in which inequalities are reproduced at the level of *everyday practices* of interaction. They become sedimented at a corporeal level, where they are repeated as habits or 'taken-for-granted know-how'. In the writings of Beauvoir and other phenomenologists, and in the work of Pierre Bourdieu and Judith Butler, we see how we learn everyday bodily patterns of behaviour which reinforce social relations of power. Moreover, both phenomenologists and post-structuralists suggest that materialist accounts of gender construction, through focusing on practices generating social divisions, fail to attend to gender *as an aspect of subjectivity*. What has not been fully explained is how gender, as an aspect of the self, is produced, or how this subjective understanding intersects with the structural gender divisions which the materialist feminists accentuate. The theorizing of gender in both phenomenology and post-structuralism emphasizes the process whereby subjects *become gendered* as the process in which subjectivities form in relation to the meanings that people have available to them. (Any account of such gendered subjectivity has to be in conversation with the psychoanalytic thought we discussed in chapter 2.) In this way, the process of becoming gendered cannot be separated from other aspects of becoming. We will engage with each of these aspects – meaning, bodily practices and the production of gendered subjectivities – in the chapters which follow.

Materialist feminists have responded to such critiques to defend the materialist approach. For example, Stevi Jackson (2001), in support of a materialist feminist perspective, argues that, firstly, materialism does not equal capitalist economic relations; secondly, it does not preclude attention to diversity; thirdly, it does not automatically ignore issues of language, culture and subjectivity; fourthly, it does not reduce women's oppression to a single cause; and, finally, it can include both overarching structures and everyday interactions. Not everything that happens to us is because of a social structure. We also need attention to everyday, micro-level interactions and how social structure is perpetuated through human practices. Hennessy and Ingraham (1997: 5) stress that, while we need language and discourse to give meaning to material conditions, materiality exists beyond the realm of the cultural and symbolic. As Hennessy attests: 'The material requirements that allow human life to continue depend on social relations that encompass *more* than language, consciousness, identity, discourse – although they depend on them too. It is the "more" that constitutes the material "outside" of language – those human relations through which needs are met – but which is only made meaningful through language' (2000: 19).

In this work, we suggest not that materialist and other approaches are in conflict but, rather, that, in order to theorize gender, we need to incorporate a range of theoretical resources. And it is just such an integration of theoretical resources that we find in the work of Simone de Beauvoir in her seminal work *The Second Sex*, to be discussed in the following chapter.

4 Simone de Beauvoir: Becoming Woman

> One is not born, but rather becomes [a] woman. No biological, psychical or economic destiny defines the figure that the human female takes on in society: it is civilization as a whole that elaborates this intermediary product between the male and the eunuch that is called feminine. Only the mediation of another can constitute an individual as an *Other*. Inasmuch as he exists for himself, the child would not grasp himself as sexually differentiated. (Beauvoir [1949] 2010: 293)
>
> But first, what is a woman? ... If the female function is not enough to define woman, and if we also reject the explanation of 'the eternal feminine,' but if we accept, even temporarily, that there are women on the earth, we then have to ask: What is a woman? (Ibid.: 3–5)

Simone de Beauvoir's *The Second Sex*, first published in 1949, is one of the most important books of the twentieth century. As Sandford points out,

> It was the single most significant text for the feminist movements that helped transform Western societies in the second half of the twentieth century ... In [it she] ... was fearless. She covered topics that her ... contemporaries professed to find scandalous (for example, abortion and lesbianism) and incurred their sanctimonious wrath for writing with clear eyed honesty – instead of sentimentality – about those subjects that they held most dear (motherhood and marriage in particular). (Sandford 2006: 53–4)

As she reports in her autobiography, Beauvoir kicked off a storm: 'Unsatisfied, frigid, priapic, nymphomaniac, lesbian, a hundred times aborted, I was everything' (1981: 197). What is particularly impressive about this text is that she wrote it without the support of a social and political women's movement and in the absence of a context of other contemporary theoretical writings exploring sexed difference. She did, however, have some writings to provide some direction. Beauvoir had returned in 1947 from a tour of America (Beauvoir [1948] 2000), where she had confronted the situation of black Americans and engaged with writings exploring it. She explicitly took Myrdal's book about the condition of black people in the US (Myrdal et al. 1944) as a model (Beauvoir 1999: 116). And, as we shall see, her analysis has points of connection with the writings of both Richard Wright and Du Bois (Du Bois [1903] 1989; Wright [1945] 1970). But in setting herself to address the position of women, and thereby the whole question of sexed difference, at the personal and social level, she was breaking new ground.

We are looking in this chapter at Beauvoir's account of sexed difference, not just because it was historically so important but because she combined attention to the biological and historical materialist factors we have discussed in chapters 1 and 3 – what she terms the objective conditions – with attention to the construction of gendered subjectivity, which we addressed in chapter 2. She attended to the materiality of the body in the way the new materialists now require. But she also realized that to explain oppression we need to pay attention to long-term economic and social structures. Beauvoir was a Marxist (see below) but recognized that Marxism did not pay attention to the lived experience of women (or men), the way they made sense of themselves and their material and social worlds. Her regard for the construction of subjectivity links her to the psychoanalysts we discussed in chapter 2, but she addressed subjectivity without utilizing Freud's model of the mind or what she regarded as his sexist assumptions. There are, however, similarities in the consideration which both Beauvoir and Freud give to the significance which is attached to bodily difference in familial settings. For her, *phenomenological* rather than psychoanalytic resources were the tools needed to theorize how gendered subjectivities came into being.

Phenomenology

Phenomenology respects the materiality of the world, including the body, but it shifts attention to *the meaning and significance* which the world has for those embodied within it. Phenomenology pays attention to the way the world is experienced. The goal of phenomenological descriptions is to enable us to rediscover the world in which we live (Merleau-Ponty [1948] 2004: 32). Phenomenology's task is to describe the world as lived and experienced by subjects, not as detached observers seeking its laws of making but as participants for which it forms our natural milieu. There are a number of key characteristics of our world to which the phenomenologists draw our attention. Our perceptions reveal a world of sensory qualities – colours, noises and tactile sensations – but the sensory qualities we encounter are qualities of everyday objects, which are perceived immediately as 'houses, the sun, mountains' (Merleau-Ponty [1945] 1962: 156). The objects we perceive are objects that are woven into our engagement with the world, objects which hold out possibilities for us: the sun for warming our face or dazzling our eyes.

Such a world requires a subject who exists within and alongside it, a subject for whom this pattern of significance can show up. The subject, for Heidegger (who characterizes it as *Dasein*; 1962 *passim*) and Merleau-Ponty, is part of the world they experience, not an observer detached from it. Such being-in-the-world is not a matter of the subject simply having a spatial position next to objects within a three-dimensional objective space, a position from which two-way causal encounters result. A subject being in the world alongside objects is not the same as the pencil being on the desk next to the computer. Being in the world requires that the world can show up for subjects in the way described above. To be a subject is to be aware of, and to have, a world of this kind available to us. For phenomenologists, our subjective character (our selfhood) is something which comes into being interdependently with the shape and significance that we find in the world. We are initiated into the possibilities that the world offers by our familial and cultural setting. And such an initiation is also simultaneously one which is the process of our becoming subjects. The possibilities we find in the world are possibilities for our self in relation to it. Central to this is the experience of the body. The subject of experience is necessarily embodied. Along with other phenomenologists, Beauvoir recognizes that 'to be present in the world implies strictly that there exists a body which is at once a material thing in the world and a point of view towards the world' (2010: 39). What is key for her is that such bodily existence, and the point of view it provides onto the experienced world, is lived differently for men and women. Consequently, how the world 'shows up' the possibilities it reveals is experienced differently.

'Woman' as situation

Phenomenology is therefore concerned with both subjectivity and meaning in ways that were not a focus in the Marxist tradition. The concern with subjectivity centres both on how the world is experienced by the subject and how this experiencing constitutes the subjectivity of the subject. For Beauvoir, phenomenology was an essential resource for understanding sexed difference, for the world showed up differently for men and women. But this was not simply a consequence of having biologically different bodies. Crucially, for Beauvoir, our sexed identity was the result of *a process*, not simply a matter of biological nature. In answer to her own question 'What is a woman?', she answers that being a woman is a *situation* (2010 *passim*). A situation for her is not simply something which is provided by nature; it is what we, collectively, in different ways, *have made* of what nature offers. The making here relates to material and social organization *but also and* interdependently to the development of meanings and signification. A situation, in this sense, is something in which we, individually, find ourselves. But it is not something entirely outside of ourselves. Our situation is the shape we find in the world when exploring the possibilities within it. It is the context in relation to which options come into view: 'my class, my race, my place, my nationality, my body, my past, my position and my relations to others are so many different situations' (Moi 1999: 65). Situations are not therefore brute givens but contexts of engagement mediated by meaning. It is the situation of sexed difference, particularly that of woman, but also that of man, that Beauvoir explores in her work, and the multiple strands which go into its making. She regarded the position of women as one of oppression. She was a phenomenologist, a Marxist and an existentialist. From her existentialism came the view that the distinctive feature of humanity was the ability of people to engage in projects of their own devising – that is, to have the potential for freedom of action. It was the curtailment of this potential which, for her, constituted oppression. Viewing women as oppressed, Beauvoir was concerned with the question of what led to and maintained this oppression, and what was needed to enhance possibilities for women to enable them to move towards liberation. But to become clear on this question she first had to 'take stock', to describe the differences between men and women, and to explain how people *become women and men*, both personally and socially. 'How will the fact of being a woman have affected our lives? ... coming out of an era of muddled controversy, this book is one attempt among others to take stock of the current state' (Beauvoir 2010: 16).

The One and the Other

Beauvoir's most famous characterization of the situation of 'woman' is that woman is *the Other*. Here she is articulating what it means to be a woman in the culture which surrounds her. To claim that woman is 'Other' is to claim that she is defined in relation to what she is *not*. Her position is in opposition to that of man, who here is *the One*, the norm. 'Humanity is male, and man defines woman, not in herself, but in relation to himself; she is not considered an autonomous being ... She is determined and differentiated in relation to man, while he is not in relation to her: she is the inessential in front of the essential. He is the Subject; he is the Absolute. She is the Other' (2010: 5–6). (There are parallels here with Lacan; see chapter 2.) This asymmetry between 'man' and 'woman', in which the man is in the privileged position, is found in the cultural meanings that are attached to each term and inscribed in the philosophies, cultural myths and literary texts which we inherit (of which more below). But the asymmetry is found not only symbolically but also, and interdependently, in the organization of work and civic life, which takes the male as the norm. It is found in men and women's lived experiences of their body and world and the possibilities for their interaction.

Woman is not the only Other.

> The category of *Other* is as original as consciousness itself. ... alterity is the fundamental category of human thought. No group ever defines itself as One without setting up the Other opposite itself. ... Village people view anyone not belonging to the village as suspicious 'others.' For the native of a country, inhabitants of other countries are viewed as 'foreigners'; Jews are the 'others' for anti-Semites, blacks for racist Americans, indigenous people for colonists, proletarians for the propertied classes. ... a fundamental hostility to any other consciousness is found in consciousness itself; the subject posits itself only in opposition; it asserts itself as the essential and sets up the other as inessential, as the object. (2010: 6–7)

When Beauvoir was writing *The Second Sex* she saw this oppositional consciousness as a universal feature of consciousness itself.[1]

Along with Sartre, Beauvoir viewed *the recognition of others* as essential to our sense of ourselves. To affirm oneself as a real, objective existent, the perspective of another is required, as this is what gives us 'the self as externalised in the form of an object' (Sandford 2006: 65). It gives us the objective features of ourselves, but it also establishes relations of conflict. Others try to define us in their terms. And we both resist such definitions and try, in turn, to define them. But Beauvoir added crucial components to this narrative. In the existentialist account, found for example in her early novel *She Came to Stay* (1943) and in Sartre's *Being and Nothingness* ([1943] 1969), the conflict is between individuals and the process is reciprocal. It moves backwards and forwards as power between people shifts. In *The Second Sex* Beauvoir develops the account to apply to social categorizations, relations between peoples as groups: 'foreigners', 'Jews', 'women', 'black people', 'the working class' – all socially positioned as the Other. (Now we could add 'refugees', 'asylum seekers', 'people on welfare'.) A whole group is defined in ways that ensure a social marginality, from which they have no power to cast an objectifying eye back on the dominant group. Beauvoir's trip to America,[2] captured in *America Day by Day* ([1948] 2000), led to an important shift in her thinking from an analysis of relations of an individual to *particular* others, to an engagement with the *social*. Travelling with Richard Wright, she comments; 'he can never forget that he is black, and that makes him conscious every minute of the whole white world from which the word "black" takes its meaning' (2000: 84).

However, for Beauvoir, 'woman is the absolute other'. In all cases of othering, apart from 'woman', Beauvoir saw the possibility of resistance and a turning of the tables, so that Jews or black people, or the proletariat could, and sometimes have, become the One, in a position to turn others into the Other. But 'between the sexes this reciprocity has not been put forward, ... one of the terms has been asserted as the only essential one, denying any relativity in regard to its correlative, defining the latter as pure alterity' (2010: 7). We may criticize Beauvoir for assigning this fundamental position to sexed difference in ways that parallel the critiques of psychoanalytic writers and some writers on patriarchy, discussed in the previous chapters. In many communities, it will be the black or the colonized, the disabled or the 'queered' person who may constitute the Absolute Other. But, even if we accept this critique (of which more below), Beauvoir's characterization of the structures of 'Othering' remains a powerful tool for capturing relations of social inequality and exclusion.

Once she has introduced the situation of women in these terms, Beauvoir took her job in *The Second Sex* to be both to describe in detail the texture and consequences of such Othering and to explain how it is brought about. *The Second Sex* is divided into two volumes, each with several parts. The first volume deals with what Beauvoir terms the objective conditions. These are conditions within which, as women and men, we find ourselves and include biological characteristics, material and economic conditions, historical positioning, and myths and cultural meanings, all contributing to the social positioning of woman as Other to man. The second volume pays attention to the formation of subjectivity, to the way in which objective conditions are *internalized* as we become women and men. This is both an articulation of subjectivity and an identification of a key strand in the reproduction of oppression. For Beauvoir is claiming that the way in which we become women and men is itself part of the conditions which maintain oppressive relations.

We will start with her account of the objective conditions.

Volume 1: The objective conditions

The data of biology

In the first chapter of *The Second Sex*, Beauvoir reviews the data of biology (2010: 21). But she does so with a warning. Such data are not to be thought of as determining individual characteristics or social life. With that warning in place, she goes on to describe what are claimed as biological characteristics of the female qua *animal* or *organism*, which, in addition to differences in reproductive role, includes claims that 'woman is weaker than man, she has less muscular strength, ... can lift less heavy weights' (2010: 66). She rehearses the facts of sexually differentiated reproduction throughout the animal kingdom:

> the fundamental difference between male and female mammals is that ... the sperm ... is separated from its body ... By contrast the ovum ... falls into the oviduct, penetrated by a foreign gamete it implants itself into the uterus ... the female ... carries the foetus in her womb for varying degrees of maturation ... inhabited by another ... both herself and other than herself ... after delivery she feeds the newborn with milk ... she takes

care of them ... she fights to defend them ... the female abdicates [her individuality] ... for the benefit of the species. (2010: 36–7)

At the same time she declares that these facts 'do not carry their meaning in themselves ... weakness is only weakness in the light of the aims man sets for himself.' So, for example, in relation to 'the burden of the generative function for women ... only society can decide' (2010: 47). For Beauvoir, the data of biology, offered as facts, lack fixity. She shows herself aware of the way in which cultural myths and metaphors influence the telling of the biological story, even as she herself offers it to us (see our discussion in chapter 1). Moreover, she shows herself consistently aware of the possibilities which the biological data leave open to us (2010: 24). On the other hand, the meanings and significance which we attach to our materiality do not float free of that materiality. The way the body is lived by us has to accommodate the data which biology variably tries to capture, facts of reproduction, menstruation, menopause.

> These biological data are of extreme importance; they ... are an essential element in women's situation ... Because the body is the instrument of our hold on the world, the world appears different to us depending on how it is grasped ... they are one of the keys to enable us to understand woman. But we refuse the idea they are a fixed destiny for her. They do not suffice to constitute the basis for a sexual hierarchy; they do not explain why woman is the Other; they do not condemn her for ever after to this subjugated role. (2010: 44–5)

Economic and social structure

Beauvoir, then, follows Marx in arguing that human beings are never left to their biological nature. The question is what, historically and culturally, they have made of this nature: 'the species realises itself. ... in society ... the question is what humanity has made of the human female' (2010: 49). To grasp this it is 'indispensable to understand the economic and social structure' (ibid.: 62). Beauvoir accepts the key components of Marx's historical materialism that we have outlined in the preceding chapter, although she makes some crucial additions to it (Shepherd 2016). In the conclusion to *The Second Sex*, she quotes Marx: 'The direct, natural and necessary relation of person to person is the relation of man to woman. From the character of this relationship follows how much man as a species-being, as man, has come to be himself and to comprehend himself' (Marx [1844] 1978: 83–4). Following which she adds, 'This could not be better said' (2010: 782). Marx is here claiming that the state of relations between men and women is the test of how human beings have made themselves and the extent to which they are realizing their potential. This Beauvoir accepts. As she was writing, she regarded the situation of women as deeply problematic. But the situation of women was historically contingent and *could* be changed.

Although Beauvoir followed Engels ([1884] 1972) in viewing the *origin* of women's oppression as probably resulting from a physical dependency in childbearing, she differed from Marx in *not* viewing its maintenance (especially once technology rendered physical strength less significant) as explicable *solely* through the workings of capitalism. Capitalism, according to her account, utilized woman's inferior position, and it is crucial to her liberation that she achieves economic independence. Her social oppression is interwoven with her *economic oppression*. Nonetheless, the experiences of women within capitalism were crucially different from those of men. 'To demand for woman all the rights, all the possibilities of the human being in general, does not mean one must be blind to her singular situation' (2010: 69). Along with oppression in relation to production, we need to pay attention to that associated with reproduction. Lack of control over reproduction is a major factor in maintaining women's oppression. For Beauvoir, lack of power and control over fertility disempowers women and denies them the choice of when, or indeed whether, to conceive a family. The material circumstances in which a woman finds herself, such as poverty and deprivation, impact on the experience of motherhood for both the mother and the child: 'The burdens that come with maternity vary greatly depending on customs: they are overwhelming if numerous pregnancies are imposed on the woman and if she must feed and raise her children without help' (2010: 64–5). Consequently, the domestic sphere is one in which men can exercise power over women.

Beauvoir, then, in a move prescient of the writings we discussed in the previous chapter, sees patriarchy and capitalism as two separate systems, both of which serve to limit a woman's individuality and freedom of choice. The needs of capitalism alone do not explain sexed inequalities. Beauvoir suggests that capitalism and patriarchy intersect, but patriarchy is also a stand-alone system that was around before capitalist society developed and will remain after its demise. Improvements in women's position, then, require economic independence, control of reproduction and social support of childcare.

Myths

> It is always difficult to describe a myth; it does not lend itself to being grasped or defined; it haunts consciousnesses without ever being posited opposite them as a fixed object. The object fluctuates so much and is so contradictory that its unity is not at first discerned: Delilah and Judith, Aspasia and Lucretia, Pandora and Athena, woman is both Eve and the Virgin Mary. She is an idol, a servant, source of life, power of darkness; she is the elementary silence of truth, she is artifice, gossip and lies; she is the medicine woman and the witch ... woman embodies nature as Mother, Spouse and Idea; these figures are sometimes confounded and sometimes in opposition, and each has a double face. (2010: 166–7)

The first chapter of *The Second Sex* to find publication (in *Les Temps modernes*) was that on myth. In this important chapter, Beauvoir initiates the discussion of what other writers have termed *discourse*, the level of meaning and images, an important part of which were the *imaginaries*, affectively laden images, which psychoanalytic writers (see chapter 2) viewed as central to the formation of our subjectivity. Beauvoir does not use the term *imaginary*, but her *myths* correspond closely to what other writers have captured with that term (Gatens 1996; Lennon 2015). In her discussion, Beauvoir is capturing the dominant imaginaries of women which have been found historically and which are reiterated within the contemporary culture she is describing. She highlights the multiple and contradictory images of women, as lovers, mothers, whores, virgins, wives, defenders of virtue, initiators into evil, bearers of a mysterious essence ('the eternal feminine'), 'the temptation of Nature, untamed against all reason ... the carnal embodiment of all moral values and their opposites, from good to bad' (2010: 219), and much more. What she makes clear is that none of these myths have their origin in actual women. 'Woman', she claims, has been defined and imagined by man. She has not been in a position to define herself (there are parallels with Irigaray here). The resultant myths, for Beauvoir, are distortions and falsifications. They are, in Marxist terms, *ideologies*, mystifying and obfuscating representations which serve to promote the interests of those in power. They are deeply damaging and form one of the key planks whereby women's oppression is maintained. There are, of course, myths of masculinity as well as of femininity. Although many of these may also be distortions, for Beauvoir, they are much less damaging, for they have also been devised by men, and very much in their favour. These are the myths of strength and virility, reason and intelligence, culture as opposed to the nature which is woman.

Myths give a normative framework to society, providing its members with views on what it is to be a proper woman or a proper man. Beauvoir claims that, if woman does not live up to the ideal of femininity, femininity is not exposed as a myth; it is the individual woman herself who is at fault: 'if the definition given is contradicted by the behaviour of real flesh-and-blood women, it is women that are wrong: it is said ... that women are not feminine. Experiential denials cannot do anything against myth' (2010: 275). Women as well as men adopt these myths and they form the context in which they make sense of their own position and envisage the possibilities open to them. Consequently, in making sense of themselves, 'they still dream through men's dreams' (ibid.: 166).

For Beauvoir, adopting Marxist terms, current myths prevented women achieving genuine human emancipation and realizing the potential of their species-being. How were they to be dislodged? For her, what was important was to make these myths evident. This is part of the job she sees herself as undertaking here. Once evident, they can be subject to reflective scrutiny and there is a possibility that their distorting character can be recognized. In this way, like Marx, Beauvoir hopes to displace ideologies with facts. But there are complications. Even for Marx, ideology could be exposed as such only in certain material conditions. The proletariat had to come together and gain a certain amount of social power to detect the ideological nature of bourgeois thought. But when Beauvoir was writing there were no such opportunities for collectives of women. Within the context of *The Second Sex*, 'they [women] even lack their own space that makes communities of American blacks, the Jews in ghettos, or the workers in Saint-Denis or Renault factories' (2010: 8). Such spaces came later with the development of second-wave feminism. Moreover, also making the unravelling of distorted myths problematic was the fact that women's (and men's) subjectivity is constituted in relation to these myths. They become women and men by embodying them.

Le Doeuff points out: 'according to *The Second Sex* there are facts and there are myths, with the myths, which appear to be embroidered upon the facts, to be stripped away so as to reduce the facts of everyday life to what they are' (2010: 91). In Beauvoir's essay on Brigitte Bardot, in the context of applauding the challenges the latter's work made to prevailing myths of the erotic and the moral, Beauvoir writes: 'As soon as a single myth is touched all myths are in danger. A sincere gaze is a fire that may spread and reduce to ashes all the shoddy disguises that camouflage reality' (1959: 58–60). But, for those writers for whom the imaginary is an essential component of our engagement with the world and cannot be dispensed with (see the discussion in chapter 2), and who in addition point out the damaging and distorting effects of current imaginaries of the female, we must collectively create different ones. Beauvoir does not explicitly endorse the task of reimagining, but her writings nonetheless recognize the all-pervasiveness of myth. Bardot is apparently offering an artless/innocent/natural female sexuality to set against the socially endorsed myths. But this is also artifice. Beauvoir points out: 'her admirers and detractors are concerned with the imaginary creature they see on the screen' (ibid.: 8). The persona of her films and public interviews, while destabilizing dominant myths, is itself mythical.

At the end of volume 1, Beauvoir has therefore laid out the objective, biological, economic and myth-making structures within which men and women are brought into being. She then moves on to describe how these impact on subjectivity.

Volume II: Lived experience

One of Beauvoir's most famous claims, which is quoted at the beginning of this chapter, is that we are not born as men or women. There is a process of *becoming* female and male selves, and this was, for her, a process of adopting and *internalizing* the objective social positions offered, alongside their justifying myths. Such internalization structures the experience of becoming woman and produces subjectivities in a way which, for Beauvoir, aids the reproduction of oppression. This process of internalization is described in volume II: 'What I will try to describe is how woman is taught to assume her condition, how she experiences this, what universe she finds herself enclosed in and what escape mechanisms are permitted her. Only then can we understand what problems women – heirs to a weighty past, striving to forge a new future – are faced with' (2010: 289).

Objectification

'Woman is defined neither by her hormones nor by mysterious instincts but by the way she grasps, through foreign consciousness, her body and her relation to the world' (2010: 77). The body, then, is central to our becoming women, but not simply as biology. It is the body *as grasped* by us, and this grasping is done via our awareness of the gaze of other people through which we come to view ourselves. Beauvoir provides a phenomenology of the body as lived at different stages of a woman's life. After a few years in which the bodies of young boys and girls are experienced in much the same way, enjoying the world and making their marks as active agents within it, the young girl's body comes to be experienced in a different way from that of the young boy. He is encouraged to climb trees and play rough games, to maintain his sense of his body as active, that by which his projects in the world can be advanced. She, in contrast, is encouraged to treat her whole person as a doll, and learns the need to please others (2010: 306). 'Through compliments and admonishments, through images and words, she discovers the meaning of the words "pretty" and "ugly"; she soon knows that to please she has to be "pretty as a picture"; she tries to resemble an image, she disguises herself, she looks at herself in the mirror, she compares herself to princesses and fairies from tales' (ibid.: 304).

Experiencing our body as an object is to experience it *as it is under the gaze of others*. In internalizing the gaze of others in this way, we experience our body as something that is our self and also that stands outside our self. Beauvoir argues that girls are brought up to experience their bodies as objects to be disciplined into compliance with a predominantly visual norm: 'the little girl pampers her doll and dresses her as she dreams of being dressed and pampered; ... she is taught that to please, she must ... make herself object; ... She is treated like a living doll' (2010: 304–5).

Beauvoir's account of the way in which women live their bodies in such an objectified way, internalizing the gaze of the other and producing their bodies as objects for others, has been one of her most important contributions to theorizing the process by which we become women. Feminist scholarship since has focused on it as part of the mechanism by which women's lesser social power is reproduced. Luna Dolezal (2010: 357) argues: 'the experience of embodiment for most women ... is one of constant body visibility, where the body's appearance and comportment is self-consciously regarded as an object for a present or imagined third-person spectator.' John Berger also makes this point in his book *Ways of Seeing*: 'A woman must continually watch herself. She is almost continuously accompanied by her own image of herself' (1972: 46). Such objectification, and the consequent disciplining by women of their own bodies according to social norms, is today reinforced by selfies, social media, Photoshop and aesthetic surgery (Alsop and Lennon 2018; Holliday and Sanchez Taylor 2006).[3]

Living bodily difference

Biology yields bodies which change at puberty, which sometimes menstruate, which are a source of both pleasurable sensations and pain, which give birth or not. But biology does not condition the way in which these events are experienced, what role they are to play in a person's life: 'the woman's body is one of the essential elements of the situation she occupies in this world. But ... it has a lived reality only as taken on by consciousness' (2010: 49). Beauvoir describes the way in which, as the girl enters puberty, her body becomes to her a source of horror and shame.

> Her breasts show through her sweater or blouse, and this body that the little girl identified with self appears to her as flesh; it is an object that others look at and see. ... The little girl feels that her body is escaping her, that it is no longer the clear expression of her individuality; it becomes foreign to her; and at the same moment, she is grasped by others as a thing: on the street, eyes follow her ... (Ibid.: 331–2)

She grants that 'boys too, at puberty, feel their body as an embarrassing presence, but because they have been proud of their virility from childhood, it is as a step towards this' that they experience bodily changes. 'Just as the penis gets its privileged value from the social context, the social context makes menstruation a malediction' (ibid.: 340).

These negative descriptions of female experiences of embodiment continue in relation to sexual initiation and motherhood. Beauvoir's phenomenology of the maternal body has been especially controversial: 'snared by nature she is plant and animal ... an incubator ... a human being, consciousness and freedom, who has become a passive instrument of life' (2010: 552). She rejects an account of motherhood which invokes a notion of maternal instinct: 'there is no such thing as maternal "instinct"; the word does not in any case apply to the human species. The mother's attitude is defined by her total situation and by the way she accepts it. It is as we have seen, extremely variable' (ibid.: 567). Given such negativity, it is important to recognize that what Beauvoir was offering was a descriptive phenomenology of female bodies as lived in specific situations (ibid.: 356–7). In the context in which she was writing, women's bodies were considered shameful and embarrassing, and menstruation was unmentionable. (The recent debates in relation to menstruation in women's tennis show how much this is still the case; George 2015.) Sexuality was framed by a double standard of morality for women and men, with myths of 'virgin' or 'whore' informing women's experiences. Such experiences also took place when abortion was illegal, contraception difficult to get hold of, and single motherhood a social and financial catastrophe. Lesbianism was discussed by Beauvoir as an option, but in a context in which it was socially ostracized. It is this situation which her writings hoped to highlight. Control for women of their own reproduction is vital, she argues, in order for women's experiences to change: 'Pregnancy and motherhood are experienced in very different ways depending on whether they take place in revolt, resignation, satisfaction or enthusiasm' (2010: 546).

The negativity manifest in Beauvoir's writing about the body in much of *The Second Sex* is countered by other writings on both sexed and pregnant embodiment. In an interview in 1976 she said that, if writing later, 'I would [have] give[n] a very frank account of my sexuality ... a sincere account and from a feminist point of view ... because it is a political not an individual issue' (Sandford 2006: 88). Moreover, her autobiographical and fictional writings are full of descriptions of joyful sexual experiences of women. Biographies and letters published after her death make clear that she had passionate and sexual relations with both women and men throughout her life. But her ability to celebrate her sensuous embodiment was, she made clear, a product of being in a very different situation to many of the women whose life experiences she was trying to describe.

Bodily habits

The consequence of living a body as proscribed for most women, in the cultural space in which Beauvoir was placed, is an *inhibited intentionality* (Young 1990), her spontaneous movements inhibited, 'lack of physical power' leading to a 'general timidity' (Beauvoir 2010: 355). 'Physically and morally she has become inferior to boys and incapable of competing with them' (ibid.: 353). Here, Beauvoir contrasts an *alienated* experience of our bodies as *objects* with a more authentic relation to the body as that by which we engage with and respond to the world, which is encouraged in boys but not in girls: 'The great advantage for the boy [is his] free movement towards the world; ... Climbing trees, fighting with his companions, ... he grasps his body as a means to dominate nature and as a fighting tool' (ibid.: 305). Girls and boys undergo something akin to training in bodily habits which structure the possibilities for interaction with their world. Habits are bodily responses that feel natural after training. They become unconscious and difficult to change. They become second nature to us. Women out of habit, rather than nature, perform actions which perpetuate their social positioning. They adopt weakness, passivity and fragility as a mode of existence, *as if* it were their biology that limits their projects.

Here Beauvoir draws on the work of other phenomenologists, such as Merleau-Ponty on the body's relation to space, as well as anticipating and influencing the work of the later theorist Pierre Bourdieu on the *habitus* (Bourdieu 1990). We experience our bodies as engaged within an environment, their possible activities moulded by and moulding the way that environment is experienced. Consequently the forming of bodily habits not only influences the way we experience our bodies; it is also the way the world takes shape for us, offering certain opportunities and not others. To a body trained to be fragile, a hill is unclimbable, a fence unjumpable, a journey hazardous (and still today, perhaps, plumbing unfathomable, cars unfixable, laboratories unnegotiable?). For the later writer Bourdieu, the habitus is 'a system of durable, transposable dispositions'. They function as the 'generative basis of structured, objectively unified practices' (1977: 72). These dispositions are a reflection of the social and material features of a particular environment in which individuals are placed, the class structure, or the power relations between men and women. We are trained how to see the world and how to behave within it in ways that simply reinforce social differentials. Only certain bodies are trained to feel comfortable in the spaces from within which power is exercised. There is some relation of 'fit' between the habitus and social structures. The sets of behaviour which are thereby engendered also work to maintain the social institutions in place. For Bourdieu, the habitus is learnt through imitation: 'practical mastery is transmitted in practice ... children are particularly attentive to the gestures and postures ... a way of walking, a tilt of the head, facial expressions, ways of sitting and using implements ... bodily hexis is a political mythology realized, *em-bodied*, turned into a permanent disposition' (1990: 87).

Bourdieu's account here echoes that of Beauvoir; 'customs cannot be deduced from biology; individuals are never left to their nature; they obey this second nature, that is, customs ... It is ... as a body subjected to taboos and laws that the subject gains consciousness of and accomplishes himself' (Beauvoir 2010: 48). Her reflections here also anticipated and influenced the work of the later feminist Iris Marion Young. In her essay 'Throwing like a girl' (1990), Young points out that the habitual ways of experiencing our bodies, whereby physical negotiation of our environment becomes possible, themselves reflect socially mediated gender difference. Girls even throw balls in a different way from boys. There are differences between Beauvoir and Bourdieu. Bourdieu has been criticized for an overly deterministic picture of the relation between our social milieu and our bodily practices.[4] Beauvoir, while stressing bodily training, leaves open the possibility of modification and change (we return to this below).

The fragility and physical weakness which Beauvoir describes as the learnt habitus of women was clearly the habitus of a privileged group of Western, white, middle- and upper-class women, even as she was writing. (See the discussion of Sojourner Truth (1851) in chapter 1: 'Look at me! Look at my arm! I have ploughed and planted, and gathered into barns, and no man could head me! And ain't I a woman? I could work as much and eat as much as a man – when I could get it – and bear the lash as well! And ain't I a woman?') Working-class women, women in rural communities and tough material circumstances, have always required physical strength to survive and are trained into it from an early age. Now, even among the privileged elite, an active body has become desirable and women's sport is given increasing prominence. There is much more emphasis on girls and women going to the gym or engaging in sporting activities (though often as a route to what is perceived to be a more attractive body). Nonetheless, although some of the bodily practices which Beauvoir describes as informing our 'becoming women' have changed since she wrote, and we are much more clearly aware of the intersectionality of these practices (see chapter 5), the recognition of learnt habits as producing gendered subjectivities and reproducing gendered hierarchies remains one of her central insights and informed the performative account of gender which we will address in chapter 6.

Life paths

When Beauvoir was writing, marriage was the normal life path for both women and men in the West, though they entered into it from very different material circumstances. With very few work opportunities open to women, and those, in both professional and labouring domains, badly paid, and with unmarried women lacking social respect: 'A girl's free choice was always restricted ... marriage was her only means of survival and the only justification of her existence' (2010: 452). Given that marriage was entered into primarily for economic reasons, Beauvoir compared it to sex work. But this similarity was sugared over by women's adoption of the myth of romantic love (ibid.: chapter 12). This asymmetry of power within marriage, and the allocation to women of all housework and childcare, led to lives of boredom, frustration and unhappiness. It also led to women remaining anxious about their attractiveness and ability to attract a man. Despite the pleasures which some women might take from domesticity and motherhood and from their attractiveness to men, such an existence was oppressive. It was conducted on men's terms, not women's. Women's power operated only through men. And men exercised this power both in public life and inside the home.

The economic dependence which Beauvoir highlighted for many women corrupted the possibilities of relations between women and men and parents and children and women and women. For sexual relations should 'be based on a free engagement that the spouses could break when they wanted to.' And motherhood should 'be freely chosen – that is, birth control and abortion would be allowed – and in return all mothers and children would be given the same rights;

maternity leave would be paid for by the society that would have responsibility for the children, which does not mean that they would be *taken* from their parents but that they would not be *abandoned* to them' (2010: 776–7). This can only be achieved through work: 'work alone can guarantee her concrete freedom' (ibid.: 737). In the context in which she was writing, the independent woman supporting herself through work was not socially accepted. She was regarded as unfeminine, as sacrificing her womanhood to gain independence. This, Beauvoir argued, was unsatisfactory. We should not have to sacrifice our womanhood in order to work. We need a changed conception of what makes a woman so that 'being woman' and 'being independent' do not sit in conflict with each other. That is, we need changes interdependently at the level of material arrangements and at the level of myths and meaning.

Beauvoir is clearly thinking primarily of the situation of middle-class European women, few of whom, at the time she was writing, worked outside of the home (Oyewumi 2000). In many other situations women laboured outside as well as inside the home, though that labour was not recognized and rewarded. She did acknowledge that working-class women did work outside, but their poor wages and subjection to men inside the home and in the workplace made their positions vulnerable and harsh. Chikwenye Ogunyemi also points out that Beauvoir's account 'does not cover the experience of the black woman ... beyond her home, where she must willy-nilly go to obtain ... survival' (Ogunyemi 1985: 76–7; cited in Gines 2017: 55). So work alone is insufficient for emancipation. And Beauvoir herself acknowledged that such work must be properly rewarded and backed up by social support of parenting.

Beauvoir's analysis of the situation of women and the changes needed to improve it has since become commonplace. In most places in Europe, and in many across the world, working women are the norm. Such work is not, however, supported by equal pay, support for childcare and full reproductive freedom (see discussion in chapter 3). In 2016 President Recep Tayyip Erdoğan of Turkey marked International Women's Day by saying a woman is 'above all a mother'.[5] As discussed in our introduction, populism of the right, aligned with conservative religious views, has revived the myth that women are primarily home-makers. In this context, Beauvoir's insistence on economic independence, social childcare, and reproductive freedoms for women retains its force and relevance.

Complicity

One of the most controversial aspects of Beauvoir's analysis of sexed difference has been her apparent suggestion that women are somehow complicit in their own oppression. 'The fact is', she says, 'that men encounter more complicity in their woman companions than the oppressor usually finds in the oppressed' (2010: 773). One of the reasons she offers for this is that 'women are willing accomplices to their masters because they stand to profit from the benefits' (ibid.: 679). This is especially true of upper-class women. She points out the very different relations in which women stand to men in comparison with how other groups stand to their oppressors. Women have relations of emotional intimacy with their fathers, husbands, brothers, sons and friends. These relations are closer than the relations they have to most other women. They both isolate women from each other and make challenges to power inequalities destabilizing of their emotional lives. 'Hence woman makes no claim for herself as subject because she lacks the concrete means, because she senses the necessary link connecting her to man without positing its reciprocity, and because she often derives satisfaction from her role as *Other*' (ibid.: 10).

Such remarks can be read as reproachful of women for failing individually to exercise their freedom to resist. It is possible to read the account of complicity as an accusation of what Beauvoir and Sartre had termed *bad faith* (Sartre 1969: 47). Women, like all humans, are *capable* of acting freely, of refusing the constraints of their situation. But to accept this is frightening, dizzying and risky. It is accepting a level of responsibility for our lives which everyone, women and men, tries to avoid. Through compliance, woman 'eludes the metaphysical risk of a freedom that must invent its goals without help' (Beauvoir 2010: 10). To disguise from themselves the option of freedom, women, like men who also try to evade such responsibilities, mystify their situation. Buying into the romance of love, the naturalness of motherhood, or the superiority of the men who lord it over her, woman avoids the risks of choosing her life for herself.

It is possible to find in these remarks a contempt for women who (unlike Beauvoir) adopt a traditional role without resistance, as well as a lack of attention to the very variable textures of women's lives within what may appear to be traditional roles, and the very variable ways in which individuals may be engaging in resistant acts.

Nonetheless, Susan James argues that Beauvoir has a much more sophisticated analysis of complicity than these remarks suggest, and one that does not have the consequence of blaming women for their position. James resists a reading of Beauvoir which views her discussions of complicity as an accusation of bad faith. 'In her arresting account, complicity is conceived as a condition of an embodied self whose abilities, and therefore options, have been formed by its social circumstances' (2003: 152) and, we might add, the bodily training and habits which we outlined above. Women do act in ways that reproduce their situation, but they do so as a consequence of such training. Consequently, Beauvoir suggests, the freedom, which she values, is not an option for most women. It does not appear to them as a possibility and so they cannot be blamed for disguising it from themselves. It is, rather, disguised from them by the workings of ideological mythologies. Changes in their social conditions are required for women to have real options and also *for these options to come into view for them*. Women are indeed capable, as are all human beings, of exercising freedom.[6] But this capacity is inhibited and obscured from them, and others, by their social training, which constructs a subjectivity for women that is in tension with such a capacity. As Gail Weiss points out, if freedom requires 'being open to new possibilities that may offer themselves for becoming other than what one is or has been, then these possibilities must themselves be capable of being imagined as potentially realizable within one's own existence or they will not be possibilities at all' (Weiss 2009: 249). Beauvoir's analysis of the way in which the becoming of woman, the development of her subjectivity, contributes in this way to her subordination is thus a key contribution to feminist theory.

Nonetheless, her account is in no way determinist. Beauvoir describes and explains women's subordination, but she insists it is historically *contingent*. There is no necessity that things should be this way. Constrained women always have some scope for agency (she follows Marx here), even though, as she shows in her description of life paths, each choice has its drawbacks. Furthermore, Beauvoir came to witness a collective agency by women which she had not anticipated. She had argued in *The Second Sex* that the isolation of women from each other would make change difficult because it was not just a matter of individual choices. When the second wave of the women's movement arrived in the early 1970s she embraced it with delight and enthusiasm (Simons 1999; Kirkpatrick 2019).

Dimensions of otherness

Beauvoir's account of women's life paths has been criticized for reflecting primarily white bourgeois society in France at the time she was writing. Elizabeth Spelman notes, 'in de Beauvoir's work, we have all the essential elements of a feminist account of "women's lives" that would not conflate "woman" with a small group of women – namely white middle-class heterosexual Christian women in western countries. Yet Beauvoir ends up producing an account which does just that' (Spelman 1988, cited in Deutscher 2008: 131). Her overall position is that women's situation varies both with material and social structures and the myths which justify them and with the ways in which they are trained into their femininity. This is why Spelman finds the narrowness of her account disappointing. *The Second Sex* does show some awareness of the differences made, particularly by class, to the life paths available, but the intersectionality of gendered positionality with other aspects of social difference is strikingly absent.

Bergoffen points out that, when Beauvoir writes that 'Humanity is male, and man defines woman, not in herself but in relation to himself' (2010: 5), she could equally 'have substituted markers of race for *man* and *woman*. The sentence would read "Thus humanity is white and white people define native people or black people, not in themselves, but as relative to them"' (Bergoffen 2009: 13). As detailed above, Beauvoir applied her account of *othering* to Jews, native peoples, black Americans and the proletariat, as well as women. It is in her analysis of racism, found first in *America Day by Day*, that, as Deutscher points out, 'Beauvoir offered her first explication of the distinction between being and becoming as it applies to embodied subjectivity' (2008: 77). In *The Second Sex* she says 'there are deep analogies between the situations of women and blacks: ... In both cases, the ruling caste bases its argument on the state of affairs it created itself. The familiar line from George Bernard Shaw sums it up: "The white American relegates the black to the rank of shoe-shine boy, and then concludes that blacks are only good for shining shoes"' (Beauvoir 2010: 12). And later in *The Second Sex*: 'Richard Wright showed in *Black Boy* how blocked from the start the ambitions of a young American black man are ... the blacks who come to France from Africa also have – within themselves as well as from outside – difficulties similar to those encountered by women'

(2010: 753). We find in Wright's and Du Bois's work, as well as in that of Beauvoir, an analysis of the transformation in our consciousness which can be brought about by encountering the look of another. Du Bois, discussing socialization, recounts the moment when 'one girl ... refused my card – refused it peremptorily, with a glance' (Du Bois [1903] 1989: 78). And Beauvoir, in turn, reports a woman saying: 'At thirteen, I walked around bare-legged, in a short dress ... A man, sniggering, made a comment about my fat calves ... I will never forget the shock I suddenly felt in seeing myself *seen*' (2010: 332). Beauvoir's phenomenology of women's experience itself was also influential on the phenomenological writer Franz Fanon, discussed in chapter 2. There we highlighted how, on his arrival in France, he discovers his blackness: '"Dirty nigger!"... I discovered myself as an object among other objects' (1968: 187–8).

Despite these closely related discussions, there remain problems with Beauvoir's discourses of both race and class. She explores raced differences and, to some extent, class differences in addition to sexed differences, but, in almost all cases, each as a discrete category. Most of her debates on raced difference, for example, concern black men. Moreover, such a discussion is not interwoven into her examination of masculinity more generally. What is not addressed is the way in which race is inter-implicated with sexed difference so that becoming man is quite a different process if you are becoming a black man, and becoming black is quite different for a man and a woman. Surprisingly, Beauvoir pays very little attention to the writings or experiences of black women. As Kathryn Gines comments, 'her emphasis on the gender oppression of white women (as if all of the women are white) and the racial oppression of Black men (as if all of the Blacks are men) ignores the multiple oppressions confronting Black women and other women of color' (Gines 2017: 49). This is not simply to ignore the fact that there are many different ways of becoming women (so, for example, some of us become strong and some fragile). It is also to ignore the ways in which the processes of becoming gendered are inseparable from the processes of becoming raced. Beauvoir highlighted the role that the doll plays in the processes of becoming objectified, but many black writers have described the consequences, if you are a black girl, of being given a doll that is white with blue eyes and blond hair (Angelou 1969; Morrison [1970] 2000). Here becoming raced and becoming gendered are painfully entangled. As Deutscher points out, 'Sex cannot be abstracted from class, age, race, or economic background and "men" and "women" arise from their mutual differentiations and relations' (2008: 163). Given her insistence on the historical contingency of the women and men whose experiences she describes, Beauvoir would, of course, agree. But in her writings the *mutual formation* of these categories is obscured. And, as a result, she does not address the way in which women, as marginalized, can also be in a position to marginalize others, constituting their own delicate bourgeois femininity in opposition to the 'vulgarity' of the working class or their own white sense of entitlement with a sense of black inferiority.

There is, however, one key dimension of difference which Beauvoir addresses both in *The Second Sex* and in her later work, in which such mutual formation is acknowledged and illuminated – namely, the dimension of *age*. Throughout *The Second Sex* she distinguishes the experiences of boys/girls/women/men at different stages of their life. The kind of material conditions, the myths and the internalized subjectivities which are derived from them, are *different* according to where in the life cycle we are positioned. We saw above her characterization of the transition from childhood to puberty. In middle age there is another transition to be handled for women, Beauvoir argues, as they can no longer rely on their sexual attractiveness to contribute to their life chances. They feel they have lost value and are exposed to disrespect. At just this point (bourgeois) men are seen as solidified in their careers and professional standing. In her later work *Old Age* (1972) Beauvoir concentrates much more on men. Her analysis concentrates particularly on the lack of *productivity* of the old and the way this has particular impact on the sense of masculinity of older men, since ideals of masculinity are defined in terms of men's roles as producers and providers. Moreover, increased bodily vulnerability detracts from the strength and virility in relation to which ideal masculinity is also characterized. In this later work it is pointed out that, released from the structures of sexual objectification, older women remain useful in society, as their domestic labour and position as carers to their families, including grandchildren, keep them more active and socially recognized as having a role. Beauvoir sees this as often a more satisfying period in women's lives. Sexed difference and aging are, therefore, woven together in her accounts in a way that she does not manage with other dimensions of difference.

Conclusions

In 1949 Simone de Beauvoir provided us with an account of the processes of becoming women and men which integrated biological bodily difference, material and economic conditions, myths and meaning, bodily habits, and the formation of subjectivity. In her attention to the biological body and its important but non-determining status, she both answered those who regarded sex difference as a natural given and paid attention to bodily specificity in a way that has been stressed more recently by the new materialists we discussed in chapter 1. She was sceptical of psychoanalysis because of its own sexism. Nonetheless, she also gave an account of subjectivity as produced in the familial and wider social realm from the significance (including the emotional salience) that is attached to bodily difference. This salience is marked by the public myths attached to both men and women. Her own Marxism gave Beauvoir an overall methodology of historical materialism, insisting on the historical specificity of oppressive relations and the centrality of economic dependency in reproducing women's subjection. She added to these three elements her phenomenological stance, which focused on our lived experience of the world and the construction of subjectivity. The model she offers of 'becoming woman' is an initiation into a situation, interweaving material conditions and bodily difference with the meanings bestowed on them. Crucial to this process is the positioning of women as 'other' to a norm which is masculine. This is a positioning which we learn to apply to ourselves by becoming aware of the gaze of other people. This complex situation is one with which we interact, and one which we internalize, yielding a subjectivity which contributes to its reproduction. Overall, it is a situation in which women's potentialities are curtailed. But the situation is not a necessity. To change it requires interventions involving all elements: biological control of fertility, economic equality, social childrearing practices, changed myths and meanings, collective political agency and individual resistance.

The Second Sex was an astonishing feat. Beauvoir weaves together different strands of theory and makes clear how multiple factors are entangled in the account we offer of becoming gendered in a way that provides a model for the approach we are following in this book. But, of course, it had its own limitations. The intersectionality of gendered positionality with other aspects of social difference is strikingly absent. As bell hooks notes: 'Influenced by the life and writing of Beauvoir, it was essential for me to move beyond her focus on women as "other" to bring together critical perspectives for understanding female identity that began from the standpoint that female identity is shaped by gender, race, and class, and never solely by sex ... we cannot understand what it means to be female or male without critically examining interlocking systems of domination' (hooks 2012: 233–5; cited in Gines 2017: 56). It is to such interlocking systems that we turn in the following chapter.

5 Intersectionality

Gender is about race is about class is about sexuality is about age is about nationality is about an entire range of social relations. (Weston 2010: 15)

The most general statement of our politics at the present time would be that we are actively committed to struggling against racial, sexual, heterosexual, and class oppression and see as our particular task the development of integrated analysis and practice based upon the fact that the major systems of oppression are interlocking. The synthesis of these oppressions creates the conditions of our lives. As Black women we see Black feminism as the logical political movement to combat the manifold and simultaneous oppressions that all women of color face. (Combahee River Collective [1977] 2015)

The most compelling and complex analyses of gender intersectionality take into consideration what I call the ability/disability system – along with race, ethnicity, sexuality, and class. (Garland-Thomson 2002: 2)

Intersectional analysis and material positionality

Intersectionality as a concept highlights the complexity of the ways in which overarching systems of oppression converge and collide to differentially inform individuals' access to resources, opportunities and social justice and to shape their sense of self. As Weston and Garland-Thomson signal (quoted above), gender is not just about gender. It is about the whole 'range of social relations' (Weston 2010: 15).

The concept of intersectionality provides us with a crucial analytical tool to make evident social differentials which might otherwise be missed. Intersectionality is about power differences, and, at its core, a politics of intersectionality is concerned with intervening to ensure a fairer redistribution of power. The key insight informing those who make use of the term is that, if we do not look at the way in which different power structures interrelate, then aspects of the working of power, and the economic and social advantages and disadvantages accruing to differing positions in society, are invisible. Here, we use the term to describe both the structural conditions within which social categories are constructed by (and intermeshed with) each other in specific historical contexts and the accompanying imaginaries which support these arrangements and inform our sense of self.

At the beginning of our discussion of historical materialism in chapter 3, we used a number of examples related to education, work, politics, health and violence to highlight the ways in which social structures and processes are gendered. If we return to some of these examples and look not through the single lens of gender but, instead, at the ways in which gendered inequalities intersect with other axes of inequality – for example, those of race and class, sexuality and differing abilities – we can see that attention purely to gender differences masks complexity and marginalizes the experiences of many women (and men), ignoring as it does the range of ways in which multiple systems of oppression interact in practice. As a concept, intersectionality moves on from *additive* models of oppression which define regimes of inequality as multiple, but distinct and separate. Rather, those who employ the term 'intersectionality' focus on how such multiple oppressions *intersect* (and mutually constitute each other) to produce specific, historically situated oppressions and inequalities that structure social relations (for example, Crenshaw 1989, 1991, 2012; Collins 1990, 2015, 2017; Yuval-Davis 2006; Collins and Bilge 2016).

We start with some examples. If we take educational attainment in England, for instance, and just look at the data through the lens of gender, exam results at GCSE and A-level have indicated for a number of years that girls are outperforming boys. With closer inspection, it is evident that class and ethnicity as well as gender have a significant impact on educational attainment. Some groups of boys – most notably boys from Chinese and Indian backgrounds – are doing well – particularly, although not exclusively, those from wealthier backgrounds. White working-class boys, working-class black Caribbean boys and white working-class girls fare particularly badly. Girls and boys from traveller backgrounds have especially low educational attainment (Department for Education and Skills

2007). A study that examines the intersection of multiple variables and offers not just a single-axis analysis is thus significant not only in illustrating the more complex intersections between oppression, social privilege and educational outcome but also in engaging with political and policy responses. The media and policy responses to the notion that boys are failing, or rather being failed by our education system, were important factors behind the move within England and Wales towards a more exam-focused assessment regime at GCSE and A-level. Boys, it was argued, were disadvantaged because of the increase in course work. Drawing often on essentialist notions of boys' learning styles, the move back to assessment via examination was seen as a way of counteracting the boys' perceived disadvantaged status within schools in terms of outcomes. More fine-tuned intersectional analysis indicates, however, that not all boys were doing badly and that ethnicity and, particularly, class were key factors shaping educational outcomes; thus, if greater parity in educational outcome across social groups is desired, other political interventions are necessary.

Likewise, an intersectional analysis of health and disability illustrates the ways in which single-axis approaches provide a simplified, partial picture of the social world. Data from the World Health Organization indicate a symbiotic relationship between poverty and disability – if you are disabled you are more at risk of poverty; if you are poor you are more at risk of disability. However, research suggests that the interrelationship between poverty and disability is more complex. An intersectional analysis conducted by Moodley and Graham (2015) indicates that women with disabilities in South Africa fare particularly badly in both education and outcome and are therefore at greater risk of poverty than men with disabilities. Employment chances of the disabled are further complicated by race: 'a White woman with a disability is as likely to be employed as a Black man without a disability ... Black people with disabilities face a double exclusion and Black women with disabilities fare the worst in terms of labour market outcomes' (2015: 28). Research from the US indicates similar interconnections. As Warner and Brown (2011: 1236) indicate: 'all demographic groups exhibiting worse functional limitation trajectories than White Men. Whereas White Men had the lowest disability levels at baseline, White Women and racial/ethnic minority Men had intermediate disability levels and Black and Hispanic Women had the highest disability levels. These health disparities remained stable with age – except among Black Women who experience a trajectory of accelerated disablement.' Again, the gender–class–race–disability nexus is key in shaping individuals' social positionality and life chances (see also Gerschick 2000; Mullings and Schulz 2006). Such intersectional data are crucial in developing scholarly and policy responses to issues of health and disability. Bowleg et al. (2012) further note that, in the US, 52 per cent of new HIV cases in 2009 were among black men and women even though they constitute just 13 per cent of the overall population. Black women, however, constituted 66 per cent of new cases. In terms of infant mortality in the US, the rate in the non-Latino black community was 2.4 times greater than that in the non-Latino white community. Raced positionality had a key impact on infant mortality rates. While class was also a factor, Bowleg (2012) notes that the infant mortality rate was still higher among highly educated black women than among non-Latino white women with lower education levels. Again, without looking at the complex intersections of a range of variables, the diverse picture of health disparities and inequalities would be obscured.

The importance of looking through an intersectional lens is also evident in tackling domestic and sexual violence (AWID 2004; Anthias 2013). There is an acknowledgement within domestic violence literature that all women, regardless of class, age, sexuality, race, and so on, can be victims of domestic and intimate partner violence. Men can also be victims of domestic violence, although data point persuasively to the greater rates of domestic violence against women. An early important move by feminist activists has been to raise public awareness of the pervasiveness of these forms of violence. However, later work has emphasized that some groups of women are more likely to experience violence and to face additional barriers in seeking to escape violent relationships. Migrant women, for example, are particularly vulnerable to domestic and sexual violence and less likely to be able to access legal and social services that might bring them protection (Pillai 2001; Menjivar and Salcido 2002; Anitha 2010, 2011; Madill and Alsop 2019). Only with attention to a multitude of intersecting factors can the complexity of violence against women be fully understood.

In her work 'Mapping the margins: intersectionality, identity politics, and violence against women of color' (1991), Crenshaw shows, in relation to the analysis of domestic violence and rape, how attending to the particular experiences of black women requires an intersectional approach which examines the ways in which racism and patriarchy are mutually constitutive of black women's experiences. Intersectionality at the level of social structure informs how women of colour in the US experience violence, anti-violence interventions and the justice system differently because of their social location as being both simultaneously female and black. As a further example, Crenshaw's analysis reflects upon the much lower conviction rates in rape cases when the victims are black women and, when convictions are achieved, the lower sentences given to the rapists of black women. She argues that this is a result, in part, of the 'sexual hierarchy in operation that holds certain female bodies in higher esteem than others' (1991: 1269). While research suggests that women engaging in 'nontraditional behaviour' are less likely to be believed in rape cases, Crenshaw argues that African-American women are less likely to be believed because 'racial identification may itself serve as a proxy for nontraditional behaviour' (ibid.: 1280). Without attention here to the intersections of gender and race (and the intersecting oppressions of patriarchy and racism), we cannot adequately understand, theorize or challenge the ways in which such sexist victim-blaming narratives are also infused with racism.

Intersectionality and lived experience

The examples above highlight the workings of the term 'intersectionality' in respect of making evident interlocking structures of social oppression and signalling the impact on individuals of being positioned within many differing strands of structural power relations.

In this chapter, we explore how the concept of intersectionality can help us theorize not only structural causes and consequences of our gendered and social positionality but also the lived experience of intersectionality and its role in constructing individual subjectivities (Brah and Phoenix 2004; Taylor et al. 2011). According to Rosemarie Garland-Thomson, feminist theory interrogates 'how subjects are multiply interpellated; in other words, how the representational systems of gender, race, ethnicity, ability, sexuality, and class mutually construct, inflect, and contradict one another ... The status of the lived body, the politics of appearance, the medicalization of the body, the privilege of normalcy' all look different from the perspective of disabled women (2002: 3–4). The relative privileges of normative femininity are often denied to disabled women: 'Cultural stereotypes imagine disabled women as asexual, unfit to reproduce, overly dependent, unattractive ... Disability thus both intensifies and attenuates the cultural scripts of femininity' (Fine and Asch 1988: 17).

We need attention to intersectionality to make sense of the differences in being gendered in different locales. What *counts as* being a man or a woman, what life opportunities result from gendered positionality, and how these factors are internalized to form our lived experience of being gendered are mediated by the other categories which intersect with gendered ones. Being a 'black man/woman', or 'gay man/woman', or 'trans man or woman' (themselves categories which also mediate each other and are mediated further by, for example, age and class and our positioning on the ability/disability axis) have different contents from being a 'white, straight, middle-class, able-bodied woman or man'. Moreover, all of these categories play out differently if they are applied in countries formed by colonialism; for colonizers brought with them, and forced the application of, categories at odds with indigenous practices (Lugones 2010; Wekker 2016). We return to this below.

These positionalities have consequences for our life opportunities both economically and in the wider social realm, which the structural data make evident. And all of this has consequences for our *lived subjectivity*, our sense of ourselves as male or female, among other identifiers. Audre Lorde writes: 'As a Black lesbian feminist comfortable with the many ingredients of my identity, and a woman committed to racial and sexual freedom of expression, I find I am constantly being encouraged to pluck out some aspect of myself and present this as a meaningful whole, eclipsing or denying the other parts of self. But this is a destructive and fragmenting way to live' (1984: 120). Lorde points here to the ways in which, at the level of individual subjectivity, the many aspects of our identities – our gender, our race, our sexuality, to name just some – are all so interwoven with each other that it is impossible in our sense of selves and in our lived experiences to split them up. It is impossible completely to separate out those bits of us that are our gender, those bits that are our sexuality, those that are our race, as they are all mutually constituting of each other. Her point is reinforced in examples given by Kath Weston:

Meet Eriko Yoshikawa, a 20-something US resident, middle-class, Japanese, able-bodied, one-time Catholic, contextually lesbian, not particularly butch but not exactly femme woman. There's very little you can understand about Eriko, or what happens to her day by day, if you insist upon examining these tags one at a time. Even she couldn't separate them. Even she had to speculate in order to explain the bad treatment she experienced at the women's bar in her California town. What made the bartender refuse to serve Eriko a second drink? Racism that would have targeted any person of color? Class resentment? A West Coast legacy of anti-Asian political agitation? Was the bartender scapegoating Japanese for the way that multinational corporations had shifted jobs out of the country? Could she have felt squeamish about public kissing? Opposed to interracial sex? Disdainful of femmes across the board? And why did most of the white women at the club immediately take Eriko for femme? The gendered effects produced by long hair? The cut of her clothing? Stereotypes that divide Asian women into Dragon Ladies and China Dolls? Three of the above? All of the above? (Weston 2010: 29)

Butler notes that the different practices of naming to which we are subjected, as people who are gendered, raced, classed, aged and carrying marks of our sexualities or abilities, etc., mean that each category is 'translated' in terms of the other – difference unsettling homogeneity. Consequently, the categories themselves are continually shifting. This all makes a difference to the way in which our social categories and their associated imaginaries 'land' and how they are taken up in the formation of our subjectivities. 'When [they do] make a landing [they] act ... in different ways, ... in multiple and sometimes contradictory ways' (Butler 2015: 5).

Intersectionality: the origins of the concept and the coining of the term

The coining of the term 'intersectionality' is often credited to the African-American civil rights advocate and feminist and critical race scholar Kimberlé Crenshaw (1989, 1991), who argues that a single-axis framework that looks at either gender or race is unable to capture the particular experiences of black women. In feminist and anti-racist identity politics, 'intra-group differences' are often ignored, with the result that black women's particular experiences are rendered invisible: 'The failure of feminism to interrogate race means that the resistance strategies of feminism will often replicate and reinforce the subordination of people of color, and the failure of anti-racism to interrogate patriarchy means that anti-racism will frequently reproduce the subordination of women' (Crenshaw 1991: 1252).

In both feminism and anti-racist politics, the specificities of black women's lives are overlooked. For Crenshaw, it was necessary to 'recast and rethink' the framework by which we explore the intersections of patriarchy and racism, not only to understand the particularities of black women's experiences and the power relations that are productive of these experiences but also to be able to intervene politically to effect change. The metaphor of the intersection is employed to show how different strands of inequality converge and enmesh to produce a combined effect. As black women, we do not experience racism *and* sexism as separate discrete strands of oppression, Crenshaw argues, but instead racism and sexism intersect and combine to shape the lives of black women in very specific ways – differently to the oppression white women may face and differently to the oppression black men may face: 'I wanted to come up with a common everyday metaphor that people could use to say: "it's well and good for me to understand the kind of discriminations that occur along this avenue, along this axis – but what happens when it flows into another axis, another avenue?"'[1]

Patricia Hill Collins (2015: 10), however, cautions against conflating the coining of the term with 'the point of origin for [the concept of] intersectionality itself'. As Nash notes:

> While intersectionality has become a scholarly buzzword, the notion that identity is formed by interlocking and mutually reinforcing vectors of race, gender, class, and sexuality has pervaded black feminist thought for decades ... Myriad feminist scholars have destabilized the notion of a universal 'woman' without explicitly mobilizing the term 'intersectionality', arguing that 'woman' itself is a contested terrain, and that the experience of 'woman' is always constituted by subjects with vastly different interests. To that end, intersectionality has provided a name to a pre-existing theoretical and political commitment. (2008: 3)

There has been a long history of black feminist activism and scholarship (including, for example, hooks 1981; Davis 1982; Lorde 1984; Collins 1990; Mirza 1997) challenging the idea that the material structures of society are operating in the same way for all women to produce a common condition of 'being a woman'. Emphasis on the diversity of women's lives, cross-cut along the lines of race, sexuality and class, undermines accounts of patriarchy based on the notion of a common womanhood. Black feminist critiques challenged the racism of mainstream white feminist thought for theorizing womanhood from the perspective of white women, thereby rendering the particular experiences of black and other groups of marginalized women invisible. Black feminists looked instead to conceptualize how women's lives were diversely informed by the intersections of gender, race and class without necessarily privileging gender as a key axis of oppression. This body of work has been foundational in expanding material analyses to take account of multiple intersecting oppressions, particularly to expound how inequalities of race, gender and class are mutually shaping. It is also from this body of work that the concept of intersectionality – now so central to contemporary analyses of gender – was born.

The statement at the start of this chapter from the Combahee River Collective, a lesbian, black feminist activist organization from the US, has been described as the 'first statement to frame identity through an intersectional lens' (Collins and Bilge 2016: 69). But attention to the principles of intersectionality has a longer history. Two centuries earlier, black female activists such as Sojourner Truth, now famous for her 'Ain't I a woman?' speech at Akron, Ohio, in 1851 (which Collins and Bilge (2016: 67) describe as 'a benchmark for intersectional sensibilities'), the abolitionist and women's rights activist Maria W. Stewart, the scholar and activist Anna Julia Cooper, and the journalist and civil rights leader Ida B. Wells, to give just some examples, were identifying how race and gender oppressions combined to shape black women's lives. They were, as Gines (2014) describes, 'proto-intersectional' thinkers.

However, it was not only black feminists who were exercised by issues of differences in gendered experience resulting from our position in other frameworks of social differentiation. The early Marxist and socialist feminists discussed in chapter 3 recognized that gender relations could not be reduced to class relations and developed dual-, multiple- and integrated system theories to try and accommodate their interrelations. As we noted in chapter 4, Beauvoir noted the locatedness of the account of 'woman' that she was offering and paid attention to the differences which resulted from age in accounting for the lived experience, normative ideals and economic possibilities for women. Judith Butler, in *Gender Trouble*, pointed out that 'the insistence upon the coherence and unity of the category of women has effectively refused the multiplicity of cultural, social and political intersections in which the concrete array of "women" are constructed' (1990a: 14). Disability theorists from the 1990s onwards explored how disability affected the gendering process and gender affected the experiences and outcomes of differing bodily abilities (Mairs 1990; Morris 1993; Gilbert 1997). Decolonial theorists challenged the constructions of what it was to be a woman that took Western feminism as its touchstone and ignored the history of colonialism (Lugones 2007; Spivak 1987; Mohanty 1986, 2003, 2013; Ortega 2016).

Crenshaw herself notes, writing with Cho and McCall, that it is not the use of the term 'intersectionality' that decides if a piece of research is intersectional but whether it has 'an intersectional way of thinking about the problem of sameness and difference and its relation to power' (Cho et al. 2013: 795). It is, they argue, about what 'intersectionality does, rather than what intersectionality is'. While much writing from differing perspectives has emphasized *differences* between women, the lack of homogeneity within our gendered categories, and the social consequences of being assigned to them, not all of this has attended to such differences in an intersectional way. What the use of the term 'intersectionality' tries to avoid is attending to these differences as *simply additive*. It is not that there is a pattern of discrimination that results from being gendered, and we simply add on to it a pattern that derives from being raced or assigned to categories of sexuality, ethnicity, class, or able-bodiedness to explain the life outcomes for people with multiple positionalities. It is rather that we cannot articulate the consequences of any of these positionalities without taking the others into account. We return to discussion of this point below.

The publication of Crenshaw's 'Mapping the margins' in 1991 represents 'a juncture when the idea of social movement politics became named and subsequently incorporated into the academy' (Collins 2015: 10). Despite the long history of the ideas that underpinned intersectionality (Anthias 2013), it is 'the term that has stuck' (Collins 2015: 2) and 'the term increasingly used by stakeholders' (Collins and Bilge 2016: 2; see also Davis 2008). Also, importantly, for Crenshaw as with other intersectional theorists (such as Collins 1990, 2015; Yuval-Davis 2006), intersectionality is not only a concept about highlighting the points where intersections occur but also a tool to explore power relations and structures of inequality. As Tomlinson noted (cited in Cho et al. 2013: 1012), it is about making clear 'which differences make a difference'. Intersectionality as a concept is not simply a theory of difference but a theory of oppression. Theories of intersectionality are not just an abstract theorizing of identity differences but born out of a political commitment to name, challenge and change power relations.

For Collins, additive models of oppression are rooted in either/or conceptualizations of oppression: you are either black or white, male or female, for example, and within this framework one is either privileged or oppressed. Collins, however, seeing gender, class and race as interlocking, invites new ways of thinking about oppression and privilege which 'opens up possibilities for a both/and conceptual stance' (1990: 225). She puts forward a nuanced understanding of power and privilege which recognizes that an individual may occupy positions of both oppression and privilege: 'In this system, for example, white women are penalized by their gender but privileged by their race. Depending on the context, an individual may be an oppressor, a member of an oppressed group, or simultaneously oppressor and oppressed' (ibid.). Collins argues that it is often easier to see our points of victimization but harder to recognize how we might 'uphold someone else's subordination' (ibid.: 229). This is a point that is explored further in Reni Eddo-Lodge's *Why I'm No Longer Talking to White People about Race*. Eddo-Lodge states: 'If feminism can understand the patriarchy, it's important to question why so many feminists struggle to understand whiteness as a political structure in the very same way' (2017: 168). Garry argues that intersectional thinking has the potential to make academics and others 'face up to dominant group members' unacknowledged privileges, including the privilege of remaining ignorant of marginalized people' (2011: 827). While Eddo-Lodge focuses on white privilege, Collins maintains that privilege may come in many forms. Middle-class African-Americans, for example, may also fail to see the privileges attached to their class position or the oppressions experienced by marginalized groups of white Americans, such as poor white women, and still 'persist in seeing poor white women as symbols of white power'. 'Oppression is filled with such contradictions', she argues, but 'a matrix of domination contains few pure victims or oppressors' (1990: 229).

Intersectionality in practice

Crenshaw makes the distinction in her analysis between *structural* intersectionality (the intersection of unequal social groups), *political* intersectionality (the intersection of political agendas and initiatives) and *representational* intersectionality (the intersection of cultural and discursive constructions) and sees these three aspects combining to produce systems of power and inequality. Most of the examples with which we opened this chapter are examples of structural intersectionality, where, for example, addressing the particular needs of those fleeing domestic violence requires us to pay attention to the intersections of gender, race and class. 'Women working in the field of domestic violence have sometimes reproduced the subordination and marginalization of women of color by adopting policies, priorities, or strategies of empowerment that either elide or wholly disregard the particular intersectional needs of women of color' (Crenshaw 1991: 1262). The point at which we mobilize politically around particular strategies is where issues of *political* intersectionality come to the fore.

A key argument within Crenshaw's analysis is that anti-racist politics often fail to attend to issues of sexism and patriarchy and that feminism fails to attend sufficiently to issues of race, with the result that 'the concerns of minority women fall into the void' (1991: 1282) as identity politics 'frequently conflates or ignores intragroup differences' (ibid.: 1242). In making a distinction between structural and political intersectionality, Crenshaw is highlighting the ways in which political initiatives such as feminism and the black civil rights movement have not paid sufficient attention to the ways in which race and gender are mutually constituted, prioritizing the experiences of white women in the former and black men in the latter, thereby failing to attend adequately to the structural and everyday inequalities black women face. 'The concept of political intersectionality highlights the fact that women of color are situated within at least two subordinated agendas ... Because women of color experience racism in ways not the same as men of color and sexism in ways not parallel to experiences of white women, antiracism and feminism are limited, even on their own terms' (ibid.: 1252). Similar points could be made regarding other aspects of our positionality that impact on relations of power. The different ways in which women who are positioned variously on the ability/disability or age spectrum experience sexism illustrate this point, as do the particular ways misogyny is directed at lesbian or trans women.

Walby and her colleagues note that this distinction between structural and political intersectionality is 'rarely addressed in the subsequent literature on intersectionality' (2012: 228). From a historical materialist perspective, making this distinction is nonetheless salient as it highlights the irreducibility of political intersectionality to structural intersectionality. As these authors indicate, 'there are many actually existing intersections in social structures, but only some of these become the focus of political and policy attention ... reasons for the selection of some intersectional strands and not others as politically relevant are significant for the analysis of intersectionality in equality policies' (ibid.: 229). There are lots of differences between people that are structurally entrenched and lots linked to issues of inequality: which ones we make the focus of action is a political issue. Crenshaw highlights, for example, the ways in which the Black Lives Matter movement in the US has focused almost exclusively on police brutality against black men and less on the many cases of police violence against black women – and even less on the fact that 'Disability – emotional, physical and mental – is one of the biggest risk factors for being killed by the police, but it is relatively suppressed in the conversation about police violence.'[2]

The third aspect of intersectionality to which Crenshaw draws our attention is *representational* intersectionality. In her analysis of black women and rape, she describes the ways in which the cultural imagery around rape is shaped by gender and race. For example, the US media gave extensive coverage to the rape of a white woman in the Central Park jogger case, and Crenshaw points to multiple cases of the rape of black women that occurred in New York around the same time that never made it into the news. As the #MeToo movement drew the world's attention to the pervasiveness of sexual violence against women, it became clear that sympathy for and the believability of women's stories were linked to their raced position, with 'instances of women of colour being forgotten or sidelined' (White 2017). Writing in *The Atlantic*, White argues, for example, that it is relevant that Harvey Weinstein chose to break his hitherto 'silence to publicly discredit Lupita Nyong'o, a black actress, when she wrote of her experience of harassment' and not the previous white women who had gone public about his behaviour.

The issue of how intersectionality is relevant to cultural representations is not limited solely to the cultural representation of rape and sexual violence, however important an issue this is; it can be applied generally to all aspects of the ways in which who is represented, how they are represented, and where they are represented are shaped by power relations informed by race, class, gender, sexuality, ability and other vectors of social inequality. For example, if we look at mainstream Hollywood films, we can see that the heroes of the narratives are generally white, more likely male (Geena Davis Institute on Gender in Media 2019), often young, usually heterosexual and nearly always able-bodied (usually reflecting also the demographics of those involved behind the scenes in the making of films.[3] Women are numerically underrepresented in lead roles, as are black and disabled characters. However, we need an intersectional analysis to show the particular ways in which systems of gendered, racial, classed and sexual hierarchies converge, firstly, in order to exclude certain groups disproportionately and, secondly, to limit and stereotype their representations when they are included.

Collins develops *her* analysis of interlocking oppressions through a 'domains of power' framework which puts forward 'four distinctive yet interconnected domains of power: interpersonal, disciplinary, cultural, and structural' (Collins and Bilge 2016: 7), 'which operate singularly and in combination in shaping the social organization of power' (Collins 2017: 22) and through which intersectional oppressions are produced. The notion of intersectionality is extended here to illustrate how different domains of power intersect at the macro-level to form an overarching system of power which produces, within specific cultural and historical contexts, a particular configuration of power that Collins terms the 'matrix of domination'. The 'domains of power' framework, Collins argues, can be used as a template to interrogate the ways in which 'the matrix of domination' – in particular, locations and time periods – works to produce specific configurations of power. Collins maintains, for example, that intersections of sexism, racism, imperialism and capitalism differ between nation-states. Some forms of power will be more pertinent in some contexts than in others. For instance, in contexts where same-sex sexual relations are prohibited by law, or taboo, being gay impacts on the lives of men and women differently to contexts in which homosexuality is legal, accepted and embraced. For women seeking to terminate a pregnancy in the UK, it matters where they live, since, as we write, Northern Ireland continues to prohibit abortion.

Patricia Zavella's analysis of the Respect ABQ Women campaign against the banning of abortion in New Mexico after twenty weeks illustrates the importance of sensitivity to the particularities of the local context in successful political campaigning. 'The organizers crafted culturally relevant, locally effective strengths-based messages that resonated with voters and promoted them in multiple sites, including Albuquerque's major newspapers and churches' (Zavella 2017: 527). Moreover, she argues, its success was built upon activism attentive to intersectional difference. 'The success was based on a broad-based cross-sectoral strategy that incorporated faith-based communities as well as organizations that work with immigrants and LGBTQ people on environmental justice or on other issues not directly related to the right to choose' (ibid.: 529).

Which inequalities does intersectionality cover? The 'etc. problem'

In her development of intersectionality theory, Crenshaw focuses her analysis on the marginalization of black women in the US with reference primarily to the mutual constitution of race and gender in their structural, political and representational oppression. Nash is critical of what she sees as 'Intersectionality's reliance on black women as the basis for its claims.' In so doing, she argues, it homogenizes the experiences of black women, sidelining their additional differences in relation to sexuality, age and disability, for instance, and consequently risks universalizing their experiences 'as transhistorical constants'. She continues:

> While Crenshaw endeavours to use black women's incapacity to comply with race/gender categories to demonstrate the inadequacy of the categories themselves, her argument shores up the conception that black women's identities are constituted exclusively by race *and* gender. That is Crenshaw focuses on black women because they are 'multiply burdened', yet her examination precludes an examination of forms of 'multiple burdens' (or the intersection of privileges and burdens) beyond race and gender. (Nash 2008: 7)

According to Nash, Crenshaw's analysis of domestic violence and rape focuses on how black women's experiences are informed by the intersection of race and gender, but she 'neglects the ways in which these experiences are also complicated by class, nationality, language, ethnicity, and sexuality' (ibid.: 9). This is not entirely fair. Crenshaw does acknowledge in her discussion in 'Mapping the margins' of domestic violence and rape that class and sexuality are interrelated factors. Throughout her work, both the impact of poverty on black women's lives and the interconnectedness with class is evident. Nonetheless, there are a range of other factors that complicate further experiences of domestic and sexual violence – whether you are disabled or able-bodied, whether you are trans or cis gender, whether or not you are migrant – are all key (see also Carbado et al. 2013).

Nash's comments do, however, raise the question of how to deal with the multitude of social factors that can be included when thinking of intersectionality. We have mentioned so far race, gender, class, ethnicity, nationality, (post-)coloniality, sexuality, age, (dis)ability, being migrant, and being cis or trans as factors that can intersect to shape structures and selves, but the list is never exhaustive; what about caste, what about the multiplicities of ways you can be a migrant – trafficked or not, documented or not documented? For fear of not being attentive to particularities of any intersectional positionality, often the list ends with 'etc.'. Butler remarks at the end of *Gender Trouble*: 'what political impetus is to be derived from the exasperated 'etc.' that so often occurs at the end of such lines?' For her, this is a mark of 'the illimitable process of signification itself' (Butler 1990a: 143), a point to which we will return below. But, here, it is at least clear that, for purposes of analysis, the etc. includes those categories which capture differences of social power. And these may be different in the different contexts identified by the theorists above. However, we do not always know in advance what they will be. Maybe we would not have predicted that disability would be a key factor in exploring police killings or prison populations, for example. For purposes of political activism, which differences are to be the basis of political engagement need to be decided by agents in very specific sociohistorical circumstances. Not all intersectional social positions lead to the formation of social groups politically engaging with inequalities of power (positions with power, for example, rarely do this). When we turn to questions of intersectionality inflecting our lived subjectivity, however, then different sets of considerations might come into play as to what circumstances it is salient to consider, tied up with personal histories as well as public structures. We will also return to this below.

Who is intersectional?

Nash raises the further question as to who is intersectional. Intersectionality has developed as an important means to make visible the usually neglected experiences of those marginalized in terms of social power. Nash suggests that, as the bulk of intersectional studies 'centred on the particular position of multiply marginalized subjects', it is unsettled as to whether 'intersectionality is a theory of marginalized subjectivity or a generalized theory of identity' (2008: 9–10). We argue for a concept of intersectionality that sees all positionalities and subjectivities as intersectional, but one that is cognizant of the varying ways in which intersectionality is imbued with power. Everyone's position in society is intersectional in some way; however, some elements of these positions are less visible and some carry less power. As Garry argues, 'Intersectionality applies to everyone, not only to members of subordinated or marginalized groups' (2011: 829). As our discussion above indicates, many writers on intersectionality are mindful of the complex and nuanced ways in which power and oppressions co-exist (for example, Collins and Bilge 2016; Garry 2011). A white middle-class woman may exercise power over her male working-class Latino gardener but may be looked over for promotion in the workplace, disadvantaged against her male colleagues.

Likewise, for Yuval-Davis (2015), intersectionality as a concept applies not just to those for whom the intersections of race, class and gender result in discrimination and social subordination but to all people. Our positions in society are moulded by such intersections, even if the result of those configurations is to be placed in a more privileged position. Yuval-Davis argues that studying inequalities is about understanding the powerful as well as the powerless (a point reiterated by Walby et al. 2012). Thus, for example, an intersectional analysis of gender, race and class applies as much to understanding the social positioning of a powerful, white male politician from a materially privileged background, such as Donald Trump, as it does to the Hispanic migrant women cleaning his hotels for minimum wage. 'As critical race and ethnicity studies point out', writes Yuval-Davis, 'not only black people are racially constructed, and feminists do remind men they too have a gender' (2015: 8).

The metaphor of the intersection

Kimberlé Crenshaw, when asked in an interview with the *New Statesman* why she used the metaphor of the intersection, explained: 'I wanted to come up with an everyday metaphor that anyone could use.'[4] That the metaphor of the intersection gained both cultural and political traction over other frameworks is testament to the success of Crenshaw's objective. As Collins and Bilge note, 'In the early twenty-first century, the term "intersectionality" has been widely taken up by scholars, policy advocates, practitioners, and activists in many places and locations' (2016: 1), as well as in international human rights discourses by agencies such as the UN (Carastathis 2014).

The simplicity of the metaphor can be seen as both its strength and its weakness. Its strength is that the metaphor of a traffic intersection is one that is visually, and conceptually, easy to grasp. It indicates that an individual is never located simply on the gender road, or the race road, or the class road, but at a crossroads where these roads collide. Our identities, social positionality and everyday experiences are thus informed by the ways in which multiple systems of oppression and privilege impact each other at this point of intersection. One is never simply black or female or working class; instead, our experiences of gender are always raced and classed. As Crenshaw notes, the roads into the point of intersection are multiple and not limited to race, class and gender but can include multiple other roads – our sexuality, our nationality, our geographical location, our religion, and so on.

However, the metaphor has come under criticism for being limited in its ability to capture the complexity and fluidity of the ways in which multiple systems of oppression constitute each other, and for being misleading in the picture it offers of the nature of our social categories. For example, Garry (2011) questions its ability to accommodate the ways in which axes of privilege and oppression work in conjunction with each other or the agency of individuals to resist oppressions; furthermore, she challenges the static picture that the metaphor of an intersection implies. She therefore shares a widely aired concern that the metaphor, in suggesting that racism, sexism, and other forms of oppression converge at an intersection, implies roads prior to the point at which the oppressions collide. Consequently, we can think about racism, sexism, class-based oppressions, heterosexism, dis-ablism, and so on, as existing separately as discrete systems of oppression prior to their interweaving. Thus, while the central tenet of intersectionality is to show the ways in which multiple systems of oppression do not work in isolation but always in conjunction with each other, the metaphor, as Carastathis also suggests, relies on the idea that the systems of oppression exist discretely prior to the point of mutual constitution, even if only theoretically. Much earlier, Anne McClintock makes the point in the following way: 'race, gender and class are not distinct realms of experience existing in splendid isolation from each other; nor can they be yoked together retrospectively like armatures of Lego. Rather they come into existence *in and through* relation to each other – if in contradictory and conflictual ways' (1995: 4–5). Paradoxically, the concept that allows us to move beyond additive models of single-axis oppressions also, at the same time, relies on the notion of discrete systems of oppression existing prior to their intersection. Carastathis (2008) points to the 'non-intersecting zones', the roads that lead up to the point of intersection, as problematic, as they presuppose that, prior to the point of intersection, race and class and gender pre-exist as distinct and separate categories, even if only in an abstract sense. She also highlights the question 'On the intersectional model, if the Black woman occupies the border, who takes residence – who is *at home* – in the non-intersecting zones?' This is additionally problematic, Carastathis argues, if, in using the example of the intersection of race and gender, it is the black woman who resides at the point of intersection. Then the non-intersecting race zone (the race road) is implicitly male and the non-intersecting gender zone (the gender road) is implicitly white.

There are serious problems with the intersectional picture. What constitutes a gendered axis of difference cannot be articulated independently of other positionalities, and no one can reside on these pure roads prior to their intersecting. Importantly, however, the intersection is put forward as a metaphor and not a model. We can pick up on some points of connection without requiring that all aspects of the metaphor be relevant. Yuval-Davis and Walby, among others, acknowledge that it is problematic if the metaphor suggests that our distinct social categories are fixed prior to any intersection rather than being given content by multiple intersections. Nonetheless, they wish to argue that *ontologically* it is in fact crucial to hold on to the ideas of racism, sexism and class-based oppressions as discrete systems which operate through each other, systems which we can theoretically abstract from their intersectional instantiations. Yuval-Davis (2015: 10) remarks: 'although in concrete situations the different social divisions constitute each other, they are irreducible to each other, each of them has a different ontological discourse of particular dynamics of power relations of exclusion and/or exploitation.' For her, the dimensions of power are irreducible to each other, but they work through each other to bring about results in the everyday lives of individuals.

Jasbir Puar (2012) raises a further issue of concern about the metaphor of interaction. She points to its lack of ability to deal with the fluidity and instability of categories and the ways in which they are in a constant process of reformation and change. She challenges the term for requiring fixed, static and retrospective categories. For Puar, categories are unstable and always in process, the point made by Butler with her insistence on the 'illiminable process of signification' (1990a: 143). Puar argues that the concept of intersectionality treats identities as objects to be analysed, 'presuming and producing static epistemological rendering of categories themselves across historical and geopolitical locations' (2012: 54). As a result, analyses of intersectionality that foreground experiences of women of colour serve only to reify their position as a marginal identity. Puar suggests that we should be looking to destabilize the category 'black women' or 'women of colour' instead of reinforcing it, as is the case in intersectionality theory. For her, and a group of broadly new materialist authors she references, 'the liminality of bodily matter cannot be captured by intersectional subject positioning .... bodies are unstable entities that cannot be seamlessly disaggregated into identity formations' (ibid.: 56).

Puar proposes that we replace the concept of the intersection with the concept of *assemblage*, derived from Deleuze and Guattari (1987). This notion stresses the complexity of change and process, which, she argues, intersectional theorists attempt to 'still and quell'. Categories such as race, gender and sexuality are considered as indicating vectors of continuing active encounters between bodies rather than entities or attributes of subjects. Using the notion of 'assemblage' stresses forces of becoming, of movement, what is beyond the here and now, rather than the picture of imposing a retrospective grid on the complexity of a social encounter.

Puar's intervention is important, but it may be possible to use theories of intersectionality without reification of the categories in the way she is suggesting. It is interesting that, in her account, the categories, though unstable, are not discarded. It is important to perceive intersectional positionalities always as positionalities in process, never fixed, their meaning always fluid. Nonetheless, to explain the social world and the inequalities therein, we need to capture moments in historical and spatial contexts where the intersections of vectors of inequality collide to produce particular and varied outcomes for different individuals/groups. Yuval-Davis is also conscious of how concepts of intersectionality can produce static accounts of social stratification – 'a snapshot of differential positionings' (2015: 24) – and stresses the 'complex, contested and constantly shifting' (ibid.: 25) nature of the categories and their interrelations. Ultimately we can read Puar as suggesting that we use/interpret intersectionality as assemblage. She quotes from Guattari regarding class, where he himself uses the term 'intersection' when outlining the problems of seeing class as a delimited sociological object: 'entities become hazy in the many interzones, the intersections .... The result is an indeterminacy that prevents the social field from being mapped out in a clear and distinct way' (Puar 2012: 59). To be alert to such matters is not necessarily to give up on any attempt at mapping. We need to use categories to highlight and oppose patterns of discrimination. The pre-discursive world does not dictate how we are to organize it discursively. Nonetheless, certain conceptualizing practices serve to make evident truths which we would miss without them. But recognizing that categories are open, without fixed reference, as well as mutually constituting, makes possible change and transformation.

Decolonial feminism

It has been widely recognized by writers on capitalist colonialism that the system brought dichotomous categories of gender, race and sexuality into colonized territories. Lugones, for example, emphasizes 'categorial, dichotomous, hierarchical logic as central to modern, colonial, capitalist thinking about race, gender, and sexuality' (Lugones 2010: 742). This had key consequences for the history of colonialism and for our understanding of gender and race. Indigenous populations did not conform to the norms of these imported categories and were not regarded as 'proper' men or women, and consequently as not fully human. Where sexual practices did not conform to a heterosexism requiring binary genders, they were also regarded as signs of degeneracy. The violence used against such populations was thus regarded as justified and was accompanied by ideological claims of a civilizing mission. 'In using the term *coloniality* I mean to name not just a classification of people in terms of the coloniality of power and gender but also the process of active reduction of people, the dehumanization that fits them for the classification, the process of subjectification, the attempt to turn the colonized into less than human beings' (ibid.: 745).

Decolonial writers have highlighted that, in many cases, the dichotomous categories of gender, sexuality and race cut across indigenous practices of classification with which they did not coincide. Oyeronke Oyewumi (1997) argues that, among the Yoruba, there was not a hierarchical and dichotomous gender system before colonization. And, 'among the Native American people, there were gynecocratic and equalitarian systems for organizing communities that were substituted by patriarchal and hierarchical systems when they were colonized' (Gonzalez-Arnal 2013: 45). Joseph Massad (2009) points out that the concept of sexuality informing the colonial project often did not coincide with local understandings, making us also currently question 'the development and adaptation of the terms *gay* or *lesbian* or the globalization of the term *queer*' (Puar 2012: 53).

This history leaves those living in, or having kinship ties to, countries emerging from a colonial legacy with a problematic relation to concepts of gender, race and sexuality. These concepts, as used within theoretical and academic discourse centring on Europe and the US, are still haunted by their colonial past and, according to Lugones (2007, 2010), still work with a colonial logic. It is not possible to resist this logic by returning to a more authentic pre-colonial past and the patterns of social life found there. For, as Pérez points out, 'There is no pure authentic original history. There are only stories, many stories' (1999: xv). Nonetheless, the echoes of alternative ways of thinking make a difference to the ways in which gendered concepts, or terms such as 'gay', 'queer' or 'trans', are employed and how they 'land', in Butler's term (2015: 5). There is a specificity to their use, an anchorage to locations in which, as highlighted by Lugones, multiple strands of sociability are *fused*.

> And thus I want to think of the colonized neither as simply imagined and constructed by the colonizer and coloniality in accordance with the colonial imagination and the strictures of the capitalist colonial venture, but as a being who begins to inhabit a fractured locus constructed doubly, perceiving doubly, relating doubly, where the sides of the locus are in tension, in conflict, and the conflict itself, its energy and moves, actively informs the subjectivity of the colonized self in multiple relation. ...
>
> As I mark the colonial translation from *chachawarmi* to man/woman, I am aware of the use of man and woman in everyday life in Bolivian communities, including in interracial discourse. The success of the complex gender norming introduced with colonization that goes into

the constitution of the coloniality of gender has turned this colonial translation into an everyday affair, but resistance to the coloniality of gender is also lived linguistically in the tension of the colonial wound. (Lugones 2010: 750)

For Lugones, the decolonial feminist's task begins by her seeing such difference. There are communalities and overlaps with the experiences of women elsewhere, but no universal structure of gendered oppression, for what it means to be a woman is not necessarily shared (Yuval-Davis 1996). What is needed, instead, is close attention to the perspectives and experiences of those in very specific locations (see also Yuval-Davis (2006, 2015) on 'situated intersectionality'). It is their material and social positions, negotiation of relations of power, and imaginary configurations that should be addressed and which decolonial writing is bringing to the fore.

Decolonial feminism and intersectionality

The anti-essentialism of these writings informs the anti-essentialism of this book. But how does it relate to the issues of intersectionality addressed in this chapter? Clearly, in both bodies of work there is a rejection of a universal definition of terms of gendered or sexed identity or a universal account of the workings of patriarchy, capitalism, colonialism, racism ++. For these theorists share a recognition that such terms are inter-articulated and structures are interlocked. However, some decolonial theorists, most notably Lugones, claim that intersectional analysis itself requires a disentangling of the strands of oppression which returns us to a 'purity' of categories (see discussion above) that cannot be pruned of their colonial heritage. It is impossible, she argues, to unpick vectors of oppression and apply universal theories of raced or gendered oppression to them, for this 'does not allow us to perceive oppressions as mixed and melted' (2005: 69–70).

A separate but connected strand of criticism claims that intersectional writings, in listing factors which mediate the operation of the categories they address, pay insufficient attention to nationality, the inherited legacy of colonialism or the consequences of movements of peoples across national boundaries.[5] Instead there is a focus on gender and race as manifest in a European and North American context.

The category 'nation' therefore appears to be the least theorized and acknowledged of intersectional categories, transmitted through a form of globalizing transparency. The United States is reproduced as the dominant site of feminist inquiry through the use of intersectionality as a heuristic to teach difference. Thus, the Euro-American bias of women's studies and history of feminism is ironically reiterated via intersectionality, eliding the main intervention of transnational and postcolonial feminist scholars since the 1990s, which has been, in part, about destabilizing the nation-centered production of the category WOC. (Kaplan and Grewal 1994: 55)

It is quite clear in the light of these critiques that the legacy of colonialism, the complex workings of national identity, and the consequences of migration are central both to individual subjectivities (of which more below) and to the interlocked objective material and cultural structures in which we find ourselves living. Moreover, these factors bear not only on geographical locations which suffered colonialism but also on those states from which colonialism originated, many of which are significantly constituted by migrant communities.

What remains in contention between intersectional theorists and at least some decolonial ones is whether it is necessary to unravel different strands in the workings of power to make evident patterns of oppression. We have followed intersectional theorists in requiring such a focus. Indeed, this book is telling a story about gender and trying to refrain from telling much more of a story about the wider complexity of the operations of power. We need a focus on gender, for example, to detect patterns of sexual violence and trafficking among migrant women (Pillai 2001; Menjívar and Salcido 2002; Anitha 2010; Madill and Alsop 2019); to highlight the consequences of the workings of machismo (Peña 1991); to uncover the specific effects of the workings of transnational capitalism on the health of women working in clothing factories or the construction industries (Hennessy 1997; Cuban 2013); or, more positively, to reveal practices of living within an environment which protects sustainability (Baskin 2017; Vashistha 2018).

In this context, we need to reflect how we might use categories within the intersectional framework. McCall identifies three approaches: anti-categorical complexity, intercategorical complexity and intra-categorical complexity. Anti-categorical approaches caution against the use of categories (such as woman/black woman/black disabled woman) because 'social life is considered too irreducibly complex ... to make fixed categories anything but simplifying social inequalities that produce inequalities in the process of producing differences' (McCall 2005: 1773). The criticisms from Lugones may seem to suggest this. An intercategorical approach is one in which the categories are used strategically with an acknowledgement that they are themselves productive of the inequalities they are used to describe but are nonetheless useful and necessary to capture a picture of the social world in which we live. We use the categories but anxiously attend to context. The first section of this chapter looking at intersectional structural inequalities is premised on an intercategorical approach. The third approach – the intra-categorical – 'tends to focus on particular social groups at neglected points of intersection' (ibid.: 1774). The work of Kimberlé Crenshaw (1989) on women of colour in US employment law, for example, displays an intra-categorical approach.

This also seems a possible response to decolonial writings, which are themselves insisting on just the specificity this requires. Gonzalez-Arnal argues that, while Lugones makes a radical criticism of the use of categories, her analysis follows intra-categorial logic, at least partly, favouring contextualization of the categories and allowing their complexity to be reflected in the analysis (Gonzalez-Arnal 2013: 20). Lugones herself says: 'As I move methodologically from Women of Color feminisms to a decolonial feminism, I think about feminism from and at the grassroots, and from and at the colonial difference, with a strong emphasis on ground, on a historicized incarnate inter-subjectivity' (Lugones 2010: 746).

Can we use gendered categories without a colonial logic? We have noted above the instability of our categories and their openness to resignification. However, we also know that our present uses are always haunted by past ones. They are also breathing in an *elsewhere and otherwise* to which these decolonial writings are drawing our attention.

Intersectionality and subjectivity

Much of our discussion thus far has focused on intersectionality as a feature of structural social inequalities of power, the intersecting of different systems of oppression. Crenshaw's analysis focuses, in the main, on intersectionality at the level of structure. Although she was concerned, ultimately, about the impact on the individual, this was in terms of access to power and justice. Likewise, while offering a structural, historical materialist conceptualization of intersectionality, Collins recognizes three levels of domination: at the individual level, at the level of community and at the 'systemic level of social institutions' (1990: 227).

It is, however, important to think further about intersectionality at the level of subjectivity and how it reveals itself in our everyday sense of ourselves. One way of discussing this matter is to point out that we all have intersectional identities. We are gendered, have sexual preferences, are raced, classed, and positioned on the ability/disability axes in a particular national and cultural location. Addressing this question in terms of identity leads to a consideration as to which of these dimensions are most important to our identity and whether these might change over time. But talking about this in terms of identities may also make too strong a demand on the elements which together constitute our subjectivity, the importance of which may shift and reassemble in different times and contexts. Identity talk can suggest an essentialism which we want to avoid, as we think of intersectionality as a way of making sense of ourselves. In this context, we may have different answers to the 'etc. problem' than that articulated above. For, although our subjective sense of self reflects the public structural relations in which we are placed, it is also consequent on our individual histories. The aspect of our complex positionality that is most salient to our sense of self is not something which can necessarily be predicted from our objective positioning. Attending to subjectivity also brings different considerations into play when we are considering the interrelations of the categories in play. As McWhorter (2004: 38 n1) points out, although various systems of oppression can be regarded as separately articulable structures which interlock, nonetheless 'they cannot be separated in the *lived experience* of hyper-oppressed subjects; that is, that "race, sex, and class are 'simultaneous factors'" in the lived experience of oppression' (emphasis added).

It is at the level of lived subjectivity that the fusion which informs Lugones's decolonial writings becomes most telling. It is where components are 'mixed and melted' and cannot be disentangled. What seems necessary, in place of claims about which aspects of our identity are most authentic, is the telling of stories which allow complexities to surface. In *Parting Ways: Jewishness and the Critique of*

Zionism (2012), Butler re-examines the character of identity, specifically Jewishness, through the prism of diaspora, dispossession and cohabitation. The term 'intersectionality' may not be a particularly happy one to capture such complexity. As we have noted above, it suggests different roads that meet, each road separately identifiable but making something more when meeting. But this is not how being of mixed heritage works – for example, in one of our cases, having an English mother and an Irish father and having been brought up in an Irish community in England. It is not possible to disentangle the English components shared with other English people and the Irish components shared with other Irish ones. Each becomes inter-implicated in the manifestation of the other. The hybridity that results bears traces of identities to which it is impossible to lay claim.

Sara Ahmed talks about her experiences of having a white English mother and a father from Pakistan and being brought up for part of her life in Australia. For her, a mixed heritage orientates us in different directions, establishing certain lines of connection, but what we must reject is any sense that the hybridity is the mixing of pure lines which we can then see as simply conjoined (Ahmed 2006: 145). According to Ahmed, such mixing gives different orientations to the whiteness and blackness, neither of which is fully claimed (ibid.: 147).

We have stressed above how the movements of peoples, which characterizes our times, has rendered inadequate nationalist, cultural and gendered categories. In the writing of Gloria Anzaldúa we have the image of the borderlands and of a *mestiza* consciousness which explores notions of subjectivity without discrete categories: 'the new *mestiza* copes by developing a tolerance for contradictions, a tolerance for ambiguity. She learns to be an Indian in Mexican culture, to be Mexican from an Anglo point of view. She learns to juggle cultures. ... Not only does she sustain contradictions, she turns the ambivalence into something else' (1987: 79). The *mestiza* consciousness which Anzaldúa is articulating is an attempt to make sense of a specific history. She was raised in the Rio Grande valley on the US–Mexican border, where indigenous Indian, Spanish, European-American and African-American peoples have produced a *mestiza* culture that is a product of this precise location. But Anzaldúa also uses the notion of *mestiza* consciousness as a metaphorical exploration of the nature of the subjectivity of us all.

Kath Weston suggests that in the face of such complexity storytelling is a means to grasp the multiple entanglements of lived experience:

> Could it be that stories do a better job than geometric models of conveying how race, class, gender, sexuality, and the like come alive? Embedded in stories are particular renditions of gender that are already raced and classed, renditions that show people in action, chasing down the curveballs that identity throws their way. The moral of the stories? Gender may assume a million shapes, but it is never just gender ...
>
> So far, class, ethnicity, sexuality, and the like have shown up primarily in the guise of identities. But these integral aspects of ... people ... are not only about identity. Sometimes they don't come close to anything coherent enough to make you say, 'I'm this' or 'I'm that'; nothing you would print out as a label and stick on your back. Yet that doesn't make them irrelevant to [the self]. (2010: 15, 32)

Yet Weston also points out that 'identities may be inseparable but ... specific identities come to the fore at specific times' (ibid.: 16). Similarly, Nash argues that we need to explain or describe 'the process and mechanisms by which subjects mobilize (or choose not to mobilize) particular aspects of their identities in particular circumstances' (2008: 11). It is not simply a matter of choice, but, depending on the situation, certain aspects of our identity are rendered more salient. For example, when Sara Ahmed travels through immigration in the US, her Pakistani Muslim heritage, as perceived through her surname by the customs official, comes to the fore: 'The name "Ahmed", a Muslim name, slows me down. It blocks my passage, even if only temporarily. I get stuck, and then move on' (2006: 162). Weston quotes a friend: 'If I went to Japan, I became more Japanese. If I was here, I was more comfortable in certain ways, but in certain situations I knew I had to shift into something else. It's like shifting gears all the time. [Here] the whole question of being a lesbian was just so much easier, compared with what I had to grow up with' (2010: 19). These shifts in our sense of self are often accompanied by shifts in our political mobilizations.

Conclusions

In this chapter, we have explored and endorsed the theoretical importance of intersectionality to any theorizing concerning gender and other dimensions of social positionality marked by relations of power. The theoretical stance which the term captures, concerning the necessary interwovenness of systems of power and privilege and the inter-articulation of our categories of social identification, has a long history, particularly in black feminist thought, but also in other theories of gender, race, class, (dis)ability and sexuality. It is central not only to looking at the objective workings of power but also in theorizing our subjective sense of self. We have explored the relation of this term to the theories of categorization found in decolonial writings. These themselves foreground a critique of essentialism (a mark of such intersectional claims), and highlighted the key role of colonialism in the history of the categorizations involved. Although there are tensions between parts of decolonial theory and some intersectional voices, our approach here has been informed by both strands of thought, and we tentatively suggest a way forward which can address the key concerns of both.

6 Judith Butler: Performativity, Precariousness and Queering

> Gender is the repeated stylization of the body, a set of repeated acts within a highly regulatory framework that congeal over time to produce the appearance of a substance. (Butler 1990a: 33)

From the 1990s onwards, the work of Judith Butler has come to occupy a central position in gender theory. In her *performative* theory of gender, she draws attention to the way mundane and everyday practices, both linguistic and other, are productive of the meaning of what it is to be a man or a woman and thereby productive of gendered selves. The nature and importance of such performativity became widely discussed with the publication of *Gender Trouble* in 1990 and has since been employed to explore not only the categories of gender but other dimensions of social difference (Tate 2005; Garland-Thomson 1997; Ahmed 2006). Butler herself has continued to develop her exploration of the emergence of subjectivity, the sedimentation of social categories and the possibilities for disrupting oppressive social norms (1993, 1997a, 1997b, 2004b, 2015). She increasingly does so in a context in which she stresses the precariousness of our existence. Such a notion highlights our vulnerability to the gaze of particular and generalized others and the public practices of naming on which we are dependent for the emergence of our own subjectivity and sense of self. Without such recognition from others we become unintelligible to them and to ourselves. Nonetheless, such identifications, and the categories in terms of which they are made, are inherently unstable, themselves precarious. It is impossible to inhabit fully the categories with which we are addressed, so our subjectivity is always incomplete, always in process. Moreover, the different practices of naming to which we are subjected, as people who are gendered, raced, classed, aged and carrying marks of our sexualities or abilities, and so on, mean that each category is 'translated' in terms of the other in just the ways discussed in the previous chapter. Given that many of the practices of social naming have oppressive consequences and render as socially unintelligible those lives which cannot easily be contained within their legitimating norms, Butler's goal in *Gender Trouble*, she explains (Ahmed 2016), was to exploit the instability of our categories, to disrupt them with signs of difference, to allow the recognition of gender (and other) complexity. Consequently, queer and trans lives would no longer be pathologized, and ways of living together, parenting and kinship could be reimagined outside the straightjacket of the heterosexual family.

Butler's strategy therefore is to destabilize and denaturalize our binary gender categories. For her, gender differentiation is an effect of *contingent* social practices. As they are contingent and not necessary, the possibility is opened up that they could be remade in different ways.

Performance and performativity

For Butler, the identifications of selves as male and female becomes constituted out of the performative acts of ourselves and others. Our gendered identifications derive not from bodily difference but from the attachment of the categories of male and female to bodies, and the consequent adoption of patterns of behaviour, which are normatively linked to those categories. A baby is born and the midwife says 'It's a girl'. She is not reporting an already determinate state of affairs but taking part in a practice which itself makes up that state of affairs. Following this declaration, the baby is wrapped in pink, held in a way that is different from the holding of boys, given cards, clothes, toys, hugs and reprimands, all of which are gender differentiated and gender differentiating. It is by a repetition of numerous acts of this kind that what it is to be male or female in our society becomes formed. The deeds or performances which serve to constitute our identities as gendered subjects range across the whole gamut of behaviours, decisions, desires and 'corporeal styles' which we associate with being male or female: playing with dolls or trucks, curling up in bed with cuddly toys, reading pony books, being immersed in car magazines, cooking meals, doing hair, enjoying nights out with the girls or the lads. Even when toys such as Lego are viewed as available for boys and girls, they are produced in different colours and in distinctly themed packs. Such practices vary according to the other categories which are being performatively enacted simultaneously with gender. Interwoven with Catholic religious practices, girls may belong to the Children of Mary, boys to the St Vincent de Paul Society, leading ultimately to only boys being allowed to be priests. In Muslim communities, girls may wear the hijab and have different access to the mosque to boys. In Sikh or Orthodox Jewish communities, boys/girls or men/women have different rules regarding hair and headcovering and roles in religious ceremonies. For Butler, it is not that there exists an originary difference between men and women to which we then attach distinct social roles. Rather, such everyday practices are what *make* such differences. They both institute and maintain our binary gendered categories.

Gendered scripts

The gendered performances in which we engage, Butler claims, are performances in accordance with a script. This script derives from ideal images of masculinity and femininity pervasive within society. These are imaginary and unachievable, but nonetheless they form the reference points in relation to which we act. They provide us with a framework of *norms* which render certain behaviours appropriate and others not, and within which we must operate if we are to be recognizably men and women. What counts as a performance of masculinity or femininity is highly contextual, and the operative norms can be very variable socially and historically and for one person over the course of their lives. In *Gender Trouble* Butler stresses, particularly, the way that gender norms are interdefined with norms of heterosexuality, so that, commonly, a proper man and a proper woman are those who engage in heterosexual practices and follow the pathway of the heterosexual family. But she also stresses that gendered norms are inter-articulated with norms of race, class, culture, age and bodily ability, so that we cannot simply isolate out what the norms of gender will be (as we made clear in our discussion in the previous chapter).

This process is messy. Lisa Käll points out: 'The unreflective process of habituation is not to be understood in the sense that we necessarily incorporate and favor habitual modes of being in seamless and uncomplicated ways. Quite to the contrary, unreflectively habituated norms and modes of being may well be, and often are, incorporated in conflicting ways, filled with tensions and different forms of disidentification and rejection' (2015: 35). This is why, even when living with shared norms, we perform our genders so differently. We may identify with or reject our mothers, for example, idolize or make a point of distancing ourselves from some public icon. Whether accepting or resisting the norms of the situation in which we are placed, they nonetheless form the context in reference to which we performatively constitute ourselves.

Käll makes her point in an article spelling out Butler's indebtedness to the phenomenological tradition, which we discussed in chapter 4. Performativity is a development of the account of sedimented bodily habits which we find in Merleau-Ponty ([1945] 1999) and which Beauvoir ([1949] 2010), in her discussion of everyday habits, put to important use in her description of the way in which we *become* women. Butler's account of the way in which social norms become incorporated as bodily practices also has parallels with the discussion of bodily *habitus* which we find in Bourdieu (1977, 1990), whose parallels with Beauvoir we have highlighted. Butler acknowledges her indebtedness in an earlier article on phenomenology, pointing out that it 'seeks to explain the mundane way in which social agents constitute social reality through language, gesture, and all manner of symbolic social signs' (Butler 1988: 519), and she points out that this apparatus is put to work by Beauvoir to show how 'bodies get crafted into genders' (ibid.: 525). She refers several times in the discussion in *Gender Trouble* to Beauvoir's claim that one is not born but rather *becomes* a woman, positioning her own work as a further exploration of that claim and signalling that it applies not only to individual becomings but also to the category of woman itself: 'If there is something right in Beauvoir's claim that one is not born, but rather *becomes* a woman, it follows that *woman* itself is a term in process, ... a constructing that cannot rightfully be said to originate or to end. As an ongoing discursive practice, it is open to intervention and resignification' (Butler 1990a: 33).

Subjectivity and subjectification

Butler, however, distances herself from Beauvoir and phenomenology in relation to the status of the subjects who adopt the bodily habits prescribed for them: 'Beauvoir ... implied ... an agent ... who somehow takes on or appropriates that gender' (1990a: 8). For Butler, this gives an ontological priority to a subject that exists and then internalizes social norms for her. A subject comes into being only as a consequence of its social positioning. We need others to position us in a cultural world so that we can have a sense of that world and of ourselves in relation to it. We develop a sense of self in response to the call 'interpellation' (1993: 121) of others.[1] We respond to their naming practices, which locate us within social categories and practices of interaction: 'this creature ... is affected by something outside of itself ... that activates and informs the subject that I am ... I am already affected before I can say "I" and ... I have to be affected to say "I" at all' (2015: 1–2).

Butler's writings here are located within a post-structuralist framework in which subjects come into being via subjection to social norms. Within these accounts the emergence of subjectivity is a process of subjectification – the making of ourselves by becoming subject to the norms which are implicit in the discourses that provide our self-understandings. Butler claims, following Foucault (1978), that 'the subject is produced through norms or by discourse more generally' (2015: 5). We mould our bodies and bend our behaviour in accordance with the 'men', 'women', 'gay' or 'straight', 'Irish' or 'Jamaican', 'able' or 'disabled', 'young' or 'old', people we take ourselves to be – but are, in fact, turning ourselves into. These discourses are not reflections of an already ordered reality; instead they are that with which reality becomes ordered. They are the means by which differences, for example between people, become produced. Discourses carry with them norms for behaviour, standards of what counts as desirable and undesirable, proper and improper. With the categories 'homosexual' and 'heterosexual' come the standards of what counts as normal sexuality and what is deviant. These are linked to other discourses concerning what constitutes a family, the position of men and women within it and the appropriate sexual behaviour for men and women. 'A norm', Butler says, 'may be said to precede us, to circulate in the world before it touches upon us ... [but] when it does make a landing it acts ... in different ways, ... in multiple and sometimes contradictory ways. ... They condition and form us, and yet they are hardly finished with that work once we start to emerge as thinking and speaking beings' (2015: 5). Here, Butler can also be seen to be engaging with the ideas of Lacan, whose work we discussed in chapter 2, for the norms which we attempt to enact are very like the Law which forms the contours of Lacan's symbolic order. Unlike Lacan, and like Foucault, however, Butler argues that the scripts can be variable and can change over time.

For Butler, gendered performances are tied up with relations of power. She shares with Foucault a conception of power which is all-pervasive, present in our everyday interactions as well as in institutional frameworks. Although there are a variety of ways in which gender can be performed, there remain certain *dominant* ideals which reinforce the power of certain groups over others. These others are treated socially as outsiders, 'the abject', and subject to social punishments. Here, Butler refers to Beauvoir's discussion of the position of women as culturally 'Other', 'outside of the universalising norms of personhood' (1990a: 11), which are male. She also cites approvingly Beauvoir's recognition that women are not the only social group for which such othering occurs. Discourses facilitate this practice of 'othering', so that positions of dominance create norms which require deviant 'others' to define themselves against: whiteness against blackness, heterosexuality against homosexuality, long-term inhabitants against immigrants, hard workers against benefit scroungers. These subordinated positionalities for both Butler and Foucault provide opportunities for resistance and for destabilization of their modes of characterization, as well as a basis for organizational groupings which can challenge the dominance of the most powerful groups.

Real genders

'Gender', says Butler, 'is a kind of persistent impersonation that passes as the real' (1990a: 14). The effect of the range of gendered performances is to make it appear that there are two distinct natures, male and female. But what we take to be 'nature' is an effect rather than a cause of our gendered acts. Butler's goal here is to show as illusory the apparent essential unity of biological sex, gender identification and heterosexuality. This is a unity which some have seen as dictated by nature (see chapter 1). If we can show that such a unity is illusory, what Butler often calls phantasmatic, then the path is cleared for reconfigurations of each of the terms. As we saw in chapter 1, Butler no more accepts sex as a biological given than gender itself: 'There is no recourse to a body that has not already been interpreted by cultural meanings, hence sex could not qualify as a prediscursive anatomical facticity' (ibid.: 8). Our understanding of material, anatomical differences is mediated through our cultural frame of meaning. Rather than gender following from biology, for Butler, our gender norms are seen as structuring our understanding of our biology.[2]

The notion of performance invokes the actor on the stage.[3] This might suggest a distinction between an identity that is, in some sense, a pretence and everyday identities that are real. But for Butler there is no such distinction; performance gives as much reality as selves contain. She points out that, if we accept that becoming gendered is a social process that is not dictated by bodily shape, then there is nothing to guarantee that the body of the one who becomes woman will necessarily be what is normally conceived of as a female body. The discussion of drag performance then becomes pivotal to her account. Drag is viewed as a parodic or exaggerated form of gender enactment, by means of which originary or authentic gender identity is exposed as itself an effect of performance. In a drag performance the apparently natural packaging of biology and gender is pulled apart. The audience, aware that it is watching a body with a certain anatomy, watches as a gendered identity is produced that is, according to regulatory gender norms, at variance with it. Then, Butler suggests, we recognize that everyday gender is just such a performance.

In *Bodies that Matter* (1993), Butler discusses Jenny Livingston's film *Paris is Burning* (1990), a documentary about drag balls in New York City attended by primarily Latino and some African-American participants in the trans community:

> The balls are contests in which the contestants compete under a variety of categories. The categories include a variety of social norms, many of which are established in white culture as signs of class, like that of the 'executive' and the Ivy League student; some of which are marked as feminine, ranging from high drag to butch queen; and some of them, like that of the 'bangie', are taken from straight black masculine street culture. [In each category the winner is the person who is most real in their class.] ... realness is the ability to compel belief, to produce the naturalized effect. This effect is itself the result of an embodiment of norms, an impersonation of a racial and class norm ... [an] ideal that remains the standard which regulates the performance, but which no performance fully approximates. (1993: 129)

What the film evidences for Butler is that the categories we attach to certain biological shapes have no necessary relation to them, so 'these variable body surfaces ... may ... become sites of transfer for properties that no longer belong properly to any anatomy' (1993: 64). The 'realness' of the performances in these contests is not in contrast to the realness of everyday raced, classed or gendered identities. It is, rather, the fact that the realness of everyday social categories is also constituted out of just the same ability to compel belief as a result of the embodiment of norms. There is nothing more to it than that. The contests involve an attempt to reach realness but actually serve to show that such realness is itself only a phantasmatic ideal. The only difference between the gender of those at the balls and others is that, in some cases, the contestants fail to embody the norm which requires a certain alignment between anatomical shape and gendered performance. Attention to the contests and categories within the film *Paris is Burning* also serves to highlight an important strength in Butler's account. The categories which inform the contest are not simply gendered categories. In each case gender is inter-articulated with race and class. The different categories therefore provide quite different performances of gender. Venus Xtravaganza, one of the participants, aspires to be 'a rich white girl'. Here the desire for a certain gender is a desire to be rescued from poverty, racism and homophobia. In this we cannot identify gender as in any way more fundamental than the whiteness and the richness to which gender is hoped to provide the route.

Precariousness

There is a political urgency to Butler's writing in *Gender Trouble* (and later). She is concerned to stress the vulnerability of those who fail to conform to social norms and to provide an account which, as noted above, removes the pathologizing gaze attached to such lives. During the making of the film discussed above, Venus, who could pass as a light-skinned woman and was working as a sex worker to pay for an operation to change her body, is murdered. For Butler, 'her life is taken presumably by a client who, upon the discovery of her "little secret", mutilates her for having seduced him' (1993: 128).

The vulnerability to social punishments and the threats of violence attach particularly to those who fail to conform to social norms. But Butler, in her later work, stresses the vulnerability and precariousness of everyone's subjectivity, formed as it is by public systems of meaning which are themselves precarious and criss-crossed by differences. We are affected by the outside, the social and familial bonds, which enable us to assume subjectivity and agency but are also injurious to us in closing down possibilities for our ways of being. 'I am affected not just by this one other or a set of others, but by a world in which humans, institutions, and organic and inorganic processes all impress themselves upon this me who is, at the outset, susceptible in ways that are radically involuntary' (2015: 6–7). This forming of ourselves is not done once but is a continuous process, intertwining both passivity and activity: 'The task is to think of being acted on and acting as simultaneous ... given over to a world in which one is formed even as one acts to bring something new into being. ... At the same time, nothing determines me ... I am not formed once and definitively .... I am still being formed as I form myself' (2015: 6).

What makes us particularly susceptible to others is our need for *recognition* by others. This notion has been central to the work of Judith Butler for many years (as well as to that of Honneth 1995, Fraser 2000 and McNay 2008) and also informed the existentialists and phenomenologists (see discussion in chapter 4). It originates in Hegel (1977). For Hegel and, in differing ways, these other writers, a self, to survive, requires recognition by another self or other selves. Without recognition from others we cannot recognize ourselves, or, in a more complex way, it is only in negotiation with others that our sense of self can emerge.

What does such recognition involve? It involves communities whose norms do not constitute us as the outsider, so that others both *notice* the distinct mode of being in the world which is central to our sense of ourselves and find that mode of being legitimate and valuable. They acknowledge and respect us. Such recognition relates to institutional, social and particular intersubjective relations. Institutional recognition rules out discriminatory practices and the facilitating of activities which are central to distinct modes of being in the world. Individual recognition requires noticing, acknowledging, respecting and including people in our everyday patterns of social interaction. People hurtle away from familial and familiar places to find ones where such recognition might be possible. Gloria Anzaldúa describes her home as unable to tolerate her lesbianism and her refusal to conform to the range of possibilities on offer to women: 'to this day I'm not sure where I found the strength to leave the source, the mother, disengage from my family, *mi terra, mi gente*, and all that picture stood for. I had to leave home so I could find myself' (Anzaldúa 1987: 16). Without such recognition, Butler suggests, life becomes unliveable (Butler 2004a; Lennon 2006), for we are not able to find our feet in the everyday practices of the varied communities in which we are placed. We will return to the question of recognition in the following chapter.

Queering

There is another strand of precariousness to which Butler draws attention, which opens up the theoretical space to explain how something that may, at one point, be unrecognizable can become woven into communal understanding (see discussion of 'the pregnant man' in chapter 7). Such possibilities derive from the precariousness of the categories themselves. Drawing on post-structuralist theories of meaning, within which Derrida (1978) is the central figure, Butler demonstrates the lack of fixity in our gendered terms. Central to post-structuralist views is the temporal dimension of meaning: the meaning of a word is dependent on a temporal history of usages. Whenever we use a term, according to Derrida, we are engaged in an act of citation. We are repeating a term, echoing its previous usages. This repeatability, termed *iterability*, makes the meanings of terms 'fluid, unstable and difficult to control' (Butler and Weed 2011: 163). For, although we can repeat the term, we do so in different contexts and circumstances, and these affect the meaning that is to be derived from it, rendering it indeterminate and not always predictable. (We use the term 'being alive', echoing its characterization of active, fit young humans and animals, but also for unconscious bodies maintained by technology, and for ancient and vulnerable trees, and perhaps for single-cell organisms and, contentiously, for groups of cells which have the potential to become organisms.)

Butler exploits this post-structuralist account of language in describing the operation of gender norms: 'The action of gender requires a performance that is repeated. This repetition is at once a reenactment and reexperiencing of a set of meanings already socially established' (Butler 1990a: 140). But these repetitions are never completely stable: 'let us remember that reiterations are never simply replicas of the same' (Butler 1993: 226). Butler stresses the subversive possibilities of citation. In different contexts and times, a repetition can take on a meaning which undermines or subverts the dominant norms. This openness of terms is central to Butler's understanding of gender and to the politics which accompanies her account. She stresses that our concepts are susceptible to change: for example, the norm which says that to be male or female we require certain body shapes can shift, so that bodies without penises can become recognizable as male. If we repeat performances in different contexts, then our categories can be subverted and new ways of both thinking and being emerge.

This process of destabilization and subversion of categories is what has become known as *queering*; and Butler is the acknowledged 'queen of queer'. Queer theory, as concerned with such processes, has thus travelled from being exclusively the domain of the theorizing of non-normative sexuality to include practices of destabilization across all categories of identity. Moreover, such queer theory, in some instances, sits uncomfortably with gay and lesbian identity politics, which reinscribe distinct categories of sexual identity (see the discussion in chapter 7). The year 1990, when *Gender Trouble* was published, was the year that Queer Nation came to public attention in the United States. Groups such as Queer Nation and Act Up (the AIDS Coalition to Unleash Power) engaged in a public and theatrical challenge to gender norms. Such groups were dissatisfied with the kind of identity politics associated with the lesbian and gay and feminist movements. For these activists, differences disrupt the coherence of all identity categories. Therefore we cannot establish firm boundaries between different groups of people. Queer Nation embraced many communities of sexual dissidents and those refusing to identify themselves by any of the available labels. They reappropriated the term 'queer' as the banner under which such *dishomogeneity* and *difference* could be claimed. The term 'queer' had been a hate word in everyday speech that had been used as a derogatory term for homosexual people. Its contemporary use within political activism, and consequently academic theory, is therefore a conscious reclaiming and resignification of the term to put it to use in a positive and productive way.

As we have pointed out above, heterosexuality occupies pride of place within the norms that govern our everyday notions of femininity and masculinity. The public visibility of gay and lesbian desire serves to undermine the supposed naturalness of heterosexual gender. For those activists reappropriating the concept 'queer', however, more is required than to make visible same-sex desire, for much gay and lesbian theorizing excluded the experiences of numbers of people who equally failed to fit within the dominant norms of heterosexuality (for example bisexual or trans people, or those who defined their sexuality in terms of practices rather than the sex of their partner). Queer theorists therefore argued for the breaking down of both sexual and gender categories, the maintenance of which creates boundaries which need to be policed. The debates historically and currently within feminist and lesbian movements concerning whether trans women are 'really' women (see introduction), and within 1990s gay and lesbian conferences concerning whether bisexual people were gay or straight, were examples of such policing in operation. Queer politics therefore works to visibly challenge norms, to show their lack of naturalness and inevitability, and to celebrate transgressions from them. This can take multiple forms: ostentatious displays of same-sex desire; disorientating juxtapositions of supposedly distinct masculine and feminine characteristics (macho men in tutus); or, less obviously, everyday acts of resistance, in which we fail to follow the expected pathways for bodies categorized as ours. The goal is to open up possibilities which our dominant discourses on sex and gender foreclose and which have also been missing from gay and lesbian and feminist movements concerned to delimit their boundaries.

Butler provides the theoretical space for just the kind of destabilizing and resignifying of our categories which queer activists have been pursuing. She uses two central examples in *Gender Trouble* of the process of queering. One is a discussion of the operation of butch/femme roles within the context of lesbian sexual practice. These roles, she argues, cannot be understood as simple repetitions of heterosexual stereotypes. Rather, the repetition and playful use of such roles within the framework of gay and lesbian sexuality serves to highlight the constructed nature of the heterosexual original: 'lesbian femmes may recall the heterosexual scene, as it were, but also displace it at the same time. In both butch and femme identities, the very notion of an original or natural identity is put into question' (1990a: 123). Butler's second example is the operation of drag, discussed above. But she also recognizes the ambivalence of the performances that drag involves. Many drag performances can involve a process of 'reidealizing' gender norms and reconsolidating them. And such *unpredictability* regarding the outcomes of practices designed to destabilize is found across all the categories we may attempt to queer.

The performativity of race

Butler's theoretical framework, which we have articulated above, has been put to work to understand not only the way gendered subjectivities are differentially produced and modified but also how other aspects of our social positionality are brought into being. In her work *Black Skins, Black Masks*, Shirley Tate explores how 'Blackness as a category is constantly recouped, transformed and reformed' (2005: 2). She quotes, with approval, Butler's remarks concerning 'the reiterative power of discourse to produce the phenomena that it regulates and constrains' (Butler 1993: 2). In her exploration of the experiences of 'light-skinned' black women, Tate shows how the public category of blackness is claimed to form and make sense of subjective positionality. But she also shows how it is reformed and remade in that claiming. Tate concentrates in her research on the everyday talk and practices of a group of women with whom she observes and interacts, and whom she also interviews. The women perform their blackness in language and everyday practices, while also challenging and reforming what it means to be black by means of them, in a double movement of being both constituted and constituting (Tate 2005: 8). As the women are light-skinned, and therefore need to ensure that others recognize their blackness, they are often especially scrupulous about espousing certain political positions, adopting cultural practices around food and clothing, making evident kinship relations and stressing their links to a history of slavery and exploitation. For example, Laura sees her African wraps as a way of manifesting her cultural identity (ibid.: 38). Sandra shifts from listening to punk to listening to soul music (ibid.: 44–5). These practices link them performatively to the black communities within which they wish to position themselves. Tate comments that there is 'a performative discourse which produces an *always already* about what a Black woman's identity is' (ibid.: 32). This discourse, in which the womanliness and the blackness are inter-articulated, is that in terms of which the women lay claim to their identities.

Nonetheless, the women who form the basis of Tate's study have kinship relations to both black and white communities and, in performatively claiming black female subjectivity, are also destabilizing an essentialist account of it. What these women are claiming is the possibility of being black women *otherwise* than in relation to a norm in which the blacker the skin the more authentic the identity. 'This happens as speakers narrate their Black womanliness as the product of dis-identification with a politics of skin' (Tate 2005: 12), a politics which within the black community has become 'a fetish which exerts its own governmentality' (ibid.: 147). Here, the performance of normatively black practices from the bodies of those with light skin can 'queer' and thereby destabilize the norms that constitute the fetish concerned. What is clear in Tate's work is both the necessity of the category of 'black woman' to the emergence of the subjectivities concerned and the impossibility of fully inhabiting the categories by which such subjectivity is enabled. In her later work *Black Beauty: Aesthetics, Stylization, Politics* (2009), Tate explores how the aesthetic practices of some young black women, for example dying their hair blond, shifts the meaning of such practices within both black and white communities.

While utilizing Butler's framework to articulate the making of raced identity, Tate nonetheless differs from her in the stress that she puts on two things, both of which have been identified as problematic in Butler's early work. Firstly, Tate stresses the importance and significance to the women she is discussing of their claimed identity as black women, a location without which they cannot speak and which, while its content is renegotiated, they are nonetheless not concerned to surpass. Secondly, such an identification is anchored in a sense of embodiment, the characteristics of which matter to almost everything that happens to them in their lives. We will discuss each in turn.

The critique of identity

One consequence of Butler's theoretical position is that political action is directed at the destabilizing of the binary gendered and sexual categories of 'man' and 'woman', 'gay' and 'straight'. The goal of such destabilization is to make visible that neither gender nor sex is a natural category – indeed, that the very idea of a 'natural' category is simply an effect of discourse. But the effect of such destabilization is often seen as being the rejection of such categories altogether (see our discussion of this issue in chapter 5). Such a conception of politics seems to put queer theory in tension with the political strategies of many activists within both feminist, gay and lesbian movements and anti-racist groups. Such activism appears to be based on shared identities and interests, often as a consequence of discriminatory practices directed at perceived members of the group, and works to remove the outsider status of these groupings and the discriminatory practices that rest on them. However, unlike, for example, the civil rights approach of the gay and lesbian movement, which sought to extend rights to lesbians and gay men, queer activists do not seek to work from within the system. 'Queer does not so much rebel against outsider status but revel in it' (Gamson 1996: 402). Butler sees political collectivities as being fraught with dangers. All such categorization, for Butler, works by creating the illusion of a unified and coherent group on the basis of exclusions, marking the boundaries of those who fail to fit into the group. This denies 'the internal complexity and indeterminacy of the term and constitutes itself only through the exclusion of some part of the constituency that it simultaneously seeks to represent' (Butler 1990a: 14). She concludes that there is no 'ontology of gender' (or race) which can be foundational to our politics.

This apparent rejection of identity categories is not always enthusiastically embraced. Harmonizing with the work of Shirley Tate discussed above, earlier writing by bell hooks (1990: 23–33) welcomes the anti-essentialism that forces the recognition that there are many black experiences: 'Such a critique allows us to affirm multiple black identities, varied black experience. It also challenges colonial imperialist paradigms of black identity which represent blackness one-dimensionally in ways that reinforce and sustain white supremacy' (ibid.: 28). Nonetheless, hooks is less happy with the refusal of blackness as a category of identity. She sees the need to identify as black both to accommodate the specific subjectivities of black people and to form a basis for political activity. Moreover, the very fragmentation of identity categories, which for Butler is a cause of celebration, is viewed by hooks as yielding 'displacement, profound alienation and despair' (ibid.: 26). The anxieties which hooks expresses here find echoes in reflections of Biddy Martin on the politics of queering (Martin 1994). Welcoming Butler's account of performativity as enabling gender norms to be less controlling, Martin nonetheless expresses reservations. The goal of transgression and destabilization can lead to a view that gender categories are purely negative, acting as traps to ensnare us. To retain one's identification as a woman or man, or, as Martin discusses at length, as 'femme', is apparently to be a victim of prohibitive norms. The implication is that to continue to use such terms is to be locked into the fixity dictated by the dominant norms governing it. Although Butler, like Foucault, recognizes the enabling as well as the disciplinary use of discourse, in her early discussion of categories of gender and sexualities it is the disciplinary effect which is foregrounded. Martin's writings, however, suggest that, without the use of such categories, 'language with which to conceive of one's sexual specificities, or to conceive of them positively', is lost (1994: 110). Lois McNay (2000: 45) accuses Butler of implying a false dualism between 'normal' and 'excluded' identities and 'dominant' (and thereby compliant) and 'resistant' responses to subjectification. Resistant responses are assumed, she claims, to originate from those in the position of the 'outside' in relation to dominant culture. For McNay, this belies the complexity of ways in which people inhabit their identity categories that makes such dualisms inappropriate. Many of us can unsettle the meanings attached to being a woman, even if we have been placed unproblematically within the category by, for example, challenging expected feminine behaviour in our everyday practices.

In addition to the need for gender and sexual categories to make sense of the specificity of subjectivity, Martin suggests that we need to utilize gender categories if we are to be able to articulate, for example, misogyny. Discussing Butler's account of the death of Venus Xtravaganza, Martin points out that Butler assumes the death was for failing to conform to gender norms. Martin points out that Venus's death could equally have been a result of her successfully passing as a woman and suffering the death that many other women face (1994: 112).[4] For many feminist writers, the urgent task is still to get sexual differences recognized and properly legislated for in the public sphere. The retention of the category 'woman' is deemed vital to fighting against gendered forms of violence, such as rape and domestic violence, or to securing gender-specific rights regarding maternity leave and reproductive choice. Anne McClintock, discussing cross-dressing, argues that the fact that it 'disrupts stable social identities does not guarantee the subversion of gender, race, or class power' (1995: 67).

It is important, however, to resist a polarization between the use of the categories and their destabilization. Tate, discussed above, insists on the necessity of both, and in this she is following Butler.

Particularly in her later work (2004b, 2015), Butler stresses the necessity of categories for the coming into being of the subject, a necessity which constitutes our primary susceptibility to what is outside of us. Butler also recognizes the need for categories in highlighting inequalities and forming coalitions of political activism. Nonetheless, as we stressed in the discussion of intersectionality, such use must be accompanied by an awareness that categorization is interwoven with 'the very operation of power' (Butler and Weed 2011: 3) and carries with it marginalities and exclusions, the undoing of which must lie at the heart of our political practices. 'Categories are still in process ... we do not yet know and cannot ever definitively know in what the human [or women] finally consists' (Butler 2004b: 37). She says: 'All ... terms have the potential to become prisons, of course, so I am often challenging them ... But I would not deny or refuse ... terms. I would only dedicate myself to not letting them become ossifying in their effects. After all, ... terms have to be living, have to become embodied in a life, have to be passed along, or passed between us, if they are to remain living, if they are to remain terms we need in order to live, to live well' (Butler in Ahmed 2016). This is the test of exploiting the precariousness of our categories in a political way. The shifts must be ones which can be passed between us, passed along, in ways that enlarge the possibilities of liveable lives (Lennon 2006).

What about the body, Judy?

Perhaps the most widespread unease felt with Butler's earlier expositions of her position was captured by the remark 'But what about the body?'. Such a query is prompted by the apparent disregard within Butler's work for any constraints on gender performance which might be set by our biological bodies. Because she emphasizes the mobility of gender and the possibilities of gender crossings, it seems as if no significance is attached to actual forms of embodiment. It is simply a dominant norm that certain kinds of gendered performances attach themselves to certain anatomical shapes, a norm which we can challenge. Surely, people often claim, the facts of reproduction, childbirth, menstruation, the production or not of semen, play some role in our gendered identities, even if not a determining one? It was just such considerations which motivated the new materialist thinking we discussed in chapter 1. Biddy Martin, while accepting that we can have no way of thinking about our bodies outside discourse, nonetheless suggests 'that the body constitute more of a drag on signification, that we pay more respect to what is given, to limits, even as we open the future to what is now unthinkable or delegitimated' (1994: 112). She argues for 'the body, the material [to be conceived of] as a drag or limit as well as a potential[, although] the kind of drag it is cannot and should not be predetermined.' The concerns she expresses here about the body also extend to the psyche. Though 'body and psyche can be said to be the effects of power, they are irreducible to it.' Martin insists that the lines of force run in both directions: 'though never constituted outside of given social/discursive relations, power also moves from bodies/psyches/minds outward' (ibid.: 119).

However, in *Bodies that Matter* (1993), Butler insists that her position was not an attempt to deny the importance of the materiality of the body but meant to undermine an opposition between such materiality and social construction. The direction from which she undermines this opposition is to point out that materiality itself is a discursive effect. What we count as matter, as material, as nature or as given is itself a product of a particular mode of conceptualizing, modes of conceptualizing which are thereby tied up with relations of power. Butler quotes with approval Spivak's remarks (first published in 1993): 'If one really thinks about the body as such, there is no possible outline of the body as such. There are thinkings of the systematicity of the body, there are value codings of the body. The body, as such, cannot be thought, and I certainly cannot approach it' (Spivak and Rooney 1994: 177). We cannot therefore investigate the question of what differences there are in 'nature' as such, because our understanding of this nature is formed by our discourses. This does not mean that there is nothing outside discourse. But what there is cannot be approached other than through its formation in terms of our concepts. We cannot sensibly ask questions about what limits are set by something quite outside what we conceptualize. We can, however, explore the limits of conceptualization by trying to conceptualize otherwise. This response does not seem entirely satisfactory, and Butler remarks in a later essay: 'I confess I am not a very good materialist. Every time I try to write about the body the writing ends up being about language' (2004b: 198).

Butler is being somewhat hard on herself here, for the body occurs in her work not simply as a blank slate inviting inscription but is also recognized as playing a constituting relation to the self. For her, the body is excessive – that is, it outruns any meaning which can be attached to it: 'though [the] referent cannot be finally named, it must be kept separate from what is namable, if only to guarantee that no name claims finally to exhaust the meaning of what we are and what we do' (1997a: 125). Consequently, any bodily practices are open to the possibility of resignification, of being taken in different ways at different times. Moreover, the point that Butler makes about the body here she also makes about the psyche, so that desire, for example, is also excessive. The possibilities of desire outrun any given performances of it.

Nonetheless, in Butler's account we do not get a sense of the body as constraining what can be said or done, a drag on signification, as Martin requires. We do not get a sense of it as itself an agent in our awareness of it in the way required by the new materialists. Butler's theorizing is in contrast with that coming, for example, from feminist theorists of disability. Within disability studies it is important to insist on the social constructedness of the binaries between 'able' and 'disabled' bodies. This accompanies the recognition that what a body is able to do is very dependent on the situation it is in and the resources that are provided for it. Butler, with Sunaura Taylor, makes this point tellingly in the film *Examined Life: Philosophy is in the Streets* (Taylor 2009). The category 'disabled' has an implied contrast with a set of people who are able bodied. Given the range of possible things our bodies are able or not able to do, and given the significance of both environment and technology to this, it seems highly contextual which bodies are to count as able or disabled.

While recognizing these points, however, some writers have also returned to the apparent bruteness of bodily facts which no social or conceptual modifications would enable us to ignore. Arms and legs may not work. Pain is part of the daily reality for many. Nancy Mairs describes living with multiple sclerosis: 'haunted by a ... mean-spirited ghost ... which trips you when you are watching where you are going, knocks glassware out of your hand, squeezes the urine out of your body before you reach the bathroom and weighs your body with a weariness no amount of rest can relieve ... it's your own body' (Mairs 1997: 298). Differences in the kinds of pains and pleasures to which our bodies are susceptible, differences in the amounts of pain endured, in degrees of physical energy and bodily strength, in age and health, in whether a body can see or hear, give a corporeal specificity to embodied experience. These have been explored by many writers (Beauvoir 2010, 1972; Mairs 1990; Inahara 2009) and are irreducible to the cultural significance with which these features are endowed.

Mairs's account, above, appears to be an articulation of a brute materiality which, for Butler, must always escape articulation. However, it also becomes clear that the way Mairs experiences her body is formed in relation to those very normalizing discourses to which Butler refers us and in relation to which the 'crippled' body, in particular the 'desiring crippled body', is banished to the realm of the rejected, often unthinkable, other. It requires just the processes of destabilization of boundaries and queering of norms which Butler describes for such bodies to be experienced by those whose bodies they are, and those that encounter them, as fully human, as capable, as desiring and desirable. Yet attention to Mairs's account does stand in tension to Butler's own. For Butler, 'there is a limit to constructedness' (Meijer and Prins 1998: 278), but this limit remains elusive. Any attempted formulation of such limits can be destabilized by the performance of what such formulations would render unthinkable. Whatever the bodily conditions may be, they exceed any account which can be provided of them, leaving open the possibility of alternative understandings. Some examples may perhaps make this clearer. Struck by the restrictions posed by certain bodies, we may articulate them as: men cannot give birth, certain kinds of disabled bodies cannot run, do sport or be objects of desire. But Butler insists that there is always an excess to what is conceptualized, that the body outruns any way we might currently have of thinking about it. This opens the possibility of alternative conceptualizations in which pregnant men and desired and desiring Olympic paraplegic bodies become thinkable. And, of course, the technologies surrounding trans experiences and the transformations in Olympic sports for many different kinds of bodies have already had exactly this outcome.

The tensions here between the two approaches to theorizing embodiment are not direct oppositions. It is, rather, the case that if we are interested in theorizing the body we have to recognize the pull from both kinds of account. We therefore need a way of thinking about the body which both recognizes its weightiness (in a way that Butler seems to ignore) and accommodates the socially mediated nature of our experience of it.

The expressive body and queer phenomenology

In her later work Butler stresses that it is through the body that we become vulnerable to our material environment and to the violence which may be inflicted on us by others: 'living in a world of beings who are ... physically dependent on one another, physically vulnerable to one another' (2004b: 22). Here there is continuity with the thoughts of the writers discussed above. Moreover, the body is also that on which the other aspects of our precariousness depend: 'it is through the body that gender and sexuality become exposed to others, implicated in social processes, inscribed by cultural norms .... In a sense, to be a body is to be given over to others ... bearing their imprint ... impressed upon by others, impressing them as well, and in ways that are not always delineable, in forms that are not fully predictable' (ibid.: 20–2). It is, 'as bodies, we are always for something more than, and other than, ourselves' (ibid.: 25).

Our bodily morphology is the point of departure for our recognition or misrecognition as raced, sexed, gendered, able-bodied. Others and we ourselves ascribe to our morphology a significance which yields a positionality in sets of social practices. Butler's thought here is close to that of phenomenologists capturing the expressive character of bodily morphology. Perceived bodily form carries intersubjective significance (Alcoff 2006; Beauvoir 2010; Lennon 2015; Merleau-Ponty 1999). We perceive certain bodily shapes as requiring/ suggesting responses of our own and others. These experiences of the significance of bodily morphology are ones into which we are initiated in our familial and wider social encounters (Beauvoir 2010). They lead to a direct or immediate perception of bodily saliences, which most often operates below the levels of reflective awareness, and is therefore difficult to dislodge (see the discussion of bodily imaginaries in chapter 2).

Once we recognize the role that the body is playing in socially constituting our subjectivity and social positionality, we realize the difficulty involved in shifting the significance which we attach to certain bodily morphologies. The political strategies of queering which Butler explores in *Gender Trouble* are an attempt to separate out bodily morphology from imaginary salience. She suggests, for example, that there will be circumstances in which we can attach the imaginary significance of the phallus to a body without a penis or an imaginary of femaleness to a body with a penis. The excessiveness of the body, the way in which it outruns any of the imaginaries in terms of which we experience it, is what makes such queering possible.

In her book *Queer Phenomenology* (2006), Sara Ahmed discusses how the process of queering takes place, given the phenomenological salience of the body. She spells out the salience of bodily morphology in relation to the pathways of interaction with the world and other people towards which different bodies *orientate* us. For her, 'orientation is about how the body, the spatial and the social are entangled' (2006: 180). We become sexed and raced by the ways in which our bodily features are taken by others, and then ourselves, to orientate us towards certain pathways, modes of inhabiting the world. Such orientations are effects of the way in which our bodily features are taken by those immediately around us and the larger social world. However, they are lived as if they originated in bodily features themselves. The material and social world is organized in a way that facilitates the pathways of privileged groups: (some) white people, (some) able-bodied people, (some) heterosexual couples, (some) men. Although the communalities of these groups seem to originate in shared bodily attributes, they are actually constituted by the shared pathways into which their bodies appear to direct them (ibid.: 124).

Such privileging can lead to feelings of *disorientation* for those whose bodies and desires do not fit these pathways. This is a disorientation felt by differently abled and aging people faced with the organization of shops and galleries and homeplaces; by women and black people in institutional, business and cultural settings where their bodily presence renders them conspicuous and the responses of others awkward and defensive; by single people faced with hotel rooms, dining rooms, etc., organized for couples; by lesbian women in the midst of family gatherings where the patterns of interaction assume heterosexual continuity of family line; by masculine-identifying teenagers in girls' schools. Without claiming that disorientation is necessarily political, Ahmed does suggest that disorientation can disturb the order of things, so that the pathways or lines our bodies are expected to follow go 'off line'. 'Queer moments happen when things fail to cohere ... to make things queer is constantly to disturb the order of things' (ibid.: 170, 161). In a link between this meaning of queer and the terms earlier used to refer to 'those who practice non normative sexualities', she recalls, 'what makes specific sexualities describable as queer in the first place ... is that they are seen as odd, bent, twisted' (ibid.: 161) – a movement of bodies away from the pathways their morphologies seem to require. But this moment of negativity also has potential. Ahmed suggests that, when a body 'becomes queer or deprived of its significance, then such a deprivation ... would not be livable simply as loss but [also] as the potential for new lines, or for new lines to gather as expressions that we do not yet know how to read. Queer gatherings are lines that gather – on the face, or as bodies around the table – to form new patterns and new ways of making sense' (ibid.: 171).

Ahmed's work integrates phenomenological attention to the expressiveness of bodily features and the importance of bodily habits with Butler's denaturalizing insistence that the imaginaries we attach to bodily forms can be destabilized. It is a discussion to which we will return in the following chapter when exploring the role of the body in relation to trans histories.

Other materialities

Butler's account of the production of gendered selves is one which concerns itself with the level of meaning, the meaning of linguistic and bodily practices. Consequently, it is not only the materiality of the body which can seem insufficiently addressed in Butler's work but also the environmental, economic and institutional materialities of people's lives – those to which we drew attention in chapter 3. In relation to the subjects of *Paris is Burning*, it has been pointed out that, outside the context of the balls, the participants remained poor and subject to racist and homophobic discrimination. When the film was a success, they wished, for example, to cash in financially on that success. However, all had signed releases which meant that they could not pursue those claims legally (Martin 1994). McNay (2000) criticizes Butler for reducing questions of gender hierarchies to questions about the construction of sexed identities, and thereby failing to attend sufficiently to material and social factors which are structuring people's lives along gendered lines. These arguments are echoed by other writers. Stevi Jackson suggests that performative accounts of gender 'ignore those material social relations which underpin the category of sex' (1995: 17). The insistence from materialist feminism on material and structural features as central to the construction of gender is an important and central one. The different kinds of paid work undertaken by, and the inequalities in pay between, women and men are examples of such material factors, as are the distinctive kinds of labour undertaken by men and women at home, especially in relation to care. Moreover, the material fact that so many women carry and care for children conditions the social possibilities available to them in quite a different way from the occasion of parenthood for most men, as does the gendered nature of public and social institutions. The insistence from the historical materialist framework, discussed in chapter 3, on the need to attend to material and structural features is an important and central one. Such materialist accounts of gender go hand in hand with materialist accounts of class and race and colonial exploitation (Mohanty 2003). If we want to understand what it is to be raced, classed or gendered, then the materialist would argue that we have to pay attention to these intersectional structural features and patterns.

We must be careful, however, not to be pushed into accepting a false dichotomy between the material and the domain of meaning. The apparent dichotomy which is being drawn here between performative identity as, in some sense, 'merely cultural' and the sphere of the legal and economic is one which Butler (1998) would herself reject. Accepting such dualism is to oversimplify a situation constituted by a complex play of interdependencies. Firstly, once we have moved away from naturalizing accounts, the material and structural divisions, despite their materiality, are social practices based on practices of social categorization. The performances whereby gender is produced do not simply carry meanings about what it is to be male and female; they are themselves material practices which serve to constitute the economic and legal frame. Moreover, these material practices are only possible because of the meanings which their participants attach to gendered categories. Material gendered divisions are dependent on our having the categories 'men' and 'women' within which to place people and on the meanings which we attach to such categories. Changes in these understandings have the consequence that the material divisions cannot function in the same way. Nonetheless, the material and institutional factors do have brute causal effects that have to be recognized, and appropriate action has to be taken to promote or to avoid them. If you have little money there is a whole range of possibilities which are not open to you. If your housing is damp you may contract certain illnesses. If certain drugs or equipment are not made available you may die in childbirth. That is, we need to recognize that the world does not simply work according to the logic of meaning (McNay 2000). However, the material practices themselves operate as 'signifying practices' (see ibid.). Not only do they have brute (i.e. unmediated) causal effects, they also have effects that are mediated through meaning. The complex set of things which means one is either male or female in a society derives at least in part from what men and women typically do and what characteristically happens to them in the social order. Transformation and destabilization of such meanings come not only from changes explicitly at the level of cultural representation but also from material changes in which, for example, men change nappies and women drive trucks, or in which wells are put into villages or money is invested in certain forms of co-operative income generation. The changes in institutional structures and everyday material practices which have been seen in the last century have been interdependent with changes in understandings of what it is to be male or female, masculine and feminine.

Conclusion

In this chapter we have looked at Judith Butler's complex work exploring the production of gendered subjectivities, its role in the facilitation of oppressive social practices, and the possibility of its destabilization. We have also considered how such work can be integrated with attention to the materiality and phenomenology of the body and with the materiality of our environments and the global and national economic and institutional structures in which we live. Each of these dimensions works in an intersectional way, as Butler herself is aware. We are never produced just as gendered beings but as raced, classed beings in specific cultural and national settings with various bodily and mental abilities. Butler's work is explicitly anti-essentialist about the necessity of binary categories of sexed difference and about the content of such categories. She insists on their variability and susceptibility to change. But she also makes clear the role played by our being recognized under categories, in the emergence of subjectivity, and in our making sense of ourselves and others in ways that make social life possible. In the following chapter we develop this theme further, by paying attention to the life histories of those for whom the fluidity of gendered categories has proved central.

7 Making Sense of our (Gendered) Selves

> I do not hold that gender is simply a social construct – one of two languages that we learn by rote from an early age. To me, gender is the poetry each of us makes of the language we are taught. (Feinburg 1998: 10)

> Hearken unto me, fellow creatures. I who have dwelt in a form unmatched with my desire, I whose flesh has become an assemblage of incongruous anatomical parts, I who achieve the similitude of a natural body only through an unnatural process, I offer you this warning: the Nature you bedevil me with is a lie. Do not trust it to protect you from what I represent, for it is a fabrication that cloaks the groundlessness of the privilege you seek to maintain for yourself at my expense. You are as constructed as me; the same anarchic Womb has birthed us both. I call upon you to investigate your nature as I have been compelled to confront mine. I challenge you to risk abjection and flourish as well as have I. Heed my words, and you may well discover the seams and sutures in yourself. (Stryker, in Stryker and Whittle 2006: 247)

The quotation above from Susan Stryker – her 'justly renowned exhortatory moment' (Rose 2016: 6) – seeks finally to destroy an account of gendered identities as simply given with our biological natures. We are all constructed, she claims. We all have 'seams' and 'sutures' in us. But the undoubted constructedness that she highlights, the way in which becoming gendered is a process we go through, is not the whole story here. The discursive categories we employ to categorize ourselves and others are not only productive of subjectivity and the structures of power within society in the way stressed by theories of performativity. They are also *answerable* to them. We turn to categories to try and make the best sense we can of our contradictory experiences and desires, experiences and desires which are also partly, but not wholly, formed by the operation of just those categories. We try to make sense of ourselves using the terms which are available in the material and socio-historical situations in which we find ourselves. But we also engage creatively with those categories to expand the possibilities for making our lives more liveable, our desires more comprehensible, and our social encounters more transparent. As Feinberg signals (in the opening quotation), we can make a poetry out of the categories we encounter. Within that project, although all our experiences are laden with meaning and can be revised in the light of alternative meanings, all interpretations are not equal. Some make more sense than others.

In this chapter we shall be exploring the use of intersecting categories of gender and sexuality in the attempt to make sense of ourselves. We do so in a context in which most present-day societies operate with a normative gender binary of male and female and an assumption that everyone fits into one side of this binary. Less pervasive, but still very widespread, is an assumption of a binary of sexuality into gay or straight, which rests on the gendered binary but criss-crosses it. In many countries, being properly gendered no longer requires being heterosexual, and legal unions of same-sex couples are recognized. At the same time, in large parts of the world, people are still prosecuted and ostracized and subject to violence and even death for such liaisons.[1] We will be particularly concerned in this chapter with those whose experiences trouble binaries of gender and sexuality in different ways.

The 'trans' umbrella

Those people who, in different ways, trouble a picture of fixed sexed difference, evident from birth, are frequently discussed as fitting under the umbrella category of *trans*. This category is important politically, socially, and for individuals to chart their life histories. But it is also problematic. Many people who may be included within the category by theorists would not necessarily include themselves in it. Valentine (2007) found that, in his work in New York (see below), those who adopt the term 'trans' most comfortably are those who change, legally, socially and sometimes bodily, their assigned sexed positionality but still embrace the categories of 'man' or 'woman'. Here 'trans' can serve to signal the route by which the social positionality of 'man' or 'woman' is achieved, signifying a subcategory with associated communalities and interests. In this way, 'trans woman or man' works like the category 'black woman or man', suggesting some shared histories and patterns of discrimination. However, even here the term has problems. As we discuss more fully below, it is often conceptualized via a spatial metaphor as the crossing of a border, suggesting discrete territories on each side and an unequivocal positioning on one side or the other. Moreover, as highlighted by the examples in the following section, such life histories are only part of a complex picture.

Nonetheless, the ubiquitousness of the term 'trans' provides an important basis for political lobbying and for the formation of communities in which people feel they can be recognized and made sense of by others. It is, consequently, used by many people to signal their own social positionality to themselves and others, sometimes replacing other historical modes of identification.[2] While we use the term, we must be alert to the diversity it covers and the theoretical pitfalls it can lead us towards. In this chapter, we are exploring the consequences for gender theory of the diverse experiences of those who might be positioned under the 'trans' umbrella. All of the gendered positionalities, which we outline below, must be accommodated when theorizing about the way categories of gender and sexuality both produce and make sense of our subjectivities.

Gendered categories

Any theorizing about sexed and gendered difference has to accommodate the fact that, currently, in some countries and cultures, it is possible for a person to change the sexed positionality which was assigned to them at birth.[3] This change is recognized both legally and socially, although both are often contested and hard fought.[4] In the UK, for example, the 2004 Gender Recognition Act lets adults officially register a change to the gender assigned at birth. The Act does not require surgery but currently does require psychiatric assessments and proof of living for two years in the desired gender. This system is regarded by many as overly medicalized. Elsewhere in the world – in Portugal, Ireland, Malta, Belgium, Norway and Denmark, for example – legislation is based on self-determination, which is a legal process, and there is no requirement for medical experts, medical treatments or diagnosis of a mental disorder for individuals to be legally recognized. Individuals who change the sexed positionality assigned to them in this way are those who most clearly fit the category of FTM (female to male) or MTF (male to female) trans people. It is important to note that this process is quite independent of where people assign themselves in terms of sexuality.

Furthermore, there are also many people who, without legally or socially changing their sexed positionality, challenge the behavioural and social norms associated with those positions and adopt some or many of those behaviours normatively associated with the other side of the binary. For example, there are masculine-identified women and feminine-identified men (see also below). Clearly, there is huge diversity here, as many people challenge the gendered norms of behaviour and social positioning to some extent, including norms of appearance, employment and social role. However, for some individuals, such a movement away from the gendered positions they are assigned in terms of body shape becomes key to how they see themselves and wish others to see them. Halberstam, for example, points to the way 'many gender-queer dykes' senses of embodiment, sexual subjectivity, and even gender legitimacy' (1998: 287) require masculine identity and practices. Yet they do not necessarily regard themselves as having an FTM trans identity. Salamon gives the example of 'the "boys" of the Lex'. These 'boys', who are found in a 'dyke bar' in San Francisco, are photographed on the club calendar as 'transgressively masculine' (2010: 6, 9); 'all of them identify as boys in some way, though the degree to which this name captures their identity varies for each of them. Some of these boys consider themselves to be women. Some relate to that category only marginally, and some do not consider themselves women at all' (ibid.: 92). What this shows, as Salamon points out, is that our categories of sexed difference operate 'not only across the categories male and female, but within them as well' (ibid.: 8).[5]

With great difficulty, a number of people are refusing gendered identity as male or female and claim a non-binary gender position. Currently, this is very difficult to sustain, for our gendered binaries are so entrenched in our socio-cultural practices that without some reference to them we become socially and legally unintelligible, sometimes even to ourselves. It is often the case that, over time, those who espouse a non-binary stance move, in their daily presentation, closer to either the masculine or feminine side of the spectrum. Nonetheless, as Salamon points out: 'Genders beyond the binary of male and female are neither fictive nor futural, but are presently embodied and lived' (2010: 72). And these genders, as lived, often outrun the language we have to describe them.

With less difficulty there are people whose sexuality is non-binary. For some people, desire does not follow the pathways of sexed difference. It is instead a response to particular others who may happen to be of either sex. For others, sexual desire may be linked to certain kinds of gendered performance, but such performance may be linked to bodies of either sex (Monro 2015).

There are also a variety of categories that people use to make sense of themselves which are intersecting categories of both gender and sexuality, and cannot neatly be claimed as either. For theorizing both gender and sexuality it is important to make a distinction between the categories. It is essential to distinguish being man or woman from being gay or straight, rather than assuming, as had been the case (in much of the Western world in the early twentieth century, for example), that a gay person was either a feminized man or a masculinized woman. This distinction is also essential in order to recognize that a change in sexed identity is compatible with being either gay or straight in this role. We must also appreciate that sexuality is the domain of desire and not simply a pattern of gender-normative or non-normative behaviour in which we have been trained (though it is also that). But, essential as these points are, it is also the case that categories both of sexed difference and of sexuality, while not equivalent, are mutually implicating, their intersections often further shown by the pathways which sexuality can open for gendered change and vice versa. So the adoption of butch roles within sexual relations can open the possibility of gendered transition. Equally it may not.

Furthermore, there are categories which intermingle aspects of gender and sexuality and cannot be neatly classified in terms of either, although they have echoes of both. Salamon's 'boys', described above, would be one example. Historically, Chinese *yinyang ren*, the *two spirited people* among Native Americans, and the *bakla* people in the Philippines,[6] anchored in both gendered roles, appearance and kinds of sexual partner, all play a complex role in society. The early twentieth-century categories employed by sexologists made use of the concept of 'the invert', which carried aspects of gendered non-conformity and same-sex desire (Nelson 2009). People made/make sense of themselves using these categories. In terms of contemporary identifications, Sally Hines reports that within her research:

Significantly, sexual categorising terms were often drawn upon to describe gender identification, while gendered codes influenced many participants' discussions of sexuality. In describing her gender identity, Gabrielle, for example, said, 'I mean words are really tricky. I guess I'd say I'm a trans lesbian' (Gabrielle, age 45); whereas, when articulating his gender identity, Del said, 'I call myself a hermaphrodyke sometimes. I've been a lesbian or a dyke. I've been a queer dyke. Queer is probably the term I feel best describes me. I could call myself a queer trannie boy. Everything is qualified in one way or another [laugh]' (Del, age 44). (Hines 2010: 150)

David Valentine, working in New York for a health initiative under the umbrella of 'trans', encountered Fiona, originally assigned as male, who identified both as a woman and gay, thus troubling our categories of 'woman' and 'gay'. Nancy and Clara cross-dress for (not only) erotic purposes, are attracted respectively to men and women when in that role, and feel, when putting their clothes away, that they are losing bits of themselves. However, in the rest of life, as white professionals, they operate as men. Rita is a Latina sex worker who has had some surgery, but for whom still having male genitalia is a selling point in the marketplace. She thinks of herself as gay, as a 'fem queen ... drag queen' (Valentine 2007: 11). All distinguish themselves from Melissa, a white trans woman who, in occupying the category woman, distinguishes herself from both cross-dressers and drag queens.

In Valentine's work it is not just the categories of binary gender and sexuality that are intersecting and becoming altered in the process. These categories are intersecting with both race and class. The sex workers he discusses, 'the Meat Market girls', named after the area in which they hang out to find customers, are mostly Latina or black (2007: 11). They are also poor. They often have surgery, which their work helps to finance, and which sometimes widens the number of their customers. Valentine's work makes clear 'that the contours of racial and classed experience can shape and reshape what gender or sexuality can mean' (ibid.: 18). This point is echoed in Susan Stryker's account of early activism countering discrimination against gender non-conforming people. She describes several 'lunch counter sit-ins' in the 1960s responding to discriminatory acts (Stryker 2008: 63). These forms of protest coincided with those employed in the civil rights struggle, as many of those involved in these sit-ins were people of colour. Stryker characterizes one of these as 'the first act of civil disobedience over antitransgender discrimination' (ibid.: 62). But the groups of people involved were quite diverse, many identifying as gay, in a movement intersecting race, class, gender and sexuality.

Valentine highlights the political and social advantages of separating the categories of gender and sexuality. The gay community, by downplaying gender non-conformity and stressing those gay lives which, in their kinship and familial relations, most closely resemble normative straight lives, have found battles, socially and politically, easier to win. Similarly, it is easier for people to accept changes of sexed positionality where the chosen sex most closely matches one side of our normative sexual binaries. What gets missed from both of these groups, though, are the historical and contemporary 'fairies and queens', butches, dykes and femmes, whose visible interwoven non-conformities of sexuality and gender trouble the binaries and the analytical distinction between sex and gender. Yet they also provide an important mirror for people to make sense of themselves and to shift the imaginaries surrounding our mainstream categories in a way that expands possibilities for everyone.

Local readings

It is important to recognize that these complex categories invoking gender and sexuality are fluid and open. They bleed into each other *and* into the normative binaries of male/female, gay/straight. The multiple gendered and sexed positions impact on the possible ways we can be male or female. Even our normative categories become less discrete and less stable, indeterminate and open to resignification, as well as to historically and culturally *local readings*, all within the workings of intersectionality (discussed in chapter 5). The factors which lead to the assignment and claiming of gendered identities vary across, and within, socio-historical moments. What we take to be constitutive of the gender we accept or yearn for can vary according to the discursive accounts of gender which we have available to us.

Here, for example, is Jan Morris, in *Conundrum*, following surgery and public adoption of the category female: 'I feel small and neat ... My blouse and skirt are light ... My shoes make my feet look more delicate than they are, besides giving me ... a suggestion of vulnerability that I rather like' (Morris 1974: 174). This model of femaleness, with its associations of smallness and lightness and vulnerability, bears little comparison to the 'african royalty' which inspires an eight-year-old mentioned by Elspeth Probyn: 'the protagonist ... is eight when she 'spied this lady ... She ain't nobody's mama – I'm sure. And she ain't wearing Sunday clothes. She got on blue jeans and a man's shirt, with the tail hanging out. She got patches on her blue jeans, and she still got her chin stuck out like she some kinda african royalty' (Probyn 1996: 109). Or compare the masculinity identified by Goffman as hegemonic in American society – 'a young, married, white, urban, northern, heterosexual, Protestant, father, of college education, fully employed, of good complexion, weight, and height' (Kimmel 1994: 125) – with that explored by Thomas McBee as he tests out the links between masculinity and aggression in the world of amateur boxing:

> There we were, two guys past our primes, circling each other in front of seventeen hundred drunk onlookers in Madison Square Garden ... All so that a guy with seventeen pounds on me could beat bruises across my face, both of us a messy mosaic of blurred senses, damp armpits ... I was a new man, the first transgender man to fight in the most storied boxing venue on earth, there to close the gap between us like the fiction that it is. (McBee 2018: 1–2)

When an insistence on local readings is added to the recognition that subjectivity is in a continual process of constitution and negotiation, then it is possible that the sexed categories in terms of which we articulate it can shift. At different points in our life histories we might make sense of ourselves differently, particularly if we stumble across more options than we were first exposed to. Patricia Zavella reports the narrative of Maria Perez. Maria, growing up in Mexico and coming to desire women, articulates her subjectivity as 'male' and adopts the macho lifestyle which goes along with it. Later, after moving to the US and finding lesbian communities with a range of possibilities for gender and sexuality, she sees herself as a woman and allows her bodily shape to change, to become rounder (see Lancaster and Leonardo 1997). Dr Pauli Murray, a ground-breaking lawyer who, in the mid-twentieth century, was a pivotal figure in African-American civil rights history, was the first to argue for a race–sex analogy in the workings of discrimination law in the United States. Throughout her life she had passionate relationships with women. She favoured what was regarded as a masculine mode of appearance and dress, asked doctors for male hormones, and explored surgical interventions. Today she may well have identified as a (trans) man, but such a category was not available to her in the 1930s and 1940s. She campaigned throughout her life, not only against segregation laws and the rights of the working class but also for the right of women to participate in public life and later in the Episcopal Church – that is, for the contours of what it was to live as a woman to be expanded. Murray was excluded from Columbia University, because at that point they did not accept women, and entered Hunter College, only for women. Later, at Howard University's law school, she was the only woman: 'On the first day, one of her professors announced to his class that he didn't know why a woman would want to go to law school ... she termed this form of degradation "Jane Crow" and spent much of the rest of her life working to end it' (Schulz 2017). Her life story shows the intersection of race and sex and class in determining her life chances. It was additionally complicated by a non-conformist presentation of gender and sexuality. What her life makes clear is that the possible positionality as a man or a woman is a matter not just of subjective identification but also of location within structures of social interaction and power. Desire and identification work alongside social positionality to render indeterminate which sets of categories would make most sense of Murray's life and subjectivity (Murray 2018; Cooper 2015; Harrison 2017).

Confronting nature

The possibility of trans identities of multiple kinds seems to put the final nail in the coffin of claims that binary sex difference is dictated by biological binaries in nature; it also makes deeply problematic the suggestion put forward, even by some feminists, that nature can tell us what counts as a 'real' woman (see discussion in introduction and chapter 1). The rejection of naturalizing accounts of gender, which seems required by the recognition of trans genders, may also seem to vindicate the version of queer theory and the performativity of gender (Butler 1990a), which we discussed in the previous chapter. Queer theory and the public visibility of trans emerged together. Within this framework trans people are portrayed as the 'gender outlaws' who challenge the dominant categorization of male and female, making evident its constructedness and opening up the possibility of both numerous forms of sex/gender/sexual identification and radical indeterminateness in positioning in the sex/gender system. For Butler in *Gender Trouble*, as for Stryker above, the changes to embodiment which are sought by those seeking bodily reassignment serve to make evident the constructedness of sexed identity, which is also constitutive of apparently more stable gender identities and displayed by other trans people in ways which do not require bodily modification. Many trans people therefore regard the advent of queer theory, with its goal of destabilizing sexual binaries, as the theoretical framework whereby trans histories can be understood. Sandy Stone, for example, argues: 'In the transsexual as text we may find the potential to map the refigured body onto conventional gender discourse and thereby disrupt it, to take advantage of the dissonances created by such a juxtaposition to fragment and reconstitute the elements of gender in new and unexpected geometries' ([1987] 1991: 352).

A radical reading of queer strategies makes identity categories altogether problematic, insisting that subjectivity is such that it can never be contained within them without the closure of possibilities. In an early article by Jack Halberstam, transsexuality becomes the marker of the fictionality of all gender categories. 'We are all transsexuals except that the referent of the trans becomes less and less clear (and more and more queer). We are all cross-dressers but where are we crossing from or to what? There is no "other" side, no "opposite" sex, no natural divide to be spanned by surgery, by disguise, by passing' (Halberstam 1994: 212). However, there are some for whom the performative theory of gender and the consequent project for queering gender and other identity categories are unsatisfactory as the only ways of making sense of trans narratives. For such writers (Prosser 1998; Namaste 2000; Bettcher and Garry 2009), the experiences of many people, trans and not, reveal the limits of queer theory's account of gendered identity. In response to Halberstam, Prosser remarks that the suggestion we are 'all transsexuals' is a way of 'not attending to the specificity of narrative' (1998: 15). In this he seems right. Not everyone who wishes to change the sexed position assigned to them at birth wants to be a gender outlaw. Many, perhaps most, people do not wish to be conspicuous. Many people, trans or not, are simply looking for a social positionality which makes best sense of their desires and yearnings, their zones of comfort and discomfort, while being enabled to get along with others in their (variable) everyday surroundings. For some this necessitates being gender outlaws, for others not. And many people who, to differing degrees, regard themselves as outlaws do not have the additional hurdle of also changing their sexed assignment.

It is worth comparing the dominant public images of trans people in the early 1990s with contemporary images in US and UK media. What is striking in both sets of images is the absence of images of trans men, more puzzling now, at a time when the majority of new referrals to gender clinics, at least in the UK,[7] are from young people assigned female at birth and wishing to change that. In 1994 Stryker, when delivering her assault on biological determinism, was dressed in what she called 'genderfuck drag': combat boots, lace, pink, crystal pendants, threadbare jeans and biker jacket with 'Queer Nation-style stickers reading SEX CHANGE, DYKE, and FUCK YOUR TRANSPHOBIA plastered on the back' (Rose 2016: 6). Now we are more familiar with the pictures of Caitlyn Jenner on the front of *Vanity Fair*, 'impeccable, Hollywood moodboarded images ... broadcast across the world' (ibid.). In contemporary images, awareness of trans lives is mediated through celebrity, and the images we have of trans women are indistinguishable from those of other celebrity women, many of whose contours have also been shaped by the surgeon's knife. What is clear is that such images are not engaged in gender fuck! Of course, everyday trans people, women and men, are much more variable, much less glamorous, and have intersectional identities which mutually constitute the kind of women or men they are. At the level of representation, alongside Jenner, we also have Laverne Cox in *Orange is the New Black*,[8] 'presenting to the world what it means to be a black, incarcerated, transsexual woman' (ibid.), and refusing surgery to make her face more feminine. For FTM trans people there is much less general visibility. But there is interest in the phenomena of trans men giving birth (Barker 2018; Cocozza 2018). What is clear is that falling under the trans umbrella and being involved in practices to destabilize gendered categories do not necessarily go together.

Trans narratives and gendered homes

Recognizing that queer theory and trans theory may not coincide, Jay Prosser, in his book *Second Skins* (1998), positions many trans people with non-trans people who may more comfortably inhabit their sexed assignment. He highlights the longing for a gender 'home', a desire for a sexed realness, a sense of belonging, which most people are able to take for granted. What emerges is a picture of people attempting to make coherent their previously fragmented lives and experiences, weaving the profound unease which they have felt with the identities which have been attributed to them into some kind of sense, finding a 'home' in which they can rest. The identification as male or female is one which makes sense of their lives: indeed, we can make sense of our lives only in terms of the categories which are on offer. Prosser points out 'the ongoing centrality of sexual difference in our worlds [with] limits to its refigurability [which has the] consequence of many subjects yearning to relocate in relation to this difference' (1998: 204). In his account, the 'realness' of trans gender, in common with the 'realness' of other genders, is predicated on the 'home' it provides and the extent to which it makes the best sense of the experiences of the subjects concerned.

Prosser suggests that trans people who identify as men or women adopt a particular kind of narrative about their life (1998: part 2). What is distinctive of their autobiographies, he argues, *is* a narrative of transition. The lives which are revealed in these texts are represented as having a teleological shape: 'transsexuality in fact appears as a narrative: a plot typically beginning in childhood recognition of cross-gendered difference and ending, again typically, with the transsexual achieving some marker of becoming, ... some degree of closure' (Prosser 1999: 90). Typically, these moments are associated with bodily transformations, to which we will return below. There are certain recurrent themes and tropes within such a plot. One key element is the feeling of being trapped in the wrong body, which, in the narratives offered, is projected back into early childhood. Other elements include posited childhood feelings of difference, of not conforming to gender stereotypes, not being sporty, not liking rough and tumble games, wanting to play with dolls, liking dressing up, or being a tomboy, not liking dolls, etc. Prosser particularly identifies in such narratives the sense of a journey, *a crossing over of borders*, of reaching a stable destination (often marked in the autobiographies he discusses by literal journeys and a literal crossing of borders, as people travel for operations or to find communities within which they can live). The narratives are, he emphasizes, an attempt to produce a coherent sense of self by means of the structure which is brought into the account of the life. What marks this structure most importantly is its *telos*, the reaching of a home of gendered realness, most commonly achieved by some degree of bodily modification which enables the possibility of social 'passing'.

The dangers of spatial metaphors

In our earlier work *Theorizing Gender*, we followed Prosser in using spatial metaphors to discuss trans identities, drawing analogies between travelling between gendered positionalities and travelling between nation-states. In each case, the travelling called into question the stability and homogeneity of the states crossed while retaining the central image of the border. But this image is problematic for a number of reasons. It invokes a moment of crossing a border, from male to female or from female to male. For those who legally alter their gendered status there is a moment when this becomes legal. For those who undergo medical and surgical procedures, there are many moments over years when these physical processes are undergone. Nonetheless, the metaphor is misleading. For many trans people, what is regarded as transition is not a change to themselves but a change in the way they are perceived by other people (Whittle 2016). In her memoir *The Argonauts*, Maggie Nelson records her own bodily processes of undergoing IVF and pregnancy alongside her partner's variable bodily changes: 'On the inside, we were two human animals undergoing transformation beside each other, bearing each other loose witness.' She quotes her transitioning partner's impatience with the idea that anyone taking hormones must be on a journey to one binary extreme or the other: 'I'm not on my way anywhere' (Nelson 2016: 103). Moreover, as Beauvoir stressed, *becoming* a man or a woman is a process for everyone, a process that develops during our upbringing and through our whole life. It is equally an ongoing process for the person who is becoming a woman, having initially been assigned to the category man, and vice versa. We become men and women of various sorts by means of differing and multiple journeys. And, of course, that is not all we become. The way we become men and women is shaped by the other categories we are also negotiating. And the historical/cultural milieu we occupy determines what *counts* as becoming a man or a woman. Thus, the notion of 'transition' can obscure the way process is involved in all genderings.

For Halberstam, the spatial metaphor 'relies on a belief in the two territories of male and female, divided by a flesh border and crossed by surgery and endocrinology' (1998: 164). Such a picture falsifies the continuities and discontinuities between a range of gendered and sexed identities – for example, the link between the experiences of FTM people and butch lesbians. In the list Prosser provides of childhood markers of trans identity, many of the recurrent motifs listed as common to trans narratives appear in the life histories of lesbian/gay and straight people who never think of changing their assigned category of sexed identity, and who may or may not find themselves comfortably inhabiting it. There seems to be a patchwork of overlapping similarities and differences here which makes a linear model with separate poles difficult to apply. Maleness and femaleness are not endpoints of a continuum but categories which are being continually constituted, contested and negotiated in the subjectivities of us all.

For Prosser, the crossing of borders is to find a home from which we have been misplaced – our real gender assumed as present, but hidden, since childhood. But there are many different stories here. The assumption of a 'real gender', originating in childhood, rules out other possibilities: 'it can't be that ... you went to ... clubs, and saw that certain ways of living were possible and desirable, and that something about your own possibilities became clear to you' (Butler 2004b: 81). Elspeth Probyn discusses, like Prosser, the use of narratives of childhood and past to articulate current subjectivity. However, she resists narratives of lives in which there 'is only one line of movement, one that goes from the present to the past in order to justify the present', seeing the present only as the effect of past causes (1996: 112). Rather, 'images ... from childhood pull us back to a space that cannot be revisited; they throw us into a present becoming, profoundly disturbing any chronological ordering of life and being' (ibid.: 103). On this account, the trans narratives which Prosser discusses in *Second Skins* would not necessarily be seen as an exploration of the past to reveal what the subject has always been; rather, they would be viewed as a reading of the past to make a narrative sense of the *present* desire to modify one's body, to belong to particular communities of men or women. Nonetheless, we argue that we must be alert to the kind of moments of clarity which may suddenly enable us to make sense of ourselves. The categories we embrace are to provide a coherence to our life, including childhood aspirations, yearnings we may feel when we see a man or woman we aspire to be like, and despair at the seeming impossibility of being differently positioned in the social world.[9]

Belongings

In later work, Prosser revised his account of the 'realness' of trans gender (Prosser 1999). Whereas, in *Second Skins*, such real gender was held out as the telos of some trans narratives marked by bodily transition, in later articles the achievement of a 'real' gender is a necessarily unachievable object of desire. What marks trans identity, he suggests, is 'the failure to be real' (1999: 85). In place of a telos there is rather a continually renegotiated desire, a yearning to be what is necessarily unattainable. In this discussion, he attributes such yearning to those whose bodies retain the marks of surgery and some trace of what cannot be reassigned. He does not address the question of the realness of non-trans gender. His discussion might suggest that the 'real' gender is unattainable only to trans men and women. Its logic, however, leads elsewhere. 'Real women' and 'real men' are fantasies to which, as Butler pointed out, we may all aspire but which no one can realize (Butler 1990a). Gender has a (variable) imaginary content which, in our diverse negotiations of our gendered positionalities, we attempt to make material in some way.

Nonetheless, the attention to gendered positionality as (desired) home, which marks Prosser's work, highlights desires for belonging that, it is arguable, are necessary to 'make life livable' (Butler 2004a, 2004b; Lennon 2006). Probyn (1996) replaces the concept of identity with that of belonging. The desire for a sense of belonging, articulated as a yearning for a home, is a theme also developed by bell hooks, who talks about the meaning of 'homeplace' for black people. In her book *Yearning* she describes the journey to her grandmother's house: 'we would have to pass that terrifying whiteness – those white faces on the porches staring us down with hate ... Oh that feeling of safety, of arrival, of homecoming when we finally reached the edges of her yard' (hooks 1990: 41). She argues for the need for such a homeplace: 'that space where we return for renewal and self-recovery, where we heal our wounds and become whole' (ibid.: 49). While our lives may have been very different to that of hooks, we can all feel the attraction, and the fantasy, of that yard.

The home which we yearn for, however, is an imaginary place, but it is an imaginary towards which we direct our actions, and it informs the choices we make and the places and people we seek out. It is a place where we can find our feet with our surroundings and the people that we encounter in them. It is a place of familiarity where we can interact with other people, effortlessly, without impediment. It is somewhere where we can live our everyday lives without feeling conspicuous. This is a space in which, in Heidegger's terms, we 'can be relieved of continual anxious alertness' (1975: 33). This is a sense of home that is impossible for many in environments which have been made inaccessible, unnegotiable, or dangerous for bodies of certain types: where our wheelchairs cannot get into buildings or along pavements; where our ambiguity rules out bathroom use; where our menstruation cycles, pregnant bodies, or sucking infants cannot be accommodated;[10] where the colour of our skin or markers of our refugee status make us unwelcome, perceived as dangerous instead of in danger.[11] This notion of home also evokes mutual intelligibility within everyday practices, our being able to conduct everyday interactions without continually explaining ourselves. Seeking this kind of home is the goal of some trans people who wish to identify simply as male or female, wanting just to be regular men and women, with whom other people in their communities can find their feet. For other trans people, it requires finding a community in which gender fluidity or a wider range of gendered categories are intelligible.

The notion of home which Prosser invokes carries with it the notion of *recognition*. As we noted in the previous chapter, this term has been central to the work of Judith Butler for many years (see, for example, Butler 2004b). We 'do not recognize ourselves at the level of feeling, desire and the body, at the moments before the mirror, in the moments before the window, in the times that one turns to psychologists, to psychiatrists, to medical and legal professionals to negotiate what may well feel like the unrecognizability of one's gender and hence the unrecognizability of one's personhood' (2004b: 58). The categories we claim for ourselves, then, must make some sense of our lives and subjectivities, our yearnings and desires, in ways in which at least some community of others can also understand and recognize.

The insistence on the possibility of recognition may seem to sit in tension with the claim, often made, that we simply know what gender we are, that it is simply a matter of an inner feeling. But inner feelings lead to claiming identifications which operate in a public space. Moreover, what we claim depends on what is available in the communities we seek to make a life within or alongside.

Categorization is dialogical and contextual. It is negotiated within social contexts. As Salamon comments: 'I claim my name and am claimed by it at once' (2010: 123). Similarly, Butler states: 'to be addressed is not merely to be recognized for what one already is, but to have the very term conferred by which the recognition of existence becomes possible' (Butler 1997a). We may be offered terms and find we can make sense of ourselves with them, or we may find we cannot make sense of ourselves and seek alternative possibilities. We can have apparent homes without such recognition. When Gloria Anzaldúa left her home, it was in hope of finding herself not alone but in relation to communities which conferred recognition on the yearnings she expressed.

The wrong body

Many people whose lives might be captured under the trans umbrella, as we have been using it, engage in some kind of bodily modification. These modifications include the taking of hormones, surgery to chests and genitals, and procedures to render faces or other bodily parts more normatively feminine or masculine. Some of these procedures are shared with non-trans people also seeking to make their appearance more normatively masculine and feminine (Alsop and Lennon 2018). We have suggested here that trans men and women lay claim to (a variety of) gendered categories in order to be enabled to take part in local, communal social practices in a way that makes them intelligible to themselves and others. The categories are employed to make life more easily liveable. The claims of those under the trans umbrella have the consequence that the content of our normative gendered categories are reconfigured in ways that reverberate through the narratives of so-called non-trans men and women, many of whom are variously embodied and who also claim the identifiers for the same purposes. The question we want to ask now is, what is the importance of the body in all this? Why is the wish for at least some kind of bodily modification so widespread?

Throughout this work we have stressed the bodiliness of our sexed identities. Despite rejecting the claim that such identities were fixed by nature, we have nonetheless accepted, with the new materialists, that the materiality of our bodies is central to our subjectivities. The ego, Freud claims, is a bodily ego, and we have followed him.

Equally we have claimed, following Beauvoir, that what is made of bodies by culture is central to grasping what is involved in being a man or a woman. While adopting much of Butler's account of gendered performativity, we also criticized her early work for its lack of attention to bodiliness, which she herself addressed with her later work on recognition and vulnerability. Prosser also stresses the bodiliness of our sexed identities, which gives rise to the desire many trans people have for bodily modification. An early Channel 4 documentary, following the pathways of young female to male protagonists, was entitled *The Wrong Body* (1998). The sense of being born into the wrong body is a recurrent motif within trans narratives. Indeed, it is the articulation of experience in this way which has often been used by psychiatrists as the criterion for a diagnosis of 'gender dysphoria'. Such a diagnosis is commonly required if people are to be allowed access to surgery and is often the basis of the claim to legally change gender. The sense of being wrongly embodied and the sense of alienation from found embodiment have dominated many accounts of trans lives. It has been pointed out how this often results in self-destructive behaviour: 'because my body was becoming more and more alien to me as I developed, there was an urge to rip off my own skin' (Raymond Thompson, quoted in Prosser 1998: 71). Such alienation is used to explain the desire to change the biological body, to bring it into line with the sexed identity that is desired. Here the changing of the flesh, the modification of the body, is taken as a necessary route to finding a gendered home. The body, on this picture, is a problem which needs to be fixed.

There are difficulties with the assumed universality of the *wrong body* account. There is the point, made by Halberstam, that many, perhaps most, people feel their body is wrong and wish to change aspects of it (1998: 172). Yet, such a general point is not all that is involved here. For reasons that will become clear below, the lack of fit to which our attention is being drawn in many trans narratives is not simply the failure to conform to a dominant norm. These norms do impact, for example, on the choices many non-trans people make with regard to cosmetic surgery and influence what *kind* of woman or man a trans person might aspire to look like. But failure to conform to norms is not all that is in play in trans desires for bodily modification. It is, rather, that the body someone has leads to their being continually wrong-footed in everyday interactions. Our bodies are read, by ourselves and others, *as expressing our social positionality*. If they express a position we are not able to occupy, then we feel the need to change them, so that they facilitate the social interactions with which we can find our feet.

Nonetheless, the relationship trans people feel towards their original embodiment is not necessarily as destructive as is articulated in the dominant paradigm. This relationship is sometimes more accepting, more accommodating, than that paradigm suggests. There is a recognition that our bodies open up possibilities and do not simply close them down, and that they can be reconfigured in transformative ways. Our bodies are what enable us to take up the world and respond to others, and, because of their materiality, the ways in which they can do this always exceed anything we can currently imagine. We will return to this below.

The expressive body

What we need to make sense of, then, is the importance of bodily modification for many trans people without retreating to a misplaced biologism in which the anatomical body is taken to be determining of sexed/gendered identity. Linda Alcoff (2006) discusses embodied identities in which people are classified by means of visible bodily markers. Embodied identities are what she terms *visible identities*, those in which bodies are divided into perceptual types, in relation to which their normative position within sets of social practices becomes immediately evident. That is, our bodies are experienced as expressing to others, and to ourselves, patterns of intersubjective relations. This is true of sexed identities,[12] 'raced' identities, which are anchored in material bodily features, identity categories surrounding disabilities, and aging. Such an account can capture the way material features of our bodies play a role in our subjective sense of self and others, without giving a biological account of such embodiment. In broad terms the classifications are phenomenological rather than biological. *Perceived bodily form* carries intersubjective significance. We perceive certain bodily shapes as requiring or suggesting responses of our own or others. That is, we perceive them directly as requiring or facilitating certain responses. Such interpersonal significance is our way of experiencing the bodies of others and ourselves as male or female and why detectable morphological differences are central to most of the practices concerned.

Bodily changes are then sought to allow others to gauge, in an immediate way, the category in which we wished to be placed. 'I want the phalloplasty because I want to be able to go swimming [which includes of course being able to use the male changing rooms]. I don't have a problem once I'm wearing my swimming costume, or when I am dressed. It's the transition period when you wonder if anyone is going to wonder' (Nataf 1996: 24). In a series of photographs taken by Jana Marcus, 'Transfigurations: the making of a man' (discussed by Salamon [2010]), Aidan discusses his response to recent chest surgery. Before having surgery 'to look like a guy', he needed to bind his breasts until they were painful, and this made it difficult to breathe. Following surgery: 'My chest is very concave where my breasts used to be, but I love that it is flat ... Yesterday it was windy outside and my shirt pressed firmly against my chest and for the first time I wasn't conscious of my breasts ... it felt amazing' (ibid.: 116).[13]

Above, we suggested that claiming a gender was positioning oneself in the context of everyday social practices. We are now suggesting that such positioning is expressed through the body. 'At homeness' in everyday social practices is made possible by bodies whose position in those practices is immediate and readable. What is highlighted by Beauvoir (as discussed in chapter 4) and others is that our bodily contours feel to us in such a way that they *make possible* certain kinds of agency and *inhibit* others, being able or not to enter a gym or a nightclub or an art gallery. For trans people who wish to change their body, the positionality which their original body expresses is not one with which they can find themselves 'at home'. It is like floundering in a language which does not feel like our own. Currently, a certain social position is expressed by means of a certain bodily shape. Consequently, some bodies, instead of facilitating engagements with the world, inhibit such possibilities. Such bodies make it difficult to engage in the world alongside others with shared intelligibility. What is desired is for aspects of a body to be changed, so that it *can* enable such shared intelligibility. For such trans subjects, therefore, the content of their own desired positionality is captured with reference to *a bodily form*.

It is important to note that it is not only bodily shape that is playing an expressive role here. The way we experience the bodies of ourselves and others does not stop at the skin. All aspects of appearance and style and the full range of bodily gestures are expressive of intersubjective possibilities, and many of these can be adopted/changed/explored without medical intervention. A given bodily morphology does not fix determinate expressive possibilities for a body. What expressive possibilities any body has is something creatively explored as it negotiates its environment. They can surprise us. Sartre discusses the performance artist Franconay, a small stout brunette woman whom we come to experience as the singer Maurice Chevalier. For that to happen, 'that black hair, we did not see as black; that body, we did not perceive as a female body, we did not see those prominent curves' (Sartre 2004: 27). Chevalier comes, Sartre suggests, *to possess* the body in front of us. Before such an encounter, we would not have anticipated that impersonating Chevalier was one of the expressive possibilities of that small stout body with its normatively female shape. But, as Butler has pointed out, along with phenomenologists before her (Butler 1993), the material of the world outruns any meaning we may attach to it and enables new ways of being. Or, as Merleau-Ponty remarks: 'the psycho-physiological equipment leaves a great variety of possibilities open' (Merleau-Ponty [1945] 1962: 189).

Transformative possibilities

The expressive possibilities of our material bodies within the material and social environments in which they are placed are both part of the situation in which we are placed and open to creative resignification. Explicit transgendered activism of the kind which Butler endorses, as well as lots of less obvious everyday activities (for example, women driving trucks, men changing nappies or cleaning), expands the expressive possibilities of differently shaped bodies. In Lieke Hettinga's words, we need to bring 'new visual grammars of the body into existence' (Hettinga 2019). However, for this to work, such activism and activities have to take place in contexts in which they can be found intelligible. The possibilities must be able to be taken up and put to use in intersubjective forms of life. We find ourselves in environments where certain kinds of bodily shape, or appearance, or gestures carry expectations. But we can respond to such assumptions in ways that develop and change these. Viewing our categories of sexed difference as expressive categories in the way suggested does allow for development and extension, to our being nudged to see the appropriateness of applying them in new circumstances. Our application of categories of male or female to trans bodies of different kinds is a consequence of perceived continuities between such bodies and other men and women, continuities anchored in the forms of life in which they participate. Such extensions allow us to make sense of sexed classification where the link between the body and reproductive role becomes muddied. There has been much publicity over recent years with regard to pregnant men.[14] At the current stage of the development of technology, these are cases of trans men who have retained a womb and often ovaries, and therefore the ability to carry a child. It would be a mistake to view our practices here, seeing some pregnant people as male and, later, as the fathers of their children, as arbitrary or purely stipulative. Practices require communities for whom the use of the term makes sense. And such communities, making possible shared modes of communal life, now exist.

These possibilities can also allow a less alienated relation to original embodiment for some trans subjects than is often assumed. Jason Barker made the feature film *A Deal with the Universe* (2018) about his own pregnancy. In the opening shot he is swimming in the London Fields lido in east London, 'his Hawaiian swim shorts flapping, his stomach a perfect, firm dome. ... it is a moment of pure levity and joy. "That swimming stuff that you see?" he says. "It felt like the first time I could ever say, 'Yeah! I actually like this body. Love it. It's brilliant'"' (Cocozza 2018). Barker had been living as a man for about twenty years when he undertook this pregnancy. Sally Hines, speaking to Cocozza, says:

> In the UK, if you look at how many people are accessing blogs and online forums and support groups, asking about healthcare because they are pregnant, or young guys thinking about the future ... There is lots of anecdotal evidence that more people are doing it. When something becomes visible, more people think it's possible ... Transition is not a straightforward A to B ... Pregnancy is not an interruption, just another part of a long and complex journey. (Ibid.)

Not all pregnant men have Barker's experience. Because of the association of pregnancy with femininity, it sometimes increases rather than decreases a sense of alienation from the body. A pregnant body is laden with social meaning and leads others to make clear assumptions about social positionality. But Barker's experience does show that such alienation is not always a necessary part of trans narratives. Moreover, the film also contributes to a reconceptualizing of masculinity. It explores strength and resilience, both associated with the male body, but it also stresses vulnerability, which Barker admits he had been fleeing while establishing his male credentials. Such trans lives widen the gendered possibilities for us all.[15]

Conclusion

What we find in trans biographies are subjects negotiating gendered positions which best make sense of their life and desires and enable shared communal practices where people interact and are made sense of by others.[16] The possibilities for negotiating intelligible subjectivities and finding possible modes of sociability are increased when our categories are reconfigured to recognize trans histories and when the categories 'man' and 'woman' normatively endorse a large range of non-dichotomous social interactions. With such reconfiguration, the possible ways of living our lives expand. For us, attention to such biographies reinforces the anti-essentialist position which we have been presenting in this work. It renders the tightening of the boundaries around what is required to be a *proper* woman (see introduction and Phipps 2016) not only politically oppressive but also theoretically indefensible.

Conclusion: The 'Truth about Gender'

In this book, we have suggested that gendered identifications are something to which we may lay claim, on our own behalf and on behalf of others. We have not attempted to provide a 'truth about gender'. That is, we have not attempted to provide a set of conditions, locally or more generally, which tell us what it is to be male or female, a man or a woman (or any of the sexed and gendered categories which have been under discussion in the previous chapters).

We have resisted all varieties of gender essentialism, whether anchored in biological theory, psychoanalytic models of the psyche, the structure of symbolic practices, deterministic views of patriarchal and capitalist structures, or patterns of social training. What we have made clear is that there are a *variety of factors in play* which have a bearing on what is involved in sexed or gendered identifications in given socio-historical locations. This multiplicity makes both the allocation of gendered categories and the consequences of such allocation open-ended and negotiable. It does not make it arbitrary. Gendered categories are public. Their use depends on a community to which they make sense. People position themselves and others within, or at a distance from, these categories in order to make sense of themselves and to signal possibilities for intersubjective relations. Such positioning has concrete material consequences for our lived opportunities within the societies in which we are placed. Some of these material consequences were spelled out in chapters 3 and 5.

The story unfolded here is a story of entanglements (Haraway 2016). Our bodily morphologies are entangled with public structures of meaning, the myths and imaginaries attaching to bodily features, social patterns of kinship, practices of intimate relations, the organization of productive and reproductive work within transnational capitalism, the legacies of colonialism, developing biological, medical and other technologies, and an immersion in, and a vulnerability to, a constantly changing material world. We are writing at a time when changing climatic conditions are destabilizing sustainable life on the planet and, together with conditions of war, producing large movements and migrations of peoples. These entanglements inform not only the existence and contents of our gendered categories but also other dimensions of differentiation with which our gendered categories intersect. The interweaving of gender with other categories has been a key aspect of the story we are telling here and a central factor undermining the essentialism we oppose.

Sites of agency

The multifactored, intersectional and entangled processes by which we become gendered are also the processes by which power differentials are established. One of the reasons we need our gendered categories or, more precisely, our intersectional categories is to make evident the workings of power, in which the distributions of wealth, land, education, health, political position and leisure are shown to privilege predominantly certain groups of men (see discussion in chapters 3 and 5). Men are also the perpetrators of most of the violent assaults, including sexual assaults, which occur globally (we return to this below). Therefore we need gender theory, both to understand features of our subjectivities and to identify what supports and sustains systems of social relations that are oppressive, and where the points of intervention might come. It is not, however, possible to consider possibilities for resistance if we isolate gender from the multifaceted positionalities within which relations of power operate (Lugones 2007, 2010).

In line with our analysis, points of intervention are multiple. They involve both the destabilizing of our binary gender system and the recognition and remaking of possibilities within it. And each of these tasks informs the other and requires interconnected interventions at the level both of meaning and of material practices. Developments in reproductive technologies, hormones and surgery widen the possibilities for bodies and for reproductive choices, at the same time that access to and control of them are problematically dependent on economic resources and legal oversight, as well as politically contested by right-wing populist and religious organizations. A diversification of heteronormative, nuclear kinship relations requires communities in which diverse relations are both legitimized and given legal and economic support. It also requires making visible the global diversity which already exists. We need to challenge the normative cultural practices and practices of bodily training within which we learn what it is to be a (certain kind of) boy or a (certain kind of) girl and are urged to discipline our bodies accordingly. As indicated in chapter 4, Beauvoir and later phenomenologists highlighted some of the practices that we encounter en route to becoming women, which can serve to narrow the possibilities that we experience the world as offering us. We return below to the problematic norms of behaviour offered en route to becoming men, in all their intersectional complexity. For women, and increasingly for young men, an ever narrower range of body images dominate our media (Gill et al. 2005), which are being challenged by campaigns to recognize and value bodily difference (Gill and Elias 2014). Such valorization of a limited range of bodily norms is implicated in colonial histories, yielding the widespread phenomenon of *colourism*, in which paler skins are privileged.[1] It impacts on non-normative bodies in women's sport (see the discussion in chapter 1) and excludes many disabled bodies from being in a position to be imagined as desirable or employable. In each of these areas, myths and imaginaries that are oppressive need to be called out and space and opportunities for making new ones created in order to multiply the imaginable possibilities for being men or women or non-binary – a key part of which comes from attention to intersectional, decolonial and trans narratives.

Changes at the level of the imaginary both require and make possible material, political and economic changes. From our perspective, within Europe, we argue for challenges to inequalities in pay, including gender pay gaps and job segregation, and to work cultures that presuppose and reward patterns of behaviour and lifestyle most closely related to a limited group of men. If women are to achieve economic parity with men, care for children and the old and vulnerable needs to be socially supported. We require resources to support migrant and refugee people that target their differential needs. We need resources to address sex trafficking. Our political groupings, judiciary, trade unions, police, arts organizations, cultural spaces and academies must reflect within their own make-up the diversity of the populations within which we live. And such diversity is not only to support greater economic equality but to create models of working within which diverse groups of people are able to fit.

In each of these directions of intervention an intersectional framework is essential. The beneficiaries (or otherwise) of particular interventions are not universal 'women' or 'men', or 'LGBTQI+' people. Rather, interventions benefit particular intersectional groupings, whose improved position may be at the cost of others. It is also the case that the urgent sites of intervention, despite the list above, are not ones which we can universalize. Some of those concerns will generalize. But what is most pressing depends on the complexity of local situations.

Gender-based violence

Violence against women is endemic across the world. As we highlighted in chapter 3, the UN estimates that '35 per cent of women worldwide have experienced either physical and/or sexual intimate partner violence or sexual violence by a non-partner at some point in their lives', and some countries have put the figure as high as 70 per cent.[2] Eighty per cent of people trafficked across the world are female,[3] and trafficked girls and women are particularly vulnerable to sexual violence (Madill and Alsop 2019). Rape in war zones remains at epidemic proportions (Palermo and Peterman 2011). Also endemic are sexual harassment and sexual assault in public spaces, schools, universities and workplaces (Russell et al. 2016; Phipps et al. 2017; House of Commons 2018; Phipps 2018; Keller et al. 2018).[4] Homophobic and transphobic violence is found in all regions of the world, but it is particularly pronounced in countries where the LGBTQI+ community lacks legal rights.[5] 'Such violence may be physical (including murder, beatings, kidnappings, rape and sexual assault) or psychological (including threats, coercion and arbitrary deprivations of liberty). These attacks constitute a form of gender-based violence, driven by a desire to punish those seen as defying gender norms' (Blondeel et al. 2017).

There have been high-profile campaigns in response to notorious cases of such violence. India has been particularly important here. The 2012 Delhi gang rape sparked global outrage and violent public protests and a sustained campaign by Indian feminists which brought changes to legislation and sentencing and public awareness. Nonetheless, despite ongoing and very public mobilization, 'rape is increasingly used as an instrument to assert power and intimidate the powerless in India' (Chup 2018). In Spain, the so-called Wolf Pack rapes in 2016 and the initial acquittals of the perpetrators concerned 'galvanised feminists in Spain like never before, turning feminism into a movement with unprecedented visibility and real political power. Immediately after the verdict, hundreds of thousands of women flooded plazas in dozens of Spanish cities to protest against the ruling, calling for Spain's sexual assault laws to be rewritten.' But these demonstrations have also provided fuel to the rising right-wing populism we described in our introduction: 'the far-right party Vox pitched itself to supporters who felt threatened by the increasing prominence of what they called "radical feminism" ... [and] became the first far-right party to win multiple seats in Spain since the death of Franco' (Beatley 2019).

In 2006, in the US, Tarana Burke initiated the MeToo campaign and hashtag which, in 2017, became used globally in the wake of numerous and widespread allegations made against the Hollywood producer Harvey Weinstein.[6] The naming and shaming of those who use sexual harassment, intimidation and assault to gain and retain power in the workplace, public services, aid agencies, universities and arts organizations has become a worldwide phenomenon. It has enabled thousands of women to break their silence, speak out and demand better. It has forced many institutions to review procedures and instigate protective structures.[7] But it is not without problems. Some voices are heard more than others, some believed more than others. There has been a vilification of accusers on social media. And the campaign, too, has led to a backlash among populist commentators and supporters.[8]

In each of these examples, from everyday sexism, unwanted touching and derogatory remarks to coercive control and sexual violence, there is a common perception. Women are imagined as *being sexually available* for men's purposes. Their sexed identity, experienced in this way, blocks interactions with them as partners, co-parents, colleagues, fellow workers, fellow activists and community leaders. Consequent responses to such violence by public shaming, policing, changes in laws, and the providing of refuges and support have to work hand in hand with both enabling and requiring shifts within this dominant imaginary.

Intersectionality is also key here. Women from within communities which are themselves vilified and under attack find it particularly difficult to speak out concerning their experiences for fear of fuelling such vilification. Angela Davis (1982) and bell hooks (1990) have both spoken out about 'the myth of the black rapist', which provoked lynching in the American South. It was also a recurrent motif in colonial India, where atrocities were justified on the grounds that the honour of English women was under threat from Indian men (Narayan 1997). The danger of assault from refugees and migrants is a recurrent theme of populist rhetoric globally. In a twist of logic, while berating feminists for calling out the abusive behaviour of men in their own communities, right-wing commentators also present these women as being particularly under threat from migration. In this context it is difficult for women within migrant groups to speak out about their own experiences (Madill and Alsop 2019).

Toxic masculinity

What has been resisted in this work are explanations of oppressive relations which employ essentialist notions of gender. Such narratives have been employed in relation to men's involvement in violence, but we reject them. Recognizing the role men play in global gender-based violence and sexual assault has led to a widespread discussion of what has been termed 'toxic masculinity'.[9] This term picks out patterns of male behaviour promoting physical, sexual and intellectual dominance. Such aggressive forms of masculinity are ones in which manhood is defined by violence, sex and status – ones in which women are devalued and homophobia is rife. Such forms are manifest in controlling and bullying relations, ranging from catcalls, derogatory remarks and unwanted touching to psychological manipulation, physical violence, and the rape and murder of women. It is also manifest in violence and aggression against LGBTQI+ people (Connell 2000, 2005, 2014; Morgan 2019; Salter 2019). Such masculinity is problematic for men as well as women. Many men are also on the receiving end of it. It is exercised against gay men and trans men, against migrant men and any men perceived 'other' to the group exercising dominance. It is exercised in particular ways by the middle classes against working-class men. It is exercised by working-class men against each other. Furthermore, even where men are not directly the target, the prevalence of models of toxic masculinities, and attempts to conform to them, damages their personal relations and mental health.

Suggestions that such patterns of domineering and abusive behaviour have an origin in hormones – for example high levels of testosterone (as discussed in chapter 1) – have long been refuted, and explanations citing evolutionary psychological frameworks have been shown to be equally problematic (Fine 2017). There are also attempts to anchor such behaviour psychoanalytically in terms of the psychic dynamic between male children and their mothers and fathers, most of which are mother-blaming and misogynistic (Phillips 2019). Even when naturalizing accounts are rejected, they can be replaced with an assumption of a determining socialization in which boys are initiated into such gender norms and trained into their bodily habitus while learning what it is to be a man (Bourdieu 2002). Men manifesting such behaviour even try to excuse themselves by pointing to a cultural milieu in which it was taught, which they could not therefore escape. They also sometimes claim that attacks on such models of masculinity are attacks on men in general and the very status of being male. As one right-wing UK journalist fumes, 'everything we told you to be, men, for the last 30 years is evil. ... Let boys be damn boys' (Young 2019).

Most gender theorists, however, accept that there are no essentialist explanations of these patterns of behaviour, and consequently that we need to drop a fatalistic 'boys will be boys' response. Instead, as with other manifestations of gendered identities, such masculinity needs to be theorized within the multiple and entangled web of factors which we have identified as formative of our gendered identities. For what is evident, alongside the pervasiveness of such patterns of behaviour, is that this is not the only way of being a man that is around. There are dangers, in these discussions, of suggesting that such damaging masculinity is the only model we encounter. There is no doubt that cultural initiation and training in damaging forms of masculinity takes place, and that to counter such masculinity we need key interventions to modify it. However, the situation is much more complex. There is a multiplicity of masculine gender norms, in some of which these toxic elements may be absent or partial. Queer and trans masculinities are of central importance here (see the discussion in chapter 7). But also key is the everyday masculinity of men taking care of their children or parents, or working happily under the direction of women, or calling out sexist behaviour in their peers, or manifesting vulnerability without shame. Masculinity is intersectional, and what constitutes it is formed in relation to other aspects of social positionality in both positive and negative ways. Connell stresses that masculinities are shaped by a myriad of interrelated factors such as nation, class, race, culture and sexuality (Connell 2000, 2005, 2014). We stress also the importance of the intersection of abilities and age. The patterns of behaviour which are manifest, and our responses to it, differ on the basis of such intersectionality.

One consequence of this is that we can challenge damaging imaginaries of 'being a man' with less damaging ones, for there are such examples around. In January 2016, Gillette, which for many years used a marketing campaign for its razors under the slogan 'the best a man can get', launched a short advertising video entitled 'The best men can be'. The advert explicitly echoed the concerns of the MeToo movement, challenging damaging male stereotypes and setting against them a masculinity with different understandings of strength and resilience (Gillette 2019). The advert provoked a large response, both positive and negative, but the making visible of such alternatives, through public culture as well as personal encounters and examples, is a condition of a shift in some masculine gender norms in less damaging directions (Obama 2019). Connell (2014), however, alerts us to the dangers of exploring masculinity simply at the level of cultural norms, without paying attention to the diverse economic and material conditions which both shape and are shaped by them. Writing in an Australian context, she contrasts the operation of coercion and domination showing up in the employment environments of wealthy white communities with the patterns of masculine behaviour that might be encountered in poor communities, without resources or respect. In the UK, the artist Grayson Perry explores manifestations of masculinity in diverse communities. The apparent tough-man masculine behaviours of north-eastern working-class areas are linked to work in the mining industries or in shipbuilding areas, but has become redundant with the disappearance of such work. It is contrasted to the domination exercised by men, with a clear sense of entitlement, in the city, an entitlement and pattern of domination over women, and men displaying masculinities of other kinds. In the housing estates of north-west England relying on food banks, with children often lacking adults empowered and enabled to look out for them, the boys' involvements with gangs and knives provided both an alternative kinship structure and a way of passing their days (Perry 2016a, 2016b). Akala, now a rapper, writer, public intellectual and educator, points out in his memoir:

> I was born poor and racialized black ... We often depended on state benefits, we lived in a council house, I ate free school meals ... The first time I saw someone being stabbed I was twelve, maybe thirteen, the same year I was searched by the police for the first time ... many of my 'uncles' ... went to prison. My upbringing was, on the face of it, typical of those of my peers who ended up meeting an early death or have spent much of their adult lives in and out of prison. (Akala 2018: 82)

If we turn our attention to the global situation, then the patterns of masculine behaviour are manifest in economic, political and imaginary contexts marked by coloniality but also haunted by alternative possibilities (Gutman and Vigoya 2005).

These complex narratives show the complexity and diversity of the circumstances in which intersectional norms of manhood are developed and uneasily occupied. It is clear that problematic aspects of masculine-gendered identifications are not going to be fixed purely by Gillette ads. Attention to material, economic and educational opportunities all matter here. Key also are communities of respect and empowerment. But, equally, damaging notions of manhood will not be changed without transformative and multiple imaginaries of how to be a man *otherwise*. The entanglements of matter and meaning, each working in intersectional ways, are required here, in the way we have argued throughout this book.

Coalition politics

An anti-essentialist approach to gender theory recognizes our complex entanglements in the material world, kinship relations, economic structures, myths and imaginaries, and practices of bodily training. Such an anti-essentialist approach has been put together, in this book, with attention to intersectionality. Our emerging gendered identifications are constituted hand in hand with other aspects of our social self. Such a theoretical framework has consequences for political agency. We have signalled above some of the many sites where it requires us to exercise such agency. This framework also requires coalition politics. Our politics can be concerned neither with a single issue nor with a single dimension of identity. Maria Lugones argues that, if we 'fragment the identity of the oppressed', then we 'disaggregate the ... springs of ... agency ... The logic of coalition is defiant of the logic of dichotomies' (2010: 755).

Here are some examples of coalitions:

- We made clear in our introduction that the emergence of right-wing populism threatens women and LGBTQI+ groups together with migrants and refugees. Opposition to such populism necessitates the working together of women concerned with the erosion of reproductive rights, sexual violence and economic disparities, alongside other groupings whose possibilities for liveable lives are under attack. It also requires us to recognize the particular vulnerability of migrant women to sexual violence, including sex trafficking.
- The Republic of Ireland provides us with examples of successful coalition politics. A series of referendums in recent years has enabled gay marriage, the right to change gender assigned at birth, and some rights to abortion. In each case it has been important to counter the social power of a conservative Catholic Church opposing each of these issues. To do this requires coalitions of all the groups involved, many of whom have overlapping members. And this overlapping group of activists is also involved in contesting the direct provision of a refugee processing system and discrimination against Irish travellers, with women contesting local elections from each of these groups (O'Leary 2019).
- Northern Ireland provides us with an additionally complex example. The tragic death in April 2019 of the journalist Lyra McKee[10] drew attention to ongoing struggles for each of the rights mentioned above, already won in the Republic, in which she was engaged. Such struggles require opposition to *both* of the dominant religious groupings, Catholic and Protestant, in the province. And this necessitates coalitions across the social and political divides. But it also requires addressing the political and economic vacuum in the region which has fuelled a return, particularly of economically deprived and directionless young men, to sectarian violence and paramilitary organizations. These complex entanglements tragically led to McKee's death.
- We are all now living on a planet the future sustainability of which is at risk, making climate change the most pressing political issue of the moment. The young environmentalist Greta Thunberg has catalysed a global movement of young people to recognize the emergency,[11] in which we have very few years left to halt the damage done to our planet and keep it capable of sustaining life.

All our possibilities for living make us vulnerable to the changes being wrought by global warming and the shrinking of biodiversity. But this issue intersects with our other concerns too. As has long been recognized, the effects of climate change are affecting poorer and richer zones of the world differentially. The damage caused by richer economies is resulting in the flooding, landslides, hurricanes, droughts and fires which are disproportionately affecting the homes and livelihoods of the poorer areas. This increases the need for migration, already fuelled by violent conflict. And women and men are differentially affected by ecological changes and by migration. There is an interconnection of ecological deterioration and oppression based on gender, race and class (Roy 1997). From the 1980s onwards, for example, the feminist Vandana Shiva established a form of ecofeminism in India which recognized the key issues for women of the availability of water, the fertility of soil and the biodiversity of crops (Shiva 2014). Across the world, women have been at the forefront of collaborative initiatives aimed at protecting these resources (Baskin 2017; Vashistha 2018), resisting an interlocked capitalism and colonialism which destroy 'everyday practices that ... habituate us to take care of the world' (Lugones 2007).

These are just some examples of feminist activism which contrast with a narrow identity politics. Forty years ago there was much talk of sisterhood, even *the* sisterhood (Morgan 1970). Our feminist groups were where we sought a home, transparency and ease of interaction, a shared politics with those whom we felt were like ourselves. It was a comforting myth, but one disrupted by class issues, issues of racism and colonialism, differences of sexuality and ability, and trans activism. Each of these areas also had its own myths of sameness blown open. This is a disruption to which we hope this book contributes. Feminism has a long history of internal criticism to prevent it settling into a comfort zone. It has been necessarily concerned with diverse communities and alliances. Feminism, we would suggest, is not a security blanket to put around people just like ourselves, but a politics where we respectfully learn to work with differences rather than to police boundaries. This is the feminist politics which the gender theory explored in this book seeks to enable. To conclude, we therefore endorse the following from Bernice Johnson Reagon's seminal paper 'Coalition politics': 'We've pretty much come to the end of the time when you can have a space that is "yours only" – just for people you want to be there ... we have just finished with that kind of isolating. There is no hiding-place. There is nowhere you can go and only be with people who are like you. It's over. Give it up' (Reagon [1983] 2000).

Questions for Further Reflection

1 What role does the body play in constituting gendered identities?

Relevant book chapters/sections:

Chapter 1
Chapter 2, 'The bodily ego'
Chapter 4, 'The data of biology', 'Living bodily difference'
Chapter 6, 'Performance and performativity', 'What about the body, Judy?'
Chapter 7, 'Confronting nature', 'The wrong body', 'The expressive body'

Further reading:

Alaimo and Hekman (2008) *Material Feminisms*: introduction.
Alcoff (2012) 'Gender and reproduction'.
Butler (1993) *Bodies that Matter*: introduction and chapter 1.
Fausto-Sterling (1993) 'The five sexes: why male and female are not enough'.
Mairs (1990) *Carnal Acts*: passim.
Stone ([1987] 1991) 'The empire strikes back: a posttranssexual manifesto'.
Tate (2009) *Black Beauty*: chapters 1 and 6.

2 How should sport deal with gender fluidity?

Relevant book chapters/sections:

Chapter 1, 'How many sexes are there?', 'The case of sport', 'Trans bodies and biology'
Chapter 5, Introduction
Chapter 7, 'Gendered categories', 'Confronting nature'

Further reading:

Cashmore (2005) *Making Sense of Sports*, 4th edn: chapter 7.
Fine (2017) *Testosterone Rex*: 'Introducing Testosterone Rex'.
Karkazis (2019) 'Stop talking about testosterone – there's no such thing as a "true sex"'.
Pape (2019) 'I was sore about losing to Caster Semenya. But this decision against her is wrong'.
Reeser (2005) 'Gender identity and sport: is the playing field level?'
Sen (2018) 'Dutee Chand proud of being first athlete to fight against hyperandrogenism rule'.

3 Why is body image a key issue for gender studies?

Relevant book chapters/sections:

Chapter 4, 'Objectification'
Chapter 6, 'Subjectivity and subjectification'
Chapter 7, 'The wrong body', 'The expressive body'

Further reading:

Alsop and Lennon (2018) 'Aesthetic surgery and the expressive body'.
Garland-Thomson (1997) *Extraordinary Bodies*.
Heyes and Jones (2009) 'Cosmetic surgery in the age of gender'.
Holliday and Sanchez Taylor (2006) 'Aesthetic surgery as false beauty'.
Jones (2013) 'Media-bodies and Photoshop'.
Moreno Figueroa and Rivers-Moore (2013) 'Beauty, race and feminist theory in Latin America and the Caribbean'.
Morrison ([1970] 2000) *The Bluest Eye*.
Tate (2009) *Black Beauty*: chapter 5.

4 What is the imaginary? What role does it play in gender theory? How can it be transformed?

Relevant book chapters/sections:

Chapter 2, 'Lacan's three orders', 'The importance of the Imaginary', 'Luce Irigaray and the feminist imaginary'
Chapter 4, 'Myths'
Chapter 5, 'Decolonial feminism'
Chapter 6, 'Gendered scripts', 'Queering', 'The performativity of race'
Chapter 7, 'The expressive body', 'Transformative possibilities'
Conclusion, 'Toxic masculinity'

Further reading:

Beauvoir ([1949] 2010) *The Second Sex*: Vol. 1, Part 3, 'Myths'.
Gatens (1996) *Imaginary Bodies*: chapter 9.
hooks (1990) *Yearning*: chapters 8 and 20.
Lennon (2015) *Imagination and the Imaginary*: chapters 6 and 7.
Lugones (2010) 'Toward a decolonial feminism'.
McClintock (1995) *Imperial Leather*: passim.

5 Why have historical materialist frameworks been central to black feminist and decolonial perspectives?

Relevant book chapters/sections:

Chapter 3, Introduction, 'Gendered societies', 'Historical materialism and globally connected inequalities', 'Conclusions'
Chapter 5, 'Intersectional analysis and material positionality', 'Decolonial feminism'

Further reading:

Anthias and Yuval-Davis (1992) *Racialized Boundaries*.
Combahee River Collective ([1977] 2015) 'A black feminist statement'.
Crenshaw (1989) 'Demarginalizing the intersection of race and sex'.
Davis (1982) *Women, Race and Class*.
Lorde (1984) *Sister Outsider*: 'Age, race, class, and sex: women redefining difference'.
Mies ([1986] 1998) *Patriarchy and Accumulation on a World Scale*.

Mohanty (2003) '"Under Western eyes" revisited: feminist solidarity through anti-capitalist struggles'.
Truth (1851) 'Ain't I a woman?'. Also read and listen to versions of Truth's speech at www.thesojournertruthproject.com.

6 Can gender equality be achieved within capitalism?

Relevant book chapters/sections:

Chapter 3, 'From Marxism to Marxist feminism', 'Second-wave Marxist feminism', 'Historical materialism and globally connected inequalities'
Chapter 4, 'Economic and social structure'

Further reading:

Acker (2004) 'Gender, capitalism and globalization'.
Acker (2006b) *Class Questions: Feminist Answers*: especially chapter 4.
Collins (1990) *Black Feminist Thought*: chapter 3.
Collins and Bilge (2016) *Intersectionality*: chapters 2 and 6.
Davis (1982) *Women, Race and Class*.
Fraser (2013) *Feminism, Capitalism, and the Cunning of History: An Introduction*.
Hennessy and Ingraham (1997) 'Introduction: reclaiming anticapitalist feminism'.
Kollontai (1909/1977) 'The social basis of the woman question'.
Skeggs (2004) *Class, Self, Culture*: chapter 1.
Walby (2011) *The Future of Feminism*: chapter 6.

7 Is there a better term than 'intersectionality' to capture the complex relations between different elements of oppression and different elements of identity?

Relevant book chapters/sections:

Chapter 5

Further reading:

Anzaldúa (1987) *Borderlands/La Frontera*.
Bilge (2013) 'Intersectionality undone: saving intersectionality studies from feminist intersectionality studies'.

Cho, Crenshaw and McCall (2013) 'Toward a field of intersectionality studies: theory, applications, and praxis'.
Collins and Bilge (2016) *Intersectionality*: chapter 3.
Lugones (2010) 'Toward a decolonial feminism'.
Ortega (2015) 'Latina feminism, experience and the self'.
Puar (2012) 'I would rather be a cyborg than a goddess'.
See also:
Curiel, Ochy: Most of this writer's work is in Spanish, but an introduction and bibliography can be found at: https://globalsocialtheory.org/thinkers/curiel-ochy/.
Wekker, Gloria, on 'white innocence', https://vimeo.com/259174248.

8 What role do bodily practices play in the production and reproduction of gender differences?

Relevant book chapters/sections:

Chapter 4, 'Bodily habits', 'Complicity'
Chapter 6, 'Performance and performativity', 'Gendered scripts', 'Real genders'

Further reading:

Beauvoir ([1949] 2010) *The Second Sex*: Vol. II, Part 1, chapter 1, 'Childhood'.
Butler (1990a) *Gender Trouble*.
McNay (2000) *Gender and Agency*.
Tate (2005) *Black Skins, Black Masks*: chapter 7.
Webber (2018) 'Sedimentation and the origins of cultural values'.
Young (1990) *Throwing Like a Girl and Other Essays in Feminist Philosophy and Social Theory*.
Young (1998) '"Throwing Like a Girl": Twenty Years Later'.

9 What role does the response of others play in the formation of our sense of (gendered) self?

Relevant book chapters/sections:

Chapter 2, 'Why Freud?', 'The bodily ego', 'Psychoanalysis: race and disability'
Chapter 4, 'The one and the other', 'Objectification', 'Dimensions of otherness'
Chapter 6, 'Precariousness'
Chapter 7, 'Gendered categories', 'The wrong body', 'The expressive body'

Further reading:

Alcoff (2006) *Visible Identities*: Part 1, Introduction; Part 3, 'The phenomenology of racial embodiment'.
Butler (2004b) *Undoing Gender*: chapter 6.
Lennon (2006) 'Making life livable'.
Lorde (1984) *Sister Outsider*.

10 Are gender and sexuality distinct?

Relevant book chapters/sections:

Chapter 5, 'Intersectional analysis and material positionality'
Chapter 6, 'Gendered scripts', 'Real genders', 'Queering'
Chapter 7, 'Gendered categories'

Further reading:

Alsop, Fitzsimons and Lennon (2002) *Theorizing Gender*: chapter 5.
Butler (1994) 'Against proper objects'.
Hines (2010) 'Sexing gender, gendering sex'.
Rubin (1993) 'Thinking sex: notes for a radical theory of the politics of sexuality'.
Rubin with Butler (1994) 'Sexual traffic'.
Valentine (2007) *Imagining Transgender*.
See also:
Curiel, Ochy: Most of this writer's work is in Spanish, but an introduction and bibliography can be found at: https://globalsocialtheory.org/thinkers/curiel-ochy/.

11 How useful is the concept of toxic masculinity in explaining gendered violence?

Relevant book chapters/sections:

Conclusion, 'Gender-based violence', 'Toxic masculinities'

Further reading:

Connell (2014) 'King hits: young men, masculinity and violence'.

Collins (2004) *Black Sexual Politics: African Americans, Gender and the New Racism*.
Crenshaw (1991) 'Mapping the margins: intersectionality, identity politics, and violence against women of color'.
Davis (1982) *Women, Race and Class*: 'Rape, racism and the myth of the black rapist'.
Morgan (2019) 'The real problem with toxic masculinity is that it assumes that there is only one way of being a man'.
Perry (2016a) *All Man*.
Perry (2016b) *The Descent of Man*.
Phipps, Ringrose, Renold and Jackson (2017) 'Rape culture, lad culture and everyday sexism: researching, conceptualizing and politicizing new mediations of gender and sexual violence'.
Young (2019) 'Piers Morgan and men's rights activists upset at "emasculating" new Gillette advert'.

Final points for discussion

After reading this book, what are your thoughts on the following questions? (You'll need to draw on arguments through the book to develop your responses.)

1. Can we imagine a world in which gendered identifications become socially insignificant?
2. As feminists, how do we build political coalitions?
3. Should feminist politics be anti-essentialist?

Notes

Introduction

1 See, for example, posts at www.facebook.com/womansplaceuk/ and www.facebook.com/DRradfem/.
2 The paedophilia claim seems quite bizarre but is found in other places, including Poland. The accusation works via a focus on education. The encouragement of gender equality and diversity in schools is seen as promoting the sexualization of children and thereby their vulnerability to assault. This is a train of thought which is damaging on very many levels. It was put forward by some Catholic bishops, following the revelation of widespread abuse over decades within the church, in order to divert attention and find another scapegoat. Though, of course, gender theory did not exist and certainly was not taught during these decades of abuse. Rather, its advent encourages children to speak out. Then, obviously, the accusation has no grasp on the means by which children become inappropriately sexualized. And, worst of all, it blames supposedly sexualized children for their own assault.
3 See the references given in note 1 above.

Chapter 1 The Data of Biology

1 See the discussion in Gatens (1996). One of the important influences on first making the distinction was the work of Robert Stoller (1968), who paid attention to both transvestite and transsexual people. For Stoller, 'a person's gender identity is primarily a result of ... [social] influences. These ... can completely override the biological fact of a person's sex and result in, for example, the situation of the transsexual [person]' (Gatens 1996: 6). Nonetheless, it is not clear that the distinction *is* adequate to capture the very diverse experiences of trans people, a point we will return to later in this book.

2 The scientific scepticism of 'binary' sex – that is, the idea that there are men and women and that they can be clearly distinguished – started even earlier. In 1968 the *Journal of the American Medical Association* carried an article by the biologist Keith L. Moore listing *nine* different components of someone's sexual identity: external genital appearance, internal reproductive organs, structure of the gonads, endocrinologic sex, genetic sex, nuclear sex, chromosomal sex, psychological sex and social sex. See also Heggie (2015).
3 Intersex Society of North America: www.isna.org/node/523.
4 There is clearly a question as to why this is, and some argue that, though women do not perform to such high levels as men, this is because of a history of exclusion and that, theoretically at least, as women and men's achievements begin to converge, they could in time equal out.
5 The reporting of this matter has been marred by an ugly sexism and racism. Castor is claimed to look masculine, on a standard of looks which privileges a certain kind of white femininity and echoes what Lugones (2010) calls the colonial logic of gender and race. Similar problems have beset the reporting of the achievements of other black female athletes, such as the tennis player Serena Williams and gymnast Gabby Douglas.
6 These writings have been called 'new materialism' to distinguish them from both reductive materialism, which sees scientific facts as determining culture, and Marxist historical materialism, which will be the focus of chapter 3.
7 There is some slippage in these discussions between biology conceived as biological facts and biology as a science. We take it that the concern is that our accounts of everyday sexed difference reflect the facts of biology, whatever these may be, and that an engagement with biology as a science is required to provide the best articulation of those facts.
8 Grosz quotes approvingly from Darwin: 'We have thus far been baffled in all our attempts to account for the differences between the races of man; but there remains one important agency, namely Sexual Selection. ... It can further be shewn that the differences between the races of man, as in colour ... &c., ... might have been expected [from] ... sexual selection' (Grosz 2008: 35).
9 This need is, of course, currently being undermined with the development of cloning.

Chapter 2 Gendered Psyches

1 One of our daughters has some webbed toes, a curiosity so far not woven into her bodily sense of self, though we can imagine circumstances in which its significance might change. Others of our children have tiny

holes in the outer ear, linking them in a criss-cross fashion across the kinship group, which they display with pride.

2   Freud's early views on homosexuality, or what he termed 'inversion', repudiate the idea prevalent at the time that inversion in men or women had any link with degeneracy. On the contrary, he insists that homosexuals are frequently indistinguishable from heterosexuals in every other way and are frequently particularly intellectually talented and ethical in their behaviour. (He believed that love of the same sex often expressed itself in the public domain as social concern.) For him, we are all potentially bisexual. There are, however, aspects of his theory which are more problematic. Freud argues that it is men's bisexual nature which frequently determines the choice of a male partner who, often in a compromise between a man and a woman, combines the characteristics of both sexes. He also views female homosexuality as a 'masculinity complex' (1915 and 1920).

3   The object-relations work of Klein (1931), Winnicott (1964), Bion (1967), Chodorow (1978) and Bollas (1992) focuses on the early relationship with the mother rather than the father as the basis for identity. Object-relations theory suggests that there can be a vital dimension of our identity that emerges intuitively and empathically within that emotional relation. Chodorow (1978) argues that mothering, which is undertaken largely by women, produces different experiences for both sexes and therefore different psychic outcomes in men and women. This in turn, she insists, leads to a male-dominated culture. Her solution to this problem is that parenting should be fully shared between men and women. Subsequently, Chodorow distanced herself from this early work because it fails to acknowledge the idea that 'masculinity' and 'femininity' exist in both men and women and depend on a Western nuclear family set-up. This work is discussed in more detail in *Theorizing Gender* (Alsop et al. 2002: 58–61).

4   When referencing Lacan's work we will use the term Imaginary, with a capital I. When referencing other uses of this term we will drop the capital.

5   This will be further discussed in the context of Beauvoir in chapter 4 and Judith Butler in chapter 6.

6   Lacan's work has played a major part in the influential work of French feminist writers such as Julia Kristeva (1977, 1982, 1984), Luce Irigaray (1985a, 1985b) and Hélène Cixous (1976). Of these writers, who are significantly different from each other (see Alsop et al. 2002: 54–6), our discussion will focus primarily on Irigaray.

7   When Freud and other psychoanalytic writers use what is translated as 'femininity', they are not using it as we often do to denote styles of behaviour or appearance. Rather, it is the state of being sexed as female.

Chapter 3 Historical Materialism

1. We invite readers to think about gendered patterns in their specific local contexts, in relation to education, employment, health, violence, the criminal justice system, and the political sphere, to see what similarities and differences arise in the UK context.
2. See Office for National Statistics, www.ons.gov.uk/employmentandlabourmarket/peopleinwork/employmentandemployeetypes/articles/familiesandthelabourmarketengland/2017#mothers-with-a-youngest-child-aged-between-three-and-four-years-old-have-the-lowest-employment-rate-of-all-adults-with-or-without-children-and-are-the-most-likely-group-to-work-part-time.
3. WISE, 'Industry led ten steps', www.wisecampaign.org.uk/resources/2016/11/women-in-the-stem-workforce-2016.
4. 'Men named "David" outnumbered all of Britain's top women CEOs last year', http://fortune.com/2017/08/04/ftse-100-ceo-pay-women/.
5. 'Election 2017: record number of female MPs', www.bbc.co.uk/news/election-2017-40192060.
6. 'Judicial diversity statistics 2017', www.judiciary.gov.uk/about-the-judiciary/who-are-the-judiciary/diversity/judicial-diversity-statistics-2017/.
7. 'Mental health statistics: suicide', www.mentalhealth.org.uk/statistics/mental-health-statistics-suicide.
8. 'Women and the criminal justice system statistics 2015', www.gov.uk/government/statistics/women-and-the-criminal-justice-system-statistics-2015; 'Homicide', www.ons.gov.uk/peoplepopulationandcommunity/crimeandjustice/compendium/focusonviolentcrimeandsexualoffences/yearendingmarch2015/chapter2homicide.
9. 'Victims', www.ons.gov.uk/peoplepopulationandcommunity/crimeandjustice/compendium/focusonviolentcrimeandsexualoffences/yearendingmarch2015/chapter2homicide#victims.
10. See United Nations, *The World's Women 2010: Trends and Statistics*, chapter 8: https://unstats.un.org/unsd/demographic-social/products/worldswomen/documents/Poverty.pdf.
11. 'Facts and figures: leadership and political participation', www.unwomen.org/en/what-we-do/leadership-and-political-participation/facts-and-figures.
12. 'Women and girls' education: facts and figures', www.unesco.org/new/en/unesco/events/prizes-and-celebrations/celebrations/international-days/international-womens-day-2014/women-ed-facts-and-figure/.
13. 'Facts and figures: ending violence against women', www.unwomen.org/en/what-we-do/ending-violence-against-women/facts-and-figures.
14. 'Fast facts: statistics on violence against women and girls', www.

endvawnow.org/en/articles/299-fast-facts-statistics-on-violence-against-women-and-girls-.html.
15. Bacchus, L. J., Ranganathan, M., Watts, C., and Devries, K., 'Recent intimate partner violence against women and health: a systematic review and meta-analysis of cohort studies', https://bmjopen.bmj.com/content/8/7/e019995.
16. In chapter 5, on intersectionality, we unpack these data further by looking at how life chances are shaped by other social factors such as ethnicity, class, age and sexuality.
17. In Kollontai's vision of an equal society, domestic labour would be brought into the sphere of social production, with childbearing separated from childrearing through communal childcare and domestic labour such as cooking and laundry also being undertaken in the public sphere.
18. In Connell's previous work (*Gender and Power*, 1987), there were three dimensions (labour, power and cathexis).

Chapter 4 Simone de Beauvoir

1. While writing *The Second Sex*, Beauvoir thought that the dialectic of the One and the Other was a universal feature of human consciousness. She saw such asymmetry as inevitable but also as reciprocal and, in principle, reversible. In later works she regarded this as a mistake. That such asymmetries emerged she saw not as a necessity of consciousness itself but, in a more Marxist vein, as the consequence of historically specific economic and social conditions. But, even when writing *The Second Sex*, she saw woman's position as the Absolute Other as historically contingent. It was her job both to describe this position and to explain why women were in this position and how it was to be changed.
2. See Deutscher (2008: 160n) for debates about Beauvoir's awareness of her own whiteness. Her acknowledgement of an awareness of her own whiteness is ambiguous. Is she viewing this as experiencing racial otherness or bringing into view her position as the oppressive One in this context? (See ibid.: 138.)
3. 'In the UK, despite recent scandals about the safety of silicone in breast implants and the country teetering on recession, the number of aesthetic surgery operations has continued to rise, in line with trends elsewhere in the developed world. In 2015 over 51,000 people in the UK had cosmetic surgery procedures in clinics registered with the British Association of Aesthetic and Plastic Surgeons alone – an increase of 13 per cent on the previous year (BAAPS 2016). Inclusion within the statistics of non-registered clinics, surgeries abroad, and excluded procedures (hair transplants, "designer vagina" surgery, and cosmetic dentistry, for example) would significantly increase numbers further. If

we add into the mix the number of non-surgical procedures performed (such as fillers), it is estimated that over 1.3 million people now undergo cosmetic work in the UK annually, creating a market worth over £2 billion' (Alsop and Lennon 2018: 97). Alsop and Lennon give an account complicating this picture and pointing out that men's bodies are also now objectified, with the two modes of objectification reinforcing male and female norms of bodily appearance.

4   See the discussion in Gilbert and Lennon (2005: chap. 6).
5   See the article in the *Gulf Times*, 8 March 2016, http://gulf-times.0mr.net/story/483780/Erdogan-says-women-are-above-all-mothers.
6   Here there is a parallel with her discussion of slavery in the *Ethics of Ambiguity*: 'The slave ... does not accept his condition through a resignation of his freedom, since he cannot even dream of any other' (Beauvoir 1976: 85).

Chapter 5 Intersectionality

1   B. Adewumni, 'Kimberlé Crenshaw on intersectionality: "I wanted to come up with an everyday metaphor that anyone could use"', *New Statesman*, 2 April 2014.
2   H. Khaleeli, '#SayHerName', *The Guardian*, 30 May 2016, www.theguardian.com/lifeandstyle/2016/may/30/sayhername-why-kimberle-crenshaw-is-fighting-for-forgotten-women.
3   G. Mumford, 'Hollywood still excludes women, ethnic minorities, LGBT and disabled people', *The Guardian*, 1 August 2017, www.theguardian.com/film/2017/aug/01/hollywood-film-women-lgbt-hispanic-disabled-people-diversity.
4   B. Adewumni, 'Kimberlé Crenshaw on intersectionality: "I wanted to come up with an everyday metaphor that anyone could use"', *New Statesman*, 2 April 2014.
5   The autobiography of Gulwali Passarlay (2015), an unaccompanied child refugee from Afghanistan, is useful to illustrate the ways in which intersectional positionality informs, and is informed by, the migratory journey. In fear for the boy's life, Gulwali's mother sent him away from Afghanistan aged twelve. Over the course of a year he made the perilous journey from Afghanistan to the UK as an unaccompanied minor. From his narrative we can see how the interplay between Gulwali's masculinity, his age, his nationality, his language, his religion and his status as an undocumented migrant were in a constant process of reformulation during his journey, being reconfigured over time within and across the various spaces he travelled.

Chapter 6 Judith Butler

1. 'Gender assignment is a kind of primary interpellation, a kind of cultural "noise"' (Butler and Athanasiou 2013: 96).
2. Here Butler takes there to be a difference between herself and Beauvoir, whom she interprets as viewing biological sex difference as a facticity even while it fails to determine the content of the category 'woman'. Our discussions in chapter 4, however, suggest that this is a misreading of Beauvoir's position.
3. Our discussion here is informed by Alsop et al. (2002: chap. 4).
4. Namaste (2009) argued that it was because trans women were working as sex workers that they were particularly vulnerable to assault and murder, so just focusing on them being trans missed the point that sex workers as a group are vulnerable to violence.

Chapter 7 Making Sense of our (Gendered) Selves

1. '72 countries criminalise same-sex relationships (and in 45 the law is applied to women as well as men); the death penalty is either "allowed", or evidence of its existence occurs, in 8 countries; in more than half the world, LGBT people may not be protected from discrimination by workplace law' (www.stonewall.org.uk/our-work/international-work-1).
2. See Johnson (1997).
3. Although most governments still deny people the right legally to change their name and gender from those that were assigned to them at birth (www.stonewall.org.uk/our-work/international-work-1).
4. G. Hinsliff, 'The Gender Recognition Act is controversial', *The Guardian*, 10 May 2018, www.theguardian.com/world/2018/may/10/the-gender-recognition-act-is-controversial-can-a-path-to-common-ground-be-found.
5. When giving talks, Stephen Whittle often picks from the audience two women with very different appearances and asks them to imagine wearing each other's clothes. Often the response is that they could not wear those clothes and remain themselves. Whittle suggests that the discomfort here reveals varieties of gendered difference operating within and not just across our binary categories.
6. Chinese *yinyang ren*: https://pride-color-schemes.tumblr.com/post/156536428710/yinyang-ren; the *two spirited* Native Americans: D. Brayboy, 'Two spirits, one heart, five genders', *Indian Country Today*, 7 September 2017, https://newsmaven.io/indiancountrytoday/archive/two-spirits-one-heart-five-genders-9UH_xnbfVEWQHWkjNn0rQQ/; the *bakla* people in the Philippines: A. de Jong, 'Bakla', www.academia.edu/5155866/Bakla._The_creation_of_a_Philippine_gay-identity.

7   C. Brinkhurst-Cuff, 'Gender identity clinic for under-18s sees number of referrals double', *The Guardian*, 11 April 2016, www.theguardian.com/society/2016/apr/11/gender-identity-clinic-under-18s-referrals-double.
8   *Orange is the New Black*, American Web television series, www.netflix.com/gb/title/70242311.
9   In the first edition of this book we also used a spatial analogy of gender crossing to accommodate those for whom the borderlands, in between two discrete territories, are home. It is a consequence of that image that those who find that neither side of the binaries of gender or sexuality makes sense of their identifications and desires are instead conceived of as occupying a borderland between discrete states, somehow stopping in the middle. But this picture of being stranded in an *in-between land* is not what is desired by many who aspire to being non-binary, even if it captures something of their current social reality. For this picture occludes, among many possibilities, that of carving out a specificity not defined in terms of the two normative groupings, neither of which is comfortable.
10 Think of Wimbledon tennis club, with its white codes of dress inhospitable to menstruating bodies, for example.
11 The body of the refugee becomes unwelcome in new homes, where for example boys/young male migrants come to be seen as dangerous rather than in danger (Madill and Alsop 2019).
12 Alcoff's own account distinguishes race and gender, as she sees gender as having an anchorage in biology which race lacks. This is discussed and evaluated in chapter 1.
13 There are parallels here with testimony from men who have cosmetic surgery to remove what are termed as 'man boobs'. See Alsop and Lennon (2018).
14 For an early discussion, see Dylan More (1998). There are a number of stories claiming to be about the first pregnant man; see https://transpregnancy.leeds.ac.uk/about/.
15 In Jackie Kay's novel *Trumpet*, in the glory of playing, Joss can accept, as a man, the girl that he has been: 'skipping along the railway line with a long cord his mother has made into a rope. In a red dress' (1998: 135).
16 Yuval-Davis points out that, although different social categories intersect in ways that are mutually constitutive, each of them has a different ontological discourse (2015: 94). Recent debates about the possibility of so-called transracial identifications highlight key differences in contemporary uses of raced and sexed categories (see McGreal 2015; Lawton 2018). Race is a category which implicates kinship, origin and ancestral history.

Conclusion

1 'Eight black women discuss the politics of skin tone', *The Guardian*, 8 April 2019, www.youtube.com/watch?v=i3rEZnxOWcw; N. Eiran, 'Colorism', Black Women of Brazil, https://blackwomenofbrazil.co/colorism-a-sad-reality-makes-dark-skinned-blacks/.
2 World Health Organization, Global and Regional Estimates of Violence against Women: Prevalence and Health Effects of Intimate Partner Violence and Non-Partner Sexual Violence, 2013, p. 2. For individual country information, see United Nations Department of Economic and Social Affairs, and the UN's Global Database on Violence against Women.
3 UN Women, 'Fast facts: statistics on violence against women and girls', www.endvawnow.org/en/articles/299-fast-facts-statistics-on-violence-against-women-and-girls-.html.
4 UN Women, 'Facts and figures: ending violence against women', www.unwomen.org/en/what-we-do/ending-violence-against-women/facts-and-figures.
5 Seventy-two countries still criminalize same-sex relationships (and in forty-five the law is applied to women as well as men). The death penalty is 'allowed', or evidence of its existence occurs, in eight countries. Most governments still deny people the right legally to change their name and gender from those that were assigned to them at birth. There are widespread laws globally against gendered discrimination or harassment at work or in services. But still, in more than half the world, LGBT people may not be protected from discrimination in the workplace or in service provision, and protections are being clawed back: www.stonewall.org.uk/our-work/international-work-1.
6 '#MeToo', www.independent.co.uk/topic/metoo-0.
7 See also *The EveryDay Sexism Project*, https://everydaysexism.com.
8 And, despite it, at the beginning of October 2018 a widely shared image made evident how women's voices still lack credibility. Dr Christine Blasey Ford was interrogated by, primarily, white middle-aged, grey-suited men concerning her claims that Brett Kavanaugh, nominated for the US Supreme Court, had assaulted her at a party when both of them were students. The questioning of Ford, a middle-class professional woman whose social history and positionality closely paralleled Kavanaugh's, in front of an audience of millions as it was transmitted around the world, was hostile and intrusive and shocking. She was not believed by the relevant officials and suffered vilification and abuse on social media. While Kavanaugh was feted and congratulated, Ford was subjected to mocking and belittlement by the president of the US at campaign rallies. She was unable to return to her house. Globally it

represented a setback to the campaign to encourage women to speak out. But it also sparked large-scale demonstrations of support for her and others who speak out, both in America and across the world.

9   Despite its widespread use within feminism, this term had its origin in 'the mythopoetic men's movement of the 1980s and '90s ... [promoting] a masculine spirituality to rescue ... the "deep masculine" – a protective "warrior" masculinity – from toxic masculinity' (Salter 2019).

10 M. Cvorak, 'Lyra McKee: video obituary', 19 April 2019, www.theguardian.com/uk-news/video/2019/apr/19/lyra-mckee-29-year-old-journalist-shot-dead-in-derry-video-obituary.

11 'This is an emergency', www.theguardian.com/environment/video/2019/apr/23/this-is-an-emergency-greta-thunberg-speaks-at-guardian-live-video.

References

Abramson, J. (2019) 'We have 102 women in Congress. It's not Trump's Washington any more', *The Guardian*, 5 January, www.theguardian.com/commentisfree/2019/jan/05/women-in-congress-new-era-not-trump-washington.

Acker, J. (1989) 'The problem with patriarchy', *Sociology* 23(2): 235–40.

Acker, J. (2004) 'Gender, capitalism and globalization', *Critical Sociology* 30(10): 17–41.

Acker, J. (2006a) 'Inequality regimes: gender, class and race in organizations', *Gender and Society* 20(4): 441–64.

Acker, J. (2006b) *Class Questions: Feminist Answers*. Oxford: Rowman & Littlefield.

Agence France-Presse (2014) 'Recep Tayyip Erdoğan: "women not equal to men"', *The Guardian*, 24 November, www.theguardian.com/world/2014/nov/24/turkeys-president-recep-tayyip-erdogan-women-not-equal-men.

Ahmed, S. (2000) *Strange Encounters: Embodied Others in Post-Coloniality*. London: Routledge.

Ahmed, S. (2006) *Queer Phenomenology: Orientations, Objects, Others*. Durham, NC: Duke University Press.

Ahmed, S. (2016) 'Interview with Judith Butler', *Sexualities* 19(4): 482–92.

AIDA (Asylum Information Database) (2018) 'Turkey: gender equality and refugee women and sexual minorities', www.asylumineurope.org/news/29-05-2018/turkey-gender-equality-and-refugee-women-and-sexual-minorities.

AIDA (Asylum Information Database) (2019) 'AIDA 2018 update: Turkey', www.asylumineurope.org/news/29-03-2019/aida-2018-update-turkey.

Akala (2018) *Natives: Race and Class in the Ruins of Empire*. London: Two Roads Press.

Alaimo, S., and Hekman, S. (2008) *Material Feminisms*. Bloomington: Indiana University Press.

Alcoff, L. M. (2006) *Visible Identities: Race, Gender, and the Self*. Oxford: Oxford University Press.

Alcoff, L. M. (2012) 'Gender and reproduction', in S. Gonzalez-Arnal, G. Jagger and K. Lennon, eds, *Embodied Selves*. Basingstoke: Palgrave Macmillan, pp. 12–28.

Alcoff, L. M., and Mendieta, E., eds (2003) *Identities: Race, Class, Gender and Nationality*. Oxford: Blackwell.

Alexander, G. M., and Hines, M. (2002) 'Sex differences in response to children's toys in nonhuman primates', *Evolution and Human Behavior* 23(6): 467–79.

Alexander, M. J., and Mohanty, C., eds (1997) *Feminist Genealogies, Colonial Legacies*. London: Routledge.

Alsop, R. (2000) *A Reversal of Fortunes? Women, Work and Change in East Germany*. Oxford: Berghahn.

Alsop, R., and Hockey, J. (2001) 'Women's reproductive lives as a symbolic resource in Central and Eastern Europe', *European Journal of Women's Studies* 8(4): 454–71.

Alsop, R., and Lennon, K. (2018) 'Aesthetic surgery and the expressive body', *Feminist Theory* 19(1): 95–112.

Alsop, R., Fitzsimons, A., and Lennon, K. (2002) *Theorizing Gender*. Cambridge: Polity.

Angelou, M. (1969) *I Know Why the Caged Bird Sings*. New York: Random House.

Anitha, S. (2010) 'No recourse, no support: state policy and practice towards South Asian women facing domestic violence', *British Journal of Social Work* 40(2): 462–79.

Anitha, S. (2011) 'Legislating gender inequalities: the nature and patterns of domestic violence experienced by South Asian women with insecure immigration status in the United Kingdom', *Violence against Women* 17(10): 1260–85.

Anthias, F. (2013) 'The intersections of class, gender, sexuality and "race": the political economy of gendered violence', *International Journal of Politics, Culture, and Society* 27(2): 153–71.

Anthias, F., and Yuval-Davis, N. (1992) *Racialized Boundaries: Race, Nation, Gender, Colour and Class and the Anti-Racist Struggle*. London: Routledge.

Anzaldúa, G. (1987) *Borderlands/La Frontera: The New Mestiza*. San Francisco: Aunt Lute Books.

Assis, M. P., and Ogando, A. C. (2018) 'Bolsonaro, "gender ideology" and hegemonic masculinity in Brazil', *Aljazeera*, 31 October, www.aljazeera.com/indepth/opinion/bolsonaro-gender-ideology-hegemonic-masculinity-brazil-181031062523759.html.

AWID (Association for Women's Rights in Development) (2004) 'Intersectionality: a tool for economic and social justice', *Women's Rights and Economic Change* 9.

BAAPS (British Association of Aesthetic and Plastic Surgeons) (2016)

SUPER CUTS 'Daddy Makeovers' and Celeb Confessions: Cosmetic Surgery Procedures Soar in Britain, https://baaps.org.uk/about/news/38/super_cuts_daddy_makeovers_and_celeb_confessions_cosmetic_surgery_procedures_soar_in_britain.

Barker, J., dir. (2018) *A Deal with the Universe*, www.imdb.com/title/tt8014038/.

Baron-Cohen, S. (2003) *The Essential Difference: Men, Women and the Extreme Male Brain*. London: Allen Lane.

Barrett, M. (1992) 'Words and things: materialism and method in contemporary feminist analysis', in M. Barrett and A. Phillips, eds, *Destabilizing Theory: Contemporary Feminist Debates*. Cambridge: Polity, pp. 201–19.

Barrett, M., and McIntosh, M. (1979) 'Christine Delphy: Towards a materialist feminism?', *Feminist Review* 1(1): 95–106.

Baskin, C. (2017) 'Ecofeminism as a revolutionary framework in India', 18 September, https://medium.com/@CateBaskin/ecofeminism-as-a-revolutionary-framework-in-india-f04061e6bfcb.

Beatley, M. (2019) 'The shocking rape trial that galvanised Spain's feminists – and the far right', *The Guardian*, 23 April, www.theguardian.com/world/2019/apr/23/wolf-pack-case-spain-feminism-far-right-vox.

Beauvoir, S. de (1943) *She Came to Stay*. London: Harper Perennial.

Beauvoir, S. de (1959) 'Brigitte Bardot and the Lolita syndrome', trans. B. Frechtman, *Esquire*, 1 August.

Beauvoir, S. de (1972) *Old Age*, trans. P. O'Brian. London: Andre Deutsch.

Beauvoir, S. de (1976) *The Ethics of Ambiguity*, trans. B. Frechtman. London: Citadel Press.

Beauvoir, S. de (1981) *Force of Circumstance*, trans. R. Howard. London: Penguin.

Beauvoir, S. de (1999) *Beloved Chicago Man: Letters to Nelson Algren 1947–64*. London: Phoenix.

Beauvoir, S. de ([1948] 2000) *America Day by Day*, trans. C. Cosman. Berkeley: University of California Press.

Beauvoir, S. de ([1949] 2010) *The Second Sex*, trans. Constance Borde and Sheila Malovany-Chevallier. London: Vintage.

Beechey, V. (1979) 'On patriarchy', *Feminist Review* 3: 66–82.

Berger, J. (1972) *Ways of Seeing*. London: Penguin.

Bergner, G. (2005) *Taboo Subjects: Race, Sex, and Psychoanalysis*. Minneapolis: University of Minnesota Press.

Bergoffen, D. (2009) 'Getting the Beauvoir we deserve', in C. Daigle and J. Golomb, eds, *Beauvoir and Sartre: The Riddle of Influence*. Bloomington: Indiana University Press, pp. 13–29.

Bettcher, T., and Garry, A. (2009) 'Introduction: transgender studies and feminism: theory, politics, and gendered realities', *Hypatia* 24(3): 1–10.

Bhabha, H. (1994) *The Location of Culture*. London: Routledge.

Bilge, S. (2013) 'Intersectionality undone: saving intersectionality studies from feminist intersectionality studies', *Du Bois Review* 10(2): 405–24.

Bion, W. (1967) *Second Thoughts: Selected Papers on Psychoanalysis*. New York: Aronson.

Bleier, R. (1984) *Science and Gender: A Critique of Biology and its Theories on Women*. New York: Pergamon Press.

Blondeel, K., Vasconcelos, S. de, García-Moreno, C., Stephenson, R., Temmerman, M., and Toskin, I. (2017) 'Violence motivated by perception of sexual orientation and gender identity: a systematic review', *Bulletin of the World Health Organization*, 23 November, www.who.int/bulletin/volumes/96/1/17-197251/en/.

Bollas, C. (1992) *Being a Character: Psychoanalysis and Self Experience*. London: Routledge.

Bourdieu, P. (1977) *Outline of a Theory of Practice*, trans. R. Nice. Cambridge: Cambridge University Press.

Bourdieu, P. (1990) *The Logic of Practice*, trans. R. Nice. Cambridge: Polity.

Bourdieu, P. (2002) *Masculine Domination*, trans. R. Nice. Cambridge: Polity.

Bowleg, L. (2012) 'The problem with the phrase women and minorities: intersectionality – an important theoretical framework for public health', *American Journal of Public Health* 102(7): 1267–73.

Bowleg, L., Teti, M., Malebranche, D. J., and Tschann, J. M. (2012) '"It's an uphill battle everyday": intersectionality, low-income black heterosexual men, and implications for HIV prevention research and interventions', *Psychology of Men & Masculinity* 14(1): 25–34.

Bradley, H. (2012) *Gender*. 2nd edn, Cambridge: Polity.

Brah, A., and Phoenix, A. (2004) 'Ain't I a woman? Revisiting intersectionality', *Journal of International Women's Studies* 5(3): 75–86.

Braidotti, R. (1994) *Nomadic Subjects: Embodiment and Sexual Difference in Contemporary Feminist Theory*. New York: Columbia University Press.

Braidotti, R. (1998) 'Sexual difference theory', in A. Jaggar and I. M. Young, eds, *A Companion to Feminist Philosophy*. Oxford: Blackwell, pp. 298–307.

Braidotti, R., with Butler, J. (1994) 'Feminism by any other name', *differences* 6(2–3): 27–61.

Brownmiller, S. (1975) *Against Our Will*. New York: Simon & Schuster.

Bruegel, I. (1979) 'Women as a reserve army of labour: a note on recent British experience', *Feminist Review* 3: 12–23.

Butler, J. (1988) 'Performative acts and gender constitution: an essay in phenomenology and feminist theory', *Theatre Journal* 40(4): 519–31.

Butler, J. (1990a) *Gender Trouble: Feminism and the Subversion of Identity*. London: Routledge.

Butler, J. (1990b) 'Gender trouble, feminist theory and psychoanalytic discourse', in L. J. Nicholson, ed., *Feminism/Postmodernism*. London: Routledge, pp. 324–41.

Butler, J. (1993) *Bodies that Matter: On the Discursive Limits of 'Sex'*. London: Routledge.
Butler, J. (1994) 'Against proper objects', *differences* 6(2–3): 1–27.
Butler, J. (1997a) *Excitable Speech: A Politics of the Performative*. London: Routledge.
Butler, J. (1997b) *The Psychic Life of Power*. Stanford, CA: Stanford University Press.
Butler, J. (1998) 'Merely cultural', *New Left Review* 227: 33–44.
Butler, J. (2004a) *Precarious Life*. London: Verso.
Butler, J. (2004b) *Undoing Gender*. London: Routledge.
Butler, J. (2010) *Frames of War*. London: Verso.
Butler, J. (2012) *Parting Ways: Jewishness and the Critique of Zionism*. New York: Columbia University Press.
Butler, J. (2015) *Senses of the Subject*. New York: Fordham University Press.
Butler, J., and Athanasiou, A. (2013) *Dispossession: The Performative in the Political*. Cambridge: Polity.
Butler, J., and Weed, E., eds (2011) *The Question of Gender: Joan W. Scott's Critical Feminism*. Bloomington: Indiana University Press.
Cameron, D. (2007) *The Myth of Mars and Venus: Do Men and Women Really Speak Different Languages?* Oxford: Oxford University Press.
Cannon, L. (2016) 'Firestonian futures and trans-affirming presents', *Hypatia* 31(2): 229–43.
Carastathis, A. (2008) 'The invisibility of privilege: a critique of intersectional models of identity', *Les Ateliers de l'éthique* 3(2): 23–38.
Carastathis, A. (2014) 'The concept of intersectionality in feminist theory', *Philosophy Compass* 9(5): 304–14.
Carbado, D. W., Crenshaw, K., Mays, V. M., and Tomlinson, B. (2013) 'Intersectionality: mapping the movements of a theory', *Du Bois Review: Social Science Research on Race* 10(2): 303–12.
Carby, H. V. (1989) *Reconstructing Womanhood: The Emergence of the Afro-American Woman Novelist*. Oxford: Oxford University Press.
Card, C., ed. (2003) *The Cambridge Companion to Simone de Beauvoir*. Cambridge: Cambridge University Press.
Cashmore, E. (2005) *Making Sense of Sports*. 4th edn, London: Routledge.
Castoriadis, C. (1994) 'Radical imagination and the social instituting imaginary', in G. Robinson and J. F. Rundell, eds, *Rethinking Imagination: Culture and Creativity*. London: Routledge, pp. 136–54.
Castoriadis, C. (1997) *World in Fragments: Writings on Politics, Society, Psychoanalysis, and the Imagination*, trans. D. A. Curtis. Stanford, CA: Stanford University Press.
Cho, S., Crenshaw, K., and McCall, L. (2013) 'Toward a field of intersectionality studies: theory, applications, and praxis', *Signs* 38(4): 785–810.
Chodorow, N. (1978) *The Reproduction of Mothering: Psychoanalysis and the Sociology of Gender*. Berkeley: University of California Press.

Chup, D. N. (2018) *Breaking the Silence about India's Women*. New Delhi: Juggernaut.
Cixous, H. (1976) 'The laugh of the Medusa', trans. K. Cohen and P. Cohen, *Signs* 1(4): 875–93.
Clisby, S., and Holdsworth, J. (2014) *Gendering Women: Identity and Mental Wellbeing through the Lifecourse*. Bristol: Policy Press.
Cocozza, P. (2018) 'The story of one man's pregnancy', *The Guardian*, 22 March, www.theguardian.com/lifeandstyle/2018/mar/22/story-one-mans-pregnancy-trans-jason-barker.
Colebrook, C. (2000) 'From radical representations to corporeal becomings: the feminist philosophy of Lloyd, Grosz, and Gatens', *Hypatia* 15(2): 76–93.
Collins, P. H. (1990) *Black Feminist Thought*. Boston: Unwin Hyman.
Collins, P. H. (2004) *Black Sexual Politics: African Americans, Gender and the New Racism*. London: Routledge.
Collins, P. H. (2015) 'Intersectionality's definitional dilemmas', *Annual Review of Sociology* 41: 1–20.
Collins, P. H. (2017) 'The difference that power makes: intersectionality and participatory democracy', *Investigaciones Feministas* 8(1): 19–39.
Collins, P. H., and Bilge, S. (2016) *Intersectionality*. Cambridge: Polity.
Combahee River Collective ([1977] 2015) 'A black feminist statement', in C. Moraga and G. Anzaldúa, eds, *This Bridge Called My Back: Writings by Radical Women of Color*. 4th edn, Albany, NY: SUNY Press, pp. 210–18.
Connell, R. W. (1987) *Gender and Power*. Cambridge: Polity.
Connell, R. W. (2000) *The Men and the Boys*. Cambridge: Polity.
Connell, R. W. (2005) 'Change among the gatekeepers: men, masculinities and gender equality in the global arena', *Signs* 30(3): 1801–25.
Connell, R. W. (2009) *Gender: In World Perspective*. 2nd edn, Cambridge: Polity.
Connell, R. W. (2014) 'King hits: young men, masculinity and violence', *The Conversation*, 21 January.
Connell, R. W., and Pearse, R. (2015) *Gender: In World Perspective*. 3rd edn, Cambridge: Polity.
Coole, D., and Frost, S., eds (2010a) *New Materialism: Ontology, Agency and Politics*. Durham, NC: Duke University Press.
Coole, D., and Frost, S. (2010b) 'Introducing the new materialisms', in D. Coole and S. Frost, eds, *New Materialism: Ontology, Agency and Politics*. Durham, NC: Duke University Press, pp. 1–46.
Cooper, B. (2015) 'Black, queer, feminist, erased from history: meet the most important legal scholar you've likely never heard of', *Salon.com*, 18 February.
Corrêa, S. (2017) 'Gender ideology: tracking its origins and meanings in current gender politics', *LSE Blogs*, https://blogs.lse.ac.uk/gender/2017/12/11/gender-ideology-tracking-its-origins-and-meanings-in-current-gender-politics/.

Corrêa, S., Paternotte, D., and Kuhar, R. (2018) 'The globalisation of anti-gender campaigns', *International Politics and Society*, 31 May, www.ips-journal.eu/topics/human-rights/article/show/the-globalisation-of-anti-gender-campaigns-2761/.

Crenshaw, K. (1989) 'Demarginalizing the intersection of race and sex: a black feminist critique of antidiscrimination doctrine, feminist theory and antiracist politics', *University of Chicago Legal Forum* 140: 139–67.

Crenshaw, K. (1991) 'Mapping the margins: intersectionality, identity politics, and violence against women of color', *Stanford Law Review* 43(6): 1241–99.

Crenshaw, K. (2012) 'Postscript', in H. Lutz, M. T. H. Vivar and L. Supik, eds, *Framing Intersectionality: Debates on a Multi-Faceted Concept in Gender Studies*. Farnham: Ashgate.

Cuban, S. (2013) *Deskilling Migrant Women in the Global Care Industry*. London: Palgrave Macmillan.

Dalla Costa, M., and James, S. (1975) *The Power of Women and the Subversion of the Community*. Bristol: Falling Wall Press.

Daly, M. (1978) *Gyn/Ecology: The Metaethics of Radical Feminists*. Boston: Beacon Press.

Darweesh, A. D., and Abdullah, N. M. (2016) 'A critical discourse analysis of Donald Trump's sexist ideology', *Journal of Education and Practice* 7(30): 87–95.

Davis, A. (1982) *Women, Race and Class*. London: Women's Press.

Davis, K. (2008) 'Intersectionality as buzzword: a sociology of science perspective on what makes a feminist theory successful', *Feminist Theory* 9(1): 67–85.

Deleuze, G., and Guattari, F. (1987) *A Thousand Plateaus*, trans. B. Massumi. Minneapolis: University of Minnesota Press.

Delphy, C. (1977) *The Main Enemy*. London: Women's Research and Resource Centre.

Department for Education and Skills (2007) *Gender and Education: The Evidence on Pupils in England*. London: Department for Education and Skills.

Derrida, J. (1978) *Writing and Difference*, trans. A. Bass. London: Routledge & Kegan Paul.

Deutscher, P. (2008) *The Philosophy of Simone de Beauvoir*. Cambridge: Cambridge University Press.

Dolezal, L. (2010) 'The (in)visible body: feminism, phenomenology, and the case of cosmetic surgery', *Hypatia* 25(2): 357–75.

Dolezal, L. (2015) *The Body and Shame: Phenomenology, Feminism, and the Socially Shaped Body*. Lanham, MD: Lexington Books.

Douglass, F. ([1845] 1982) *Narrative of the Life of Frederick Douglass, an American Slave*. New York: Penguin.

Du Bois, W. E. B. ([1903] 1989) *The Souls of Black Folk*. New York: Penguin.
Dylan More, S. (1998) 'The pregnant man – an oxymoron?', *Journal of Gender Studies* 7(3): 319–28.
Ebert, T. (1996) *Ludic Feminism and After: Postmodernism, Desire and Labor in Late Capitalism*. Ann Arbor: University of Michigan Press.
Ebert, T. (1999) 'Alexandra Kollontai and red love', *Solidarity*, www.solidarity-us.org/node/1724.
Eddo-Lodge, R. (2017) *Why I'm No Longer Talking to White People about Race*. London: Bloomsbury.
Einhorn, B. (1993) *Cinderella Goes to Market*. London: Verso.
Engels, F. ([1884] 1972) *The Origins of the Family, Private Property and the State*. London: Lawrence & Wishart.
Fanon, F. (1968) *Black Skin, White Masks*. London: MacGibbon & Kee.
Fanon, F. (2001) 'The lived experience of the black man', *Black Skin, White Masks*. London: MacGibbon & Kee, pp. 89–119; repr. in R. Bernasconi, ed., *Race*. Oxford: Blackwell, pp. 184–202.
Fausto-Sterling, A. (1992) *Myths of Gender: Biological Theories about Women and Men*. New York: Basic Books.
Fausto-Sterling, A. (1993) 'The five sexes: why male and female are not enough', *Sciences* 33(2): 20–5.
Fausto-Sterling, A. (2000) *Sexing the Body: Gender Politics and the Construction of Sexuality*. New York: Basic Books.
Fehr, C. (2011) 'Feminist philosophy of biology', in E. N. Zalta, ed., *The Stanford Encyclopedia of Philosophy*, http://plato.stanford.edu/archives/fall2011/entries/feminist-philosophy-biology.
Feinberg, L. (1998) *Trans Liberation: Beyond Pink or Blue*. Boston: Beacon Press.
Field, K. L. (1982) 'Alexandra Kollontai: precursor of Eurofeminism', *Dialectical Anthropology* 6(3): 229–44.
Fine, C. (2012) *Delusions of Gender*. London: Icon Books.
Fine, C. (2017) *Testosterone Rex*. London: Icon Books.
Fine, M., and Asch, A. (1988) 'Disability beyond stigma: social interaction, discrimination, and activism', *Journal of Social Issues* 44(1): 3–21.
Firestone, S. (1970) *The Dialectic of Sex: The Case for Feminist Revolution*. New York: William Morrow.
Foucault, M. (1978) *The History of Sexuality*, Vol. 1: *An Introduction*. London: Penguin.
Fox, G. (2019) 'Meet the neuroscientist shattering the myth of the gendered brain', *The Observer*, 24 February, www.theguardian.com/science/2019/feb/24/meet-the-neuroscientist-shattering-the-myth-of-the-gendered-brain-gina-rippon.
Fraser, N. (2000) 'Rethinking recognition', *New Left Review* 3 (May–June).
Fraser, N. (2013) *Feminism, Capitalism, and the Cunning of History: An Introduction*, https://halshs.archives-ouvertes.fr/halshs-00725055/document.

Fraser, N., and Bartky, S. L., eds (1992) *Revaluing French Feminism: Critical Essays on Difference, Agency, and Culture*. Bloomington: Indiana University Press.

Freud, A., ed. (1986) *Sigmund Freud: The Essentials of Psychoanalysis*. Harmondsworth: Penguin.

Freud, S. (1914) 'On narcissism: an introduction', SE 14: 67–104.

Freud, S. (1915) 'A case of paranoia running counter to the psycho-analytic theory of the disease', SE 14: 261–72.

Freud, S. (1920) 'The psychogenesis of a case of homosexuality in a woman', SE 18: 145–76.

Freud, S. (1923) *The Ego and the Id*, SE 19: 12–68; PFL 2.

Freud, S. (1933) 'Femininity', *New Introductory Lectures on Psychoanalysis*, SE 22: 112–35; PFL 2; repr. in R. Minsky, ed. (1996) *Psychoanalysis and Gender: An Introductory Reader*. Abingdon: Routledge, pp. 215–35.

Freud, S. (1953–65) *The Standard Edition of the Complete Psychological Works of Sigmund Freud*, 24 vols, trans. J. Strachey et al. London: Hogarth Press and the Institute of Psycho-Analysis [SE].

Freud, S. (1973–) *Pelican Freud Library*, 14 vols. Harmondsworth: Penguin [PFL].

Gamson, J. (1996) 'Must identity movements self-destruct? A queer dilemma', in S. Seidman, ed., *Queer Theory/Sociology*. Oxford: Blackwell, pp. 395–420.

Garland-Thomson, R. (1997) *Extraordinary Bodies: Figuring Physical Disability in American Culture and Literature*. New York: Columbia University Press.

Garland-Thomson, R. (2002) 'Integrating disability, transforming feminist theory', *NWSA Journal* 14(3): 1–32.

Garry, A. (2011) 'Intersectionality, metaphors, and the multiplicity of gender', *Hypatia* 26(4): 826–50.

Gatens, M. (1996) *Imaginary Bodies: Ethics, Power and Corporeality*. London: Routledge.

Geena Davis Institute on Gender in Media (2019) *The Geena Benchmark Report 2007–2017*, https://seejane.org/wp-content/uploads/geena-benchmark-report-2007-2017-2-12-19.pdf.

George, R. (2015) 'My period may hurt: but not talking about menstruation hurts more', *The Guardian*, 22 January, www.theguardian.com/commentisfree/2015/jan/22/period-menstruation-heather-watson-taboo.

Gerschick, T. J. (2000) 'Toward a theory of disability and gender', *Signs* 25(4): 1263–8.

Gilbert, P. (1997) 'The evolution of social attractiveness and its role in shame, humiliation, guilt and therapy', *Psychology and Psychotherapy* 70(2): 113–47.

Gilbert, P., and Lennon, K. (2005) *The World, the Flesh and the Subject: Continental Themes in Philosophy of Mind and Body*. Edinburgh: Edinburgh University Press.

Gill, R., and Elias, A. S. (2014) '"Awaken your incredible": love your body discourses and postfeminist contradictions', *International Journal of Media and Cultural Politics* 10(2): 179–88.

Gill, R., Henwood, K., and McLean, C. (2005) 'Body projects and the regulation of normative masculinity', *Body & Society* 11(1): 37–62.

Gillette (2019) 'We believe: the best men can be', www.youtube.com/watch?v=koPmuEyP3a0.

Gines, K. T. (2014) 'Race women, race men and early expressions of proto-intersectionality, 1830s–1930s', in N. Goswami, M. M. O'Donovan and L. Yount, eds, *Why Race and Gender Still Matter: An Intersectional Approach*. New York: Routledge, pp. 13–26.

Gines, K. (2017) 'Simone de Beauvoir and the race/gender analogy in *The Second Sex* revisited', in L. Hengehold and N. Bauer, eds, *A Companion to Simone de Beauvoir*. Oxford: Wiley Blackwell, pp. 47–58.

Glatz, C. (2015) 'Pope Francis: gender theory is the problem, not the solution', *National Catholic Reporter*, 15 April, www.ncronline.org/blogs/francis-chronicles/pope-francis-gender-theory-problem-not-solution.

Gonzalez-Arnal, S. (2013) 'Interseccionalidad y diversidad: en defensa de un modelo de análisis categorial no opresivo que respeta la diferencia', in M. Zapata Galindo, S. García Peter and J. Chan de Ávila, eds, *La interseccionalidad en debate*. Berlin: Lateinamerika-Institut der Freien Universität, pp. 45–55.

Gonzalez-Arnal, S., Jagger, G., and Lennon, K. (2012) *Embodied Selves*. Basingstoke: Palgrave Macmillan.

Graff, A. (2014) 'Report from the gender trenches: war against "genderism" in Poland', *European Journal of Women's Studies* 21(4): 431–42.

Grosz, E. (1994) *Volatile Bodies: Towards a Corporeal Feminism*. Bloomington: Indiana University Press.

Grosz, E. (2008) 'Darwin and feminism: preliminary investigations for a possible alliance', in S. Alaimo and S. Hekman, eds, *Material Feminisms*. Bloomington: Indiana University Press.

Gutman, M. C., and Vigoya, M. V. (2005) 'Masculinities in Latin America', in M. S. Kimmel, J. Hearn and R. W. Connell, eds, *Handbook of Studies on Men and Masculinity*. London: Sage, pp. 114–28.

Halberstam, J. (1994) 'F2M: the making of female masculinity', in L. Doan, ed., *The Lesbian Postmodern*. New York: Columbia University Press, pp. 210–28.

Halberstam, J. (1998) *Female Masculinity*. Durham, NC: Duke University Press.

Haraway, D. J. (1991) *Simians, Cyborgs and Women: The Reinvention of Nature*. London: Routledge.

Haraway, D. J. (1997) *Modest_Witness@Second_Millennium.FemaleMan©_Meets_OncoMouse™: Feminism and Technoscience*. London: Routledge.

Haraway, D. J. (2008) 'Otherworldly conversations, terran topics, local terms', in S. Alaimo and S. Hekman, eds, *Material Feminisms*. Bloomington: Indiana University Press, pp. 157–87.

Haraway, D. J. (2016) *Staying with the Trouble: Making Kin in the Chthulucene*. Durham, NC: Duke University Press.

Harding, S. (1992) *Whose Science, Whose Knowledge? Thinking from Women's Lives*. Ithaca, NY: Cornell University Press.

Harding, S., ed. (1993) *The 'Racial' Economy of Science: Towards a Democratic Future*. Bloomington: Indiana University Press.

Harding, S. (1998) *Is Science Multicultural? Postcolonialisms, Feminisms, and Epistemologies*. Bloomington: Indiana University Press.

Harrison, P. (2017) 'Why Pauli Murray, why now?', *Radcliffe Institute for Advanced Study, Harvard University*, www.radcliffe.harvard.edu/news/in-news/why-pauli-murray-why-now.

Hartmann, H. I. (1979) 'The unhappy marriage of Marxism and feminism: towards a more progressive union', *Capital and Class* 8: 1–33.

Hegel, G. W. F. (1977) *Phenomenology of Spirit*, trans. J. N. Findlay. Oxford: Clarendon Press.

Heggie, V. (2015) 'Nature and sex redefined – we have never been binary', *The Guardian*, 19 February, www.theguardian.com/science/the-h-word/2015/feb/19/nature-sex-redefined-we-have-never-been-binary.

Heidegger, M. (1962) *Being and Time*, trans. E. Macquarrie and J. Robinson. Oxford: Blackwell.

Heidegger, M. (1975) 'Building, dwelling, thinking', in *Poetry, Language, Thought*, trans. A. Hofstadter. New York: Harper & Row.

Heinämaa, S. (2003) *Toward a Phenomenology of Sexual Difference*. Lanham, MD: Rowman & Littlefield.

Hennessy, R. (1993) *Materialist Feminism and the Politics of Discourse*. London: Routledge.

Hennessy, R. (2000) *Profit and Pleasure. Sexual Identities in Late Capitalism*. London: Routledge.

Hennessy, R., and Ingraham, C. (1997) 'Introduction: reclaiming anticapitalist feminism', in R. Hennessy and C. Ingraham, eds, *Materialist Feminism: A Reader in Class, Difference and Women's Lives*. London: Routledge, pp. 1–16.

Herbert, J. (2015) *Testosterone: Sex, Power and the Will to Win*. Oxford: Oxford University Press.

Herdt, G., ed. (1994) *Third Sex, Third Gender: Beyond Sexual Dimorphism in Culture and History*. New York: Zone Books.

Hettinga, L. (2019) 'Against accommodation: disability and trans* visual poetics', *Gender and Cultures of In/Equality in Europe* workshop, Utrecht, 7–9 March.

Heyes, C., and Jones, M. (2009) 'Cosmetic surgery in the age of gender', in C. Heyes and M. Jones, eds, *Cosmetic Surgery: A Feminist Primer*. Farnham: Ashgate.

Hines, S. (2006) 'What's the difference? Bringing particularity to queer studies of transgender', *Journal of Gender Studies* 15(1): 49–66.

Hines, S. (2010) 'Sexing gender, gendering sex: towards an intersectional analysis of transgender', in Y. Taylor, S. Hines and M. E. Casey, eds, *Theorizing Intersectionality and Sexuality*. Basingstoke: Palgrave Macmillan, pp. 140–62.

Hines, S. (2019) 'The feminist frontier: on trans and feminism', *Journal of Gender Studies* 28(2): 145–57.

Hinsliff, G. (2018a) 'I am not prepared to tell trans women they are less valid', *The Guardian*, 9 February, www.theguardian.com/commentisfree/2018/feb/09/transgender-women-labour-shortlists-gender-discrimination.

Hinsliff, G. (2018b) 'The Gender Recognition Act is controversial – can a path to common ground be found?', *The Guardian*, 10 May, www.theguardian.com/world/2018/may/10/the-gender-recognition-act-is-controversial-can-a-path-to-common-ground-be-found.

Holliday, R., and Sanchez Taylor, J. (2006) 'Aesthetic surgery as false beauty', *Feminist Theory* 7(2): 179–95.

Honneth, A. (1995) *The Struggle for Recognition: The Moral Grammar of Social Conflicts*, trans. J. Anderson. Cambridge: Polity.

hooks, b. (1981) *Ain't I a Woman? Black Women and Feminism*. London: Pluto Press.

hooks, b. (1984) *Feminist Theory from Margin to Centre*. Boston: South End Press.

hooks, b. (1990) *Yearning: Race, Gender, and Cultural Politics*. Boston: South End Press.

hooks, b. (1991) 'Theory as liberatory practice', *Yale Journal of Law & Feminism* 4(1), https://digitalcommons.law.yale.edu/cgi/viewcontent.cgi?article=1044&context=yjlf.

hooks, b. (2012) 'True philosophers: Beauvoir and bell', in S. M. Mussett and W. S. Wilkerson, eds, *Simone de Beauvoir in Western Thought: Plato to Butler*. New York: SUNY Press, pp. 227–36.

House of Commons, Women and Equalities Committee (2018) *Sexual Harassment in the Workplace*. London: House of Commons.

Howie, G. (2010) 'Sexing the state of nature: Firestone's materialist manifesto', in M. Merck and S. Sandford, eds, *Further Adventures of the Dialectic of Sex: Critical Essays on Shulamith Firestone*. Basingstoke: Palgrave Macmillan, pp. 215–34.

Hurst, G. (2018) 'Minister Penny Mordaunt orders research into rise of gender referrals for girls', *The Times*, 17 September, www.thetimes.co.uk/article/research-into-rise-of-girl-gender-referrals-w6b5v6fx5.

Inahara, M. (2009) *Abject Love: Undoing the Boundaries of Physical Disability*. Munster: VDM.

Irigaray, L. (1985a) *Speculum of the Other Woman*, trans. G. Gill. Ithaca, NY: Cornell University Press; extracts repr. in R. Minsky, ed. (1996)

Psychoanalysis and Gender: An Introductory Reader. Abingdon: Routledge, pp. 289–93.

Irigaray, L. (1985b) *This Sex Which is not One*, trans. C. Porter with C. Burke. Ithaca, NY: Cornell University Press.

Irigaray, L. (1993) *Sex and Genealogies*, trans. G. Gill. New York: Columbia University Press.

Irigaray, L. (1994) *Thinking the Difference: For a Peaceful Revolution*, trans. K. Montin. London: Athlone Press.

Jackson, S. (1995) 'Gender and heterosexuality: a materialist feminist analysis', in M. Maynard and J. Purvis, eds, *(Hetero)sexual Politics*. London: Taylor & Francis, pp. 11–26.

Jackson, S. (1997) 'Classic review – *Against Our Will*', *Trouble and Strife* 35, www.troubleandstrife.org/articles/issue-35/classic-review-against-our-will/.

Jackson, S. (2001) 'Why a materialist feminism is (still) possible – and necessary', *Women's Studies International Forum* 24(3–4): 283–93.

Jagger, G. (2015) 'The new materialism and sexual difference', *Signs* 40(2): 321–42.

James, S. (2003) 'Complicity and slavery in *The Second Sex*', in C. Card, ed., *The Cambridge Companion to Simone de Beauvoir*. Cambridge: Cambridge University Press, pp. 149–67.

Jaschik, S. (2017) 'Judith Butler on being attacked in Brazil', *Inside Higher Ed*, 13 November, www.insidehighered.com/news/2017/11/13/judith-butler-discusses-being-burned-effigy-and-protested-brazil.

Johnson, M. (1997) *Beauty and Power: Transgendering and Cultural Transformation in the Southern Philippines*. Oxford: Berg.

Jonason, P. K. (2007) 'An evolutionary psychology perspective on sex differences in exercise behaviors and motivations', *Journal of Social Psychology* 147(1): 5–14.

Jones, M. (2013) 'Media-bodies and Photoshop', in F. Attwood, V. Campbell, I. Q. Hunter and S. Lockyer, eds, *Controversial Images: Media Representations on the Edge*. Basingstoke: Palgrave Macmillan, pp. 19–35.

Jordan-Young, R. M. (2010) *Brain Storm: The Flaws in the Science of Sex Differences*. Cambridge, MA: Harvard University Press.

Jordan-Young, R. M., and Karkazis, K. (2019) *Testosterone: An Unauthorized Biography*. Cambridge, MA: Harvard University Press.

Käll, L. F. (2015) 'A path between voluntarism and determinism tracing elements of phenomenology in Judith Butler's account of performativity', *lambda nordica* 2–3: 23–48.

Kantola, J., and Lombardo, E. (2019) 'Populism and feminist politics: The cases of Finland and Spain', *European Journal of Political Research*, 28 February.

Kaplan, C., and Grewal, I., eds (1994) *Scattered Hegemonies: Postmodernity and Transnational Feminist Practices*. Minneapolis: University of Minnesota Press.

Karkazis, K. (2019) 'Stop talking about testosterone – there's no such thing as a "true sex"', *The Guardian*, 6 March, www.theguardian.com/commentisfree/2019/mar/06/testosterone-biological-sex-sports-bodies.

Kay, J. (1998) *Trumpet*. London: Picador.

Keller, J., Mendes, K., and Ringrose, J. (2018) 'Speaking "unspeakable things": documenting digital feminist responses to rape culture', *Journal of Gender Studies* 27(1): 22–36.

Kimmel, M. S. (1994) 'Masculinity as homophobia: fear, shame and silence in the construction of gender identity', in H. Brod and M. Kaufmann, eds, *Theorizing Masculinities*. Thousand Oaks, CA: Sage, pp. 119–41.

Kirkpatrick, K. (2019) *Becoming Beauvoir: A Life*. London: Bloomsbury Academic.

Klein, M. (1931) *The Psychoanalysis of Children*. London: Hogarth Press.

Kollontai, A. (1977) *Alexandra Kollontai: Selected Writings*, ed. A. Holt. London: Allison & Busby.

Kollontai, A. ([1909] 1977) 'The social basis of the woman question', in *Alexandra Kollontai: Selected Writings*, ed. A. Holt. London: Allison & Busby.

Kollontai, A. ([1921] 1977) 'Sexual relations and the class struggle', in *Alexandra Kollontai: Selected Writings*, ed. A. Holt. London: Allison & Busby.

Koyama, E. (2006) 'Whose feminism is it anyway? The unspoken racism of the trans inclusion debate', in S. Stryker and S. Whittle, eds, *The Transgender Studies Reader*. New York: Routledge, pp. 698–705.

Kristeva, J. (1977) *About Chinese Women*. London: Marion Boyars.

Kristeva, J. (1982) *Powers of Horror: An Essay on Abjection*. New York: Columbia University Press.

Kristeva, J. (1984) *Revolution in Poetic Language*, trans. M. Waller. New York: Columbia University Press.

Kruks, S. (2012) 'Theorising oppression', in *Simone de Beauvoir and the Politics of Ambiguity*. Oxford: Oxford University Press, pp. 56–92.

Kuhar, R., and Paternotte, D., eds (2017) *Anti-Gender Campaigns in Europe: Mobilizing Against Equality*. London: Rowman & Littlefield.

Lacan, J. (1978) *The Four Fundamental Concepts of Psycho-Analysis*, ed. J.-A. Miller, trans. A. Sheridan. New York: W. W. Norton.

Lacan, J. (2005) *Ecrits*, trans. B. Fink. New York: W. W. Norton.

Lancaster, R. N., and Leonardo, M. di (1997) *The Gender/Sexuality Reader: Culture, History, Political Economy*. London: Routledge.

Lane, R. (2009) 'Trans as bodily becoming; rethinking the biological as diversity, not dichotomy', *Hypatia* 24(3): 136–57.

Laplanche, J., and Pontalis, J. B. (1985) *The Language of Psychoanalysis*. London: Hogarth Press.

Laqueur, T. (1990) *Making Sex: Body and Gender from the Greeks to Freud*. Cambridge, MA: Harvard University Press.

Lawton, G. (2018) 'Is this "black" theatre director actually using white privilege?', *The Guardian*, 6 November, www.theguardian.com/

commentisfree/2018/nov/06/black-anthony-lennon-theatre-director-white-mixed-race.
Le Doeuff, M. (2010) 'Beauvoir the mythoclast', *Paragraph* 33(1): 90–104.
Lenin, V. I. (1966) *On the Emancipation of Women*. New York: International.
Lennon, K. (2006) 'Making life livable: transsexuality and bodily transformation', *Radical Philosophy* 140: 26–34.
Lennon, K. (2015) *Imagination and the Imaginary*. Abingdon: Routledge.
Lennon, K. (2018) 'Expressing the world: Merleau-Ponty and feminist debates on nature/culture', in C. Fischer and L. Dolezal, eds, *New Feminist Perspectives on Embodiment*. Basingstoke: Palgrave Macmillan, pp. 125–44.
Livingston, J. (dir.) (1990) *Paris is Burning*. Miramax.
Lloyd, E. (2003) 'Violence against science: rape and evolution', in C. Travis, ed., *Evolution, Gender, and Rape*. Cambridge, MA: MIT Press, pp. 235–62.
Lokaneeta, J. (2001) 'Alexandra Kollontai and Marxist feminism', *Economic and Political Weekly* 36(7): 1405–12.
Lorde, A. (1984) *Sister Outsider: Essays and Speeches*. Berkeley, CA: Crossing Press.
Lugones, M. (2003) *Pilgrimages/Peregrinajes: Theorizing Coalition against Multiple Oppressions*. Oxford: Rowman & Littlefield.
Lugones, M. (2005) 'Multiculturalismo radical y feminismos de mujeres de color', *Revista Internacional de Filosofía Política* 25: 61–76.
Lugones, M. (2007) 'Heterosexualism and the colonial/modern gender system', *Hypatia* 22(1): 186–209.
Lugones, M. (2010) 'Toward a decolonial feminism', *Hypatia* 25(4): 742–59.
Maas, A. H. E. M., and Appelman, Y. E. A. (2010) 'Gender differences in coronary heart disease', *Netherlands Heart Journal* 18(12): 598–602.
McBee, T. P. (2018) *Amateur: A True Story about What Makes a Man*. Edinburgh: Canongate Books.
McCall, L. (2005) 'The complexity of intersectionality', *Signs* 30(3): 1771–800.
McClintock, A. (1995) *Imperial Leather: Race, Gender and Sexuality in the Colonial Contest*. London: Routledge, pp. 235–54.
McDowell, L. (1999) *Gender, Identity and Place: Understanding Feminist Geographies*. Minneapolis: University of Minnesota Press.
McGreal, C. (2015) 'Rachel Dolezal: I wasn't identifying as black to upset people. I was being me', *The Guardian*, 13 December, www.theguardian.com/us-news/2015/dec/13/rachel-dolezal-i-wasnt-identifying-as-black-to-upset-people-i-was-being-me.
McNay, L. (2000) *Gender and Agency*. Cambridge: Polity.
McNay, L. (2008) *Against Recognition*. Cambridge: Polity.
McWhorter, L. (2004) 'Sex, race, and biopower: a Foucauldian genealogy', *Hypatia* 19(3): 38–62.
Madill, E., and Alsop, R. (2019) *Evaluation of the Empower Women Project*. London: Shpresa Programme, https://empowerwomentoolkit.org.

Mairs, N. (1986) 'On being a cripple', *Plaintext Essays*. Tucson: University of Arizona Press.
Mairs, N. (1990) *Carnal Acts*. Boston: Beacon Press.
Mairs, N. (1997) 'Carnal acts', in K. Conboy, N. Medina and S. Stanbury, eds, *Writing on the Body: Female Embodiment and Feminist Theory*. New York: Columbia University Press, pp. 293–309.
Martin, B. (1988) 'Feminism, criticism and Foucault', in I. Diamond and L. Quinby, eds, *Feminism and Foucault: Reflections on Resistance*. Boston: Northeastern University Press, pp. 3–19.
Martin, B. (1994) 'Sexuality without gender and other queer utopias', *Diacritics* 24(2–3): 104–21.
Martin, E. (1987) *The Woman in the Body: A Cultural Analysis of Reproduction*. Milton Keynes: Open University Press.
Marx, K. ([1844] 1978) 'Economic and philosophic manuscripts', in *The Marx–Engels Reader*, ed. R. C. Tucker. 2nd edn, New York: W. W. Norton.
Marx, K. ([1859] 2013) *A Contribution to the Critique of Political Economy*. 2nd edn, Chicago: Charles H. Kerr.
Marx, K., and Engels, F. ([1848] 2017) *The Communist Manifesto*. London: Pluto Press.
Massad, J. (2009) 'How not to study gender in the Arab world', Lecture at Oberlin College, October.
Mead, M. (1949a) *Coming of Age*. New York: Mentor.
Mead, M. (1949b) *Male and Female: A Study of the Sexes in a Changing World*. New York: William Morrow.
Meijer, I. C., and Prins, B. (1998) 'How bodies come to matter: an interview with Judith Butler', *Signs* 23(2): 275–86.
Menjívar, C., and Salcido, O. (2002) 'Immigrant women and domestic violence: common experiences in different countries', *Gender and Society* 16(6): 898–920.
Meret, S., and Siim, B. (2013) 'Gender, populism and politics of belonging: discourses of right-wing populist parties in Denmark, Norway and Austria', in B. Siim and M. Mokre, eds, *Negotiating Gender and Diversity in an Emergent European Public Sphere*. Basingstoke: Palgrave Macmillan, pp. 78–96.
Merleau-Ponty, M. ([1945] 1962) *Phenomenology of Perception*, trans. C. Smith. London: Routledge.
Merleau-Ponty, M. ([1948] 2004) *The World of Perception*, trans. O. Davis. London: Routledge.
Mies, M. ([1986] 1998) *Patriarchy and Accumulation on a World Scale: Women in the International Division of Labour*. London: Zed Books.
Millett, K. (1970) *Sexual Politics*. London: Hart-Davis.
Minsky, R., ed. (1996) *Psychoanalysis and Gender: An Introductory Reader*. Abingdon: Routledge.

Mirza, H. S., ed. (1997) *Black British Feminism: A Reader*. London: Routledge.
Mitchell, J. (1974) *Psychoanalysis and Women*. Harmondsworth: Penguin.
Mohanty, C. T. (1986) 'Under Western eyes: feminist scholarship and colonial discourses', *boundary* 2(12): 333–58.
Mohanty, C. T. (2003) '"Under Western eyes" revisited: feminist solidarity through anticapitalist struggles', in Mohanty, *Feminism without Borders: Decolonizing Theory, Practicing Solidarity*. Durham, NC: Duke University Press, chapter 9.
Mohanty, C. T. (2013) 'Transnational feminist crossings: on neoliberalism and radical critique', *Signs* 38(4): 967–91.
Moi, T. (1999) *What is a Woman?* Oxford: Oxford University Press.
Moi, T. (2008) *Simone de Beauvoir: The Making of an Intellectual Woman*. 2nd edn, Oxford: Oxford University Press.
Monro, S. (2015) *Bisexuality: Identities, Politics, and Theories*. Basingstoke: Palgrave Macmillan.
Moodley, J., and Graham, L. (2015) 'The importance of intersectionality in disability and gender studies', *Agenda* 29(2): 24–33.
Moreno Figueroa, M. G., and Rivers-Moore, M. (2013) 'Beauty, race and feminist theory in Latin America and the Caribbean', *Feminist Theory* 14(2): 131–6.
Morgan, A. (2019) 'The real problem with toxic masculinity is that it assumes that there is only one way of being a man', *The Conversation*, 7 February.
Morgan, R., ed. (1970) *Sisterhood is Powerful*. London: Random House.
Morris, J. (1974) *Conundrum*. New York: Harcourt, Brace, Jovanovich.
Morris, J. (1993) 'Feminism and disability', *Feminist Review* 43(1): 57–70.
Morrison, T. ([1970] 2000) *The Bluest Eye*. New York: Knopf.
Mullings, L., and Schulz, A. J. (2006) 'Intersectionality and health: an introduction', in A. J. Schulz and L. Mullings, eds, *Gender, Race, Class and Health: Intersectional Approaches*. San Francisco: Jossey-Bass, pp. 3–17.
Murray, J. (2017) 'Be trans, be proud – but don't call yourself a "real woman"', *Sunday Times*, 5 March, www.thetimes.co.uk/article/be-trans-be-proud-but-dont-call-yourself-a-real-woman-frtld7q5c.
Murray, P. (2018) *Song in a Weary Throat: Memoir of an American Pilgrimage*. New York: Liveright.
Myrdal, G., Sterner, R., and Rose, A. (1944) *An American Dilemma: The Negro Problem and Modern Democracy*. New York: Harper.
Namaste, V. (2000) *Invisible Lives: The Erasure of Transsexual and Transgendered People*. Chicago: University of Chicago Press.
Namaste, V. (2009) 'Undoing theory: the "transgender question" and the epistemic violence of Anglo-American feminist theory', *Hypatia* 24(3): 11–32.
Narayan, U. (1997) *Dislocating Cultures: Identities, Traditions, and Third-World Feminism*. London: Routledge.
Nash, J. C. (2008) 'Rethinking intersectionality', *Feminist Review* 89: 1–15.

Nataf, Z. I. (1996) *Lesbians Talk Transgender*. London: Scarlett Press.
Nelson, E. S., ed. (2009) *Encyclopedia of Contemporary LGBTQ Literature of the United States*, 2 vols. Santa Barbara, CA: Greenwood Press.
Nelson, M. (2016) *The Argonauts*. London: Melville.
Oakley, A. (1985) *Sex, Gender and Society*. Aldershot: Arena.
Obama, B. (2019) 'President Obama on what it means to "be a man"', *Now This*, February, www.youtube.com/watch?v=mbkgYVYoXjw.
Ogunyemi, C. (1985) 'Womanism: the dynamics of the contemporary black female novel in English', *Signs* 11(1): 63–80.
O'Leary, N. (2019) 'Ireland's feminist revolution', *Politico*, 27 March, www.politico.eu/article/ireland-feminist-revolution/.
Ortega, M. (2015) 'Latina feminism, experience and the self', *Philosophy Compass* 10(4): 244–54.
Ortega, M. (2016) *In-Between: Latina Feminist Phenomenology, Multiplicity and the Self*. New York: SUNY Press.
Ortega, M., and Alcoff, L. M., eds (2009) *Constructing the Nation: A Race and Nationalism Reader*. New York: SUNY Press.
Oudshoorn, N. (1994) *Beyond the Natural Body: An Archaeology of Sex Hormones*. London: Routledge.
Oyewumi, O. (1997) *The Invention of Women: Making an African Sense of Western Gender Discourses*. Minneapolis: University of Minnesota Press.
Oyewumi, O. (2000) 'Family bonds/conceptual binds: African notes on feminist epistemologies', *Signs* 25(4): 1093–8.
Palermo, T., and Peterman, A. (2011) 'Undercounting, overcounting and the longevity of flawed estimates: statistics on sexual violence in conflict', *Bulletin of the World Health Organization* 89: 924–5, www.who.int/bulletin/volumes/89/12/11-089888/en/.
Pape, M. (2019) 'I was sore about losing to Caster Semenya. But this decision against her is wrong', *The Guardian*, 1 May, www.theguardian.com/commentisfree/2019/may/01/losing-caster-semenya-decision-wrong-women-testosterone-iaaf.
Parashar, S. (2011) 'Feminism and postcolonialism: (en)gendering encounters', *Postcolonial Studies* 19(4): 371–7.
Passarlay, G. (2015) *The Lightless Sky: My Journey to Safety as a Child Refugee*. London: Atlantic Books.
Peña, M. (1991) 'Class, gender, and machismo: the "treacherous-woman" folklore of Mexican male workers', *Gender & Society* 5(1): 30–46.
Pérez, E. (1999) *The Decolonial Imaginary: Writing Chicanas into History*. Bloomington: Indiana University Press.
Perry, G. (2016a) *Grayson Perry: All Man*. Channel 4.
Perry, G. (2016b) *The Descent of Man*. London: Allen Lane.
Peto, A. (2016) 'How Hungary and Poland have silenced women and stifled human rights', *The Conversation*, 16 October, https://theconversation.

com/how-hungary-and-poland-have-silenced-women-and-stifled-human-rights-66743.
Phillips, A. (2019) 'Unforgiven', *London Review of Books* 41(5): 3–6.
Phipps, A. (2016) 'Whose personal is more political? Experience in contemporary feminist politics', *Feminist Theory* 17(3): 303–21.
Phipps, A. (2018) 'Reckoning up: sexual harassment and violence in the neoliberal university', *Gender and Education*, 6 June.
Phipps, A., Ringrose, J., Renold, E., and Jackson, C. (2017) 'Rape culture, lad culture and everyday sexism: researching, conceptualizing and politicizing new mediations of gender and sexual violence', *Journal of Gender Studies* 27(1): 1–8.
Pilcher, J. (1999) *Women in Contemporary Britain*. London: Routledge.
Pillai, S. (2001) 'Domestic violence in New Zealand: an Asian immigrant perspective', *Economic and Political Weekly* 36(11): 965–74.
Pollert, A. (1996) 'Gender and class revisited: or, the poverty of patriarchy', *Sociology* 30(4): 639–59.
Probyn, E. (1996) *Outside Belongings*. London: Routledge.
Prosser, J. (1998) *Second Skins: The Body Narratives of Transsexuality*. New York: Columbia University Press.
Prosser, J. (1999) 'Exceptional locations; transsexual travelogues', in K. More and S. Whittle (eds), *Reclaiming Genders: Transsexual Grammars at the Fin de Siècle*. London: Cassell, pp. 83–117.
Puar, J. K. (2012) 'I would rather be a cyborg than a goddess', *philoSOPHIA* 2(1): 49–66.
Ratliff, K. A., Redford, L., and Conway, J. (2019) 'Engendering support: hostile sexism predicts voting for Donald Trump over Hillary Clinton in the 2016 U.S. presidential election', *Group Processes & Intergroup Relations* 22(4): 578–93.
Reagon, B. J. ([1983] 2000) 'Coalition politics: turning the century', in B. Smith, ed., *Home Girls: A Black Feminist Anthology*. New Brunswick, NJ: Rutgers University Press, pp. 343–56.
Redecker, E. von (2018) 'Symbolic glue', *Radical Philosophy* 2(03), www.radicalphilosophy.com/reviews/individual-reviews/symbolic-glue.
Reeser, J. C. (2005) 'Gender identity and sport: is the playing field level?', *British Journal of Sports Medicine* 39(10): 695–9.
Rippon, G. (2019) *The Gendered Brain*. London: Vintage.
Robinson, V., and Richardson, D. (2015) *Introducing Gender and Women's Studies*. 4th edn, Basingstoke: Palgrave Macmillan.
Roelofs, R. (2018) 'Alexandra Kollontai: socialist feminism in theory and practice', *International Critical Thought* 8(1): 166–75.
Rose, H., and Rose, S. (2011) 'Never mind the bollocks', *London Review of Books* 33(9): 17–18 [review of Jordan-Young, *Brain Storm*].
Rose, J. (2016) 'Who do you think you are?', *London Review of Books* 38(9): 3–13.

Rose, S. (2004) 'Chat-up-lines', *The Guardian*, 21 August, www.theguardian.com/books/2004/aug/21/featuresreviews.guadianreview4.
Roughgarden, J. (2004) *Evolution's Rainbow: Diversity, Gender, and Sexuality in Nature and People*. Berkeley: University of California Press.
Roy, A. (1997) *The God of Small Things*. London: Flamingo.
Rubin, G. (1993) 'Thinking sex: notes for a radical theory of the politics of sexuality', in H. Abelove, M. A. Barale and D. M. Halperin, eds, *The Lesbian and Gay Studies Reader*. London: Routledge, pp. 3–44.
Rubin, G., with Butler, J. (1994) 'Sexual traffic', *differences* 6(2–3): 62–100.
Russell, L., Alsop, R., Bradshaw, L., Clisby, S., and Smith, K. (2016) *The State of Girls' Rights in the UK*. London: Plan International.
Salamon, G. (2010) *Assuming a Body: Transgender and Rhetorics of Materiality*. New York: Columbia University Press.
Salter, M. (2019) 'The problem with a fight against toxic masculinity', *The Atlantic*, 27 February, www.theatlantic.com/health/archive/2019/02/toxic-masculinity-history/583411/.
Sandford, S. (2006) *How to Read Beauvoir*. London: Granta Books.
Sartre, J.-P. ([1943] 1969) *Being and Nothingness*, trans. H. Barnes. London: Routledge.
Sartre, J.-P. (2004) *The Imaginary*, trans. J. Webber. London: Routledge.
Schilder, P. (1950) *The Image and the Appearance of the Human Body*. Madison: International Universities Press.
Schulz, K. (2017) 'The many lives of Pauli Murray', *New Yorker*, 10 April.
Scott, J. W. (2018) 'Gender studies under threat worldwide, says subject pioneer', *Times Higher Education Supplement*, 4 December.
Sen, R. (2018) 'Dutee Chand proud of being first athlete to fight against hyperandrogenism rule', *India Today*, 15 September.
Seneviratne, P. (2018) 'Marxist feminism meets postcolonial feminism in organizational theorizing: issues, implications and responses', *Journal of International Women's Studies* 19(2): 186–96.
Shepherd, A. (2016) *De Beauvoir and The Second Sex: A Marxist Interpretation*. PhD thesis, University of Hull, https://hydra.hull.ac.uk/assets/hull:14016a/content.
Shiva, V. (2014) *The Vandana Shiva Reader (Culture of the Land)*. Lexington: Kentucky University Press.
Simons, M. A. (1999) *Beauvoir and "The Second Sex": Feminism, Race and the Origins of Existentialism*. London: Rowman & Littlefield.
Skeggs, B. (2004) *Class, Self, Culture*. London: Routledge.
Spelman, E. (1988) *Inessential Women: Problems of Exclusion in Feminist Thought*. Boston: Beacon Press.
Spivak, G. C. (1987) *In Other Worlds: Essays in Cultural Politics*. London: Routledge.
Spivak, G. C., with Rooney, E. (1994) 'In a word: interview', in N. Schor and

E. Weed, eds, *The Essential Difference*. Bloomington: Indiana University Press.

Stoller, R. J. (1968) *Sex and Gender*. London: Hogarth Press.

Stone, A. (2006) *Luce Irigaray and the Philosophy of Sexual Difference*. Cambridge: Cambridge University Press.

Stone, A. (2007) *An Introduction to Feminist Philosophy*. Cambridge: Polity.

Stone, S. ([1987] 1991) 'The Empire strikes back: a posttranssexual manifesto', in J. Epstein and K. Straub, eds, *Body Guards: The Cultural Politics of Gender Ambiguity*. New York: Routledge; https://sandystone.com/empire-strikes-back.pdf.

Stryker, S. (2008) *Transgender History*. Berkeley, CA: Seal Press.

Stryker, S., and Aizura, A. Z., eds (2013) *The Transgender Studies Reader 2*. London: Routledge.

Tate, S. A. (2005) *Black Skins, Black Masks: Hybridity Dialogism Performativity*. Aldershot: Ashgate.

Tate, S. A. (2009) *Black Beauty: Aesthetics, Stylization, Politics*. Farnham: Ashgate.

Taylor, A. (dir.) (2009) *Examined Life: Philosophy is in the Streets*. ICA Films.

Taylor, Y., Hines, S., and Casey, M., eds (2011) *Theorizing Intersectionality and Sexuality*. Basingstoke: Palgrave Macmillan.

Tong, R. (1989) *Feminist Thought: A Comprehensive Introduction*. London: Unwin Hyman.

Travis, C. B. (2003) *Evolution, Gender, and Rape*. Cambridge, MA: MIT Press.

Truth, S. (1851) 'Ain't I a woman?', speech delivered at the Women's Convention in Akron, Ohio, www.feminist.com/resources/artspeech/genwom/sojour.htm.

Valentine, D. (2007) *Imagining Transgender*. Durham, NC: Duke University Press.

Valentino, N. A., Wayne, C., and Oceno, M. (2018) 'Mobilizing sexism: the interaction of emotion and gender attitudes in the 2016 US presidential election', *Public Opinion Quarterly* 82(S1): 799–821.

Van den Wijngaard, M. (1997) *Reinventing the Sexes: The Biomedical Construction of Femininity and Masculinity*. Bloomington: Indiana University Press.

Van Houtte, M. (2004) 'Why boys achieve less at schools than girls: the difference between boys' and girls' academic culture', *Educational Studies* 30(2): 159–73.

Vashistha, S. (2018) 'Village women empower themselves with ecofeminism in India', *Ecoideaz*, www.ecoideaz.com/showcase/village-women-empower-themselves-with-ecofeminism-in-india.

Verloo, M. (2018) 'Gender knowledge, and opposition to the feminist project: extreme-right populist parties in the Netherlands', *Politics and Governance* 6(3): 20–30.

Walby, S. (1990) *Theorizing Patriarchy*. Oxford: Blackwell.
Walby, S. (1997) *Gender Transformations*. London: Routledge.
Walby, S. (2011) *The Future of Feminism*. Cambridge: Polity.
Walby, S., Armstrong, J., and Strid, S. (2012) 'Intersectionality: multiple inequalities in social theory', *Sociology* 46(2): 224–40.
Walker, S. (2018) '"We won't keep quiet again": the women taking on Viktor Orbán', *The Guardian*, 21 December, www.theguardian.com/world/2018/dec/21/hungary-female-politicians-viktor-orban.
Warner, D. F., and Brown, T. H. (2011) 'Understanding how race/ethnicity and gender define age-trajectories of disability: an intersectionality approach', *Social Science & Medicine* 72(8): 1236–48.
Webber, J. (2018) 'Sedimentation and the origins of cultural values', in *Rethinking Existentialism*. Oxford: Oxford University Press.
Weedon, C. (1987) *Feminist Practice and Poststructuralist Theory*. Oxford: Blackwell.
Weiss, G. (1999) *Body Images: Embodiment as Intercorporeality*. London: Routledge.
Weiss, G. (2009) 'Freedom f/or the other', in C. Daigle and J. Golomb, eds., *Beauvoir and Sartre: The Riddle of Influence*. Bloomington: Indiana University Press, pp. 241–54.
Weiss, G. (2015) 'The normal, the natural, and the normative: implications of Merleau-Ponty's work for feminist theory, critical race theory, and disability studies', *Continental Philosophy Review* 48(1): 77–93.
Wekker, G. (2016) *White Innocence: Paradoxes of Colonialism and Race*. Durham, NC: Duke University Press.
Weston, K. (2010) 'Me, myself and I', in Y. Taylor, S. Hines and M. E. Casey, eds, *Theorizing Intersectionality and Sexuality*. Basingstoke: Palgrave Macmillan, pp. 15–36.
White, G. B. (2017) 'The glaring blind spot of the "Me Too" movement', *The Atlantic*, 22 November, www.theatlantic.com/entertainment/archive/2017/11/the-glaring-blind-spot-of-the-me-too-movement/546458/.
Whitford, M. (1991) *Luce Irigaray: Philosophy in the Feminine*. London: Routledge.
Whitford, M., ed. (1992) *The Irigaray Reader*. Oxford: Blackwell.
Whittle, S. T. (2016) 'Non-binary – is it a timely end to gender identity as we know it?', keynote speech at the Borderlands research conference, Hull Centre for Gender Studies, November 2016.
Whittle, S. T., and Turner, L. (2009) *Transphobic: Hate Crime in the European Union*. London: Press for Change.
Winnicott, D. (1964) *The Child, the Family and the Outside World*. Harmondsworth: Penguin.
Wright, R. ([1945] 1970) *Black Boy*. Harlow: Longman.
Yeates, N. (2004) 'Global care chains', *International Feminist Journal of Politics* 6(3): 369–91.

Yilmaz, F. (2012) 'Right-wing hegemony and immigration: how the populist far-right achieved hegemony through the immigration debate in Europe', *Current Sociology* 60(3): 368–81.

Young, I. M. (1981) 'Beyond the unhappy marriage: a critique of the dual systems theory', in L. Sargent, ed., *Women and Revolution*. Boston: South End Press, pp. 43–70.

Young, I. M. (1990) *Throwing Like a Girl and Other Essays in Feminist Philosophy and Social Theory*. Bloomington: Indiana University Press.

Young, I. M. (1998) '*Throwing Like a Girl*: twenty years later', in D. Welton, ed., *Body and Flesh: A Philosophical Reader*. Oxford: Blackwell, pp. 286–91.

Young, I. M. (2005) *On Female Body Experience: 'Throwing Like a Girl' and Other Essays*. New York: Oxford University Press.

Young, S. (2019) 'Piers Morgan and men's rights activists upset at "emasculating" new Gillette advert', *The Independent*, 15 January, www.independent.co.uk/life-style/piers-morgan-gillette-advert-reaction-gmb-mens-rights-activists-toxic-masculinity-metoo-a8728756.html.

Yuval-Davis, N. (1996) *Gender and Nation*. London: Sage.

Yuval-Davis, N. (2006) 'Intersectionality and feminist politics', *European Journal of Women's Studies* 13(3): 193–209.

Yuval-Davis, N. (2015) 'Situated intersectionality and social inequality', *Raisons politiques* 58(2): 91–100.

Zavella, P. (2017) 'Intersectional praxis in the movement for reproductive justice: the Respect ABQ Women campaign', *Signs* 42(2): 509–33.

Index

A Deal with the Universe 197
abortion, access to 9, 135–6, 208
Abramson, J. 10
Acker, J. 81, 84
Act Up (AIDS Coalition to Unleash Power) 161
aesthetic surgery 193, 222n3, 225n13
age 119, 130
agency, sites of 200–2, 207
Ahmed, Sara 148, 149, 152, 172–3
AIDA (Asylum Information Database) 10
Akala 206–7
Alaimo, Stacy 38, 39
Alcoff, Linda 33, 34, 38, 42, 194
animal studies 27–8
Anzaldúa, Gloria 148, 159–60
Assis, M. P. 9
Australia 9, 206

bad faith 115
Barad, Karen 41
Bardot, Brigitte 107
Barker, Clara 14
Barker, Jason 197
Baron-Cohen, Simon 23, 28
Barrett, Michèle 93
Beatley, M. 203
Beauvoir, Simone de 2–3, 17
   age 119, 130
   bad faith 115
   becoming a woman/man 102, 107–8, 116, 118, 120, 188
   bodily habits 58, 94, 111–13, 154
   Butler and 4, 154–5, 156
   capitalism and patriarchy 204–5
   complicity 115–16
   data of biology 16, 22, 102–3
   dimensions of otherness 117–19
   economic and social structure 103–5
   existentialism 99, 101
   Freud and 97
   historical materialism 5, 71
   life paths 113–14
   lived experience 107–14
   living bodily difference 109–10
   Marxism 97, 103–4, 120
   masculinity and 106, 119
   myths 17, 105–7, 113, 116, 120
   objectification 108–9, 119
   objective conditions 17, 102–7
   phenomenology 4, 97–8, 171
   race and 97, 101, 114, 117–19
   'woman' as situation 99–100
   woman as *the Other* 100–2, 121, 156
Beechey, Veronica 79, 81
behavioural sex differences 23–4
belonging 190–2
Bergner, Gwen 67, 68, 69
Bergoffen, D. 117
Bilge, Sirma 130, 131, 135, 139
biology 1, 3, 16, 23–4, 82
   animal studies 27–8
   chromosomes 33–5
   control of reproduction 104, 110
   gender essentialism and 3, 22, 53, 64
   hormones *see* hormones
   puberty 109
   reproduction 22–3, 33–4, 38, 42–3, 102–3
   sexed categories as natural kinds 22–3
   sexual difference *see* sexual difference
   trans bodies and 37–8
biophobia 39
black feminism 5, 17–18, 122, 129–30, 150; *see also* intersectionality
Black Lives Matter 134
Bleier, Ruth 29
bodily ego 45, 47–9, 65, 192
bodily habits 58, 94, 111–13, 154
bodily modification
   cosmetic surgery 193, 222n3, 225n13
   hormones and 38, 188, 192
   trans people 38, 181, 188, 192, 195
Bohr, Niels 41
Bolsonaro, Jair 9, 11
Bourdieu, Pierre 94, 111–12, 154, 205

boxing 183
Braidotti, Rosi 64
brain 6, 20, 28–30
Brazil 9, 10, 11–12
Brownmiller, Susan 81
Bruegel, Irene 80
Burke, Tarana 203
Butler, Judith 5–6, 18, 94
   Beauvoir and 4, 154–5, 156
   the body 167–73
   in Brazil 11–12
   critique of identity 164–7
   on drag 157, 162–3
   gendered scripts 153–4
   intersectionality and 130–1, 137, 141, 143, 147–8
   on naming 128, 151–2, 155
   on *Paris is Burning* 157–8, 173
   performance and performativity 18, 152–3, 174, 185
   performativity of race 163–4
   precariousness 158–60, 167, 171
   queering 160–3
   real genders 156–8
   recognition by others 18, 159–60, 191, 192
   sexual difference 58, 64, 70
   subjectivity and subjectification 154–6
   vulnerability to others 5, 18, 158

Cameron, Deborah 24, 26–7, 28
Cannon, L. 82
capitalism
   class relations 76
   female labour 79–80
   modes of production 71, 76–7, 79, 82–3
   patriarchy and 82–5, 104–5
   race and 84–5
   relations of production 76, 77, 78, 82, 84
Carastathis, A. 139, 140
care industry 91–2
Castoriadis, Cornelius 60, 61, 62–3
castration anxiety 44, 50, 63
Catholic Church 9, 12, 153, 218n
Chand, Dutee 36
Chevalier, Maurice 196
Chodorow, Nancy 220n3
chromosomes 33–5
cis gender, definition of 7
class
   educational attainment and 123–4
   Marxist theory 76
   masculinity and 84, 206–7
   materialist feminism 90
   middle and upper class 31, 112
   working class 31, 61, 84, 112, 114, 123–4, 206–7
   see also intersectionality

Clinton, Hillary 8
coalition politics 207–9
Cocozza, P. 197
Colebrook, Claire 38
Collins, Patricia Hill 129, 130, 131, 132, 135, 139, 147
colonialism 5, 90, 92, 142, 204
   decolonial feminism 5, 142–6
   intersectional analysis 127
colonizing gestures 66–7
colourism 201
Combahee River Collective 122, 130
complicity 115–16
Connell, Raewyn 87–90, 94, 206
Coole, D. 72, 90
Cooper, Anna Julia 130
Corrêa, S. 12
cosmetic surgery 193, 222n3, 225n13
Cox, Laverne 186
Crenshaw, Kimberlé 5, 126, 128–9, 131, 132–4, 136–7, 138–9, 146
criminalization of same-sex relationships 224n1, 226n5
Cuban, S. 91–2
culture
   nature/culture distinction 38–40
   new materialism and 38–40
   social practices 93–4
cyborgs 41

Daly, M. 81
Darwinian ideas 39–40
Davis, Angela 79, 204
decolonial feminism 5, 142–4
   intersectionality and 144–6
Delphy, Christine 82–3
Derrida, Jacques 160
Deutscher, P. 117, 118–19
dimensions of otherness 117–19
disability
   intersectional analysis 124–5, 127, 131
   multiple sclerosis 169–70
   psychoanalysis and 67–9
discrimination legislation 2, 93, 178
Dolezal, Luna 109
domestic violence 166
   intersectional analysis 125–6, 133, 136
   see also gender-based violence
Douglas, Gabby 219n5
Douglass, Frederick 69
drag 157, 162–3, 181, 186
Du Bois, W. E. B. 97, 118
dual-systems theories 83–5

Eddo-Lodge, Reni 132
educational attainment 6
earnings and 72

intersectional analysis 123–4
literacy 75
Engels, Friedrich 76, 77, 104
entanglements 41–3, 199–200
environmentalism 208–9
Erdoğan, Recep Tayyip 10, 114
evolutionary psychology 25–8
existentialism 99, 101, 159
expressive body 171–2, 194–6

Fanon, Franz 61, 68, 118
Fausto-Sterling, Anne 26, 29–30, 33–4, 35, 40
Fehr, C. 25
Feinberg, L. 176, 177
femininity 1, 21, 30–1, 33
    Beauvoir and 106
    disabled women and 127
    Freud on 50–1, 63
    Gatens on 62
    gendered scripts 153
feminism
    black feminism 5, 17–18, 122, 129–30, 150
    decolonial feminism 5, 142–6
    Marxist feminism 76–9
    materialist feminism 16, 90, 93–5, 173–4
    second-wave Marxist feminism 78, 79–80
    trans women and 13–15
Fine, Cordelia 20, 21, 27, 28, 29, 205
Finland 9
Firestone, Shulamith 82
Ford, Christine Blasey 226n8
Foucault, Michel 155, 156, 166
Francis, Pope 12
Franconay, Claire 196
Fraser, Nancy 66, 67
Freud, Sigmund 16, 44, 45–54, 70
    Beauvoir and 97
    bodily ego 45, 47–9, 65, 192
    castration anxiety 44, 50, 63
    femininity and 50–1, 63
    gender essentialism and 45, 53, 70
    on homosexuality 52
    id, ego, superego 47
    Oedipal complex/crisis 47, 49–51, 52, 56, 69
    penis envy 44, 46, 50–1, 53, 63
    sexual difference and 49–54
    the unconscious 46–7, 50, 51, 52, 63
    see also psychoanalysis
Frost, S. 72, 90

Garland-Thomson, Rosemarie 68, 122, 126
Garry, Ann 132, 138, 139
Gatens, Moira 61–2
gaze of others 118
    Beauvoir 108–9
    male gaze 63

gender
    defining 1–2, 151
    see also sex/gender distinction
gender dysphoria 193
gender essentialism 3, 6–7
    attacks on gender theory and 12–13
    biology and 3, 22, 53, 64
    Butler and 18
    Freud and 45, 53, 70
    Lacan and 53, 70
    right-wing populism 6–7
gender ideology 8, 11, 12
gender pay gaps 72, 74, 173, 201
Gender Recognition Act 2004 2, 178
gender regimes 85–7
gender theory 2–4, 21
    attacks on 10–13
    terminology 2–3
gender-based violence 73, 75, 166, 202–4
    domestic violence 125–6, 133, 136, 166
    intersectional analysis 125–6, 133, 134–5, 136, 203–4
    migrant women 10, 125, 145, 204, 208
    patriarchy and 81
    right-wing populism and 203, 204
    toxic masculinity 204–7
    see also rape
George, R. 110
Gill, R. 201
Gillette 206, 207
Gines, Kathryn 118, 130
global financial crisis 2008 23
globalization 90–2
Goffman, Erving 183
Gonzalez-Arnal, S. 146
Graff, A. 12
Greece 9
Grewal, I. 145
Grosz, Elizabeth 39–40, 64
Guattari, Félix 141, 142
Gutman, M. C. 207

Halberstam, Jack 185, 188–9, 193
Haraway, Donna 4, 41–3, 199
Hartmann, Heidi 81, 83–4, 85
health
    gender and 73
    intersectional analysis 124–5
    mental health problems 73
Hegel, G. W. F. 159
Heggie, Vanessa 37
Heidegger, Martin 98, 191
Hekman, Susan 38, 39
Hennessy, Rosemary 72, 90, 91, 95
Herbert, J. 23
hermaphrodites 34
Hettinga, Lieke 196

Hines, Sally 180–1, 197
Hinsliff, Gaby 14
historical materialism 5, 16–17, 71–2, 92
    Beauvoir and 5, 71
    Connell on gender 87–90
    gender regimes 85–7
    gendered societies 72–6
    globally connected inequalities 90–2
    materiality of the body 89
    patriarchy and 80–3
    Walby on gender 85–7
Hollywood films 135
home 190–2
    gender homes 186–7
hooks, bell 11, 68, 121, 165, 190, 204
hormones 20–1, 23, 24, 33
    bodily modification and 38, 188, 192
    sport and 36–7
    toxic masculinity 205
Hungary 9, 12
Hurst, G. 6
hyperandrogenism rule 36

ideology
    'gender ideology' 8, 11, 12
    Marx and 76, 94, 105–6
    myths 105–6
imaginary, the
    class differences and 61
    Irigaray and 61, 62–4, 65, 66
    Lacan and 45, 54, 55, 59–62, 66
    race and 61
    see also Castoriadis; myths; toxic masculinity
India 202–3, 204
Ingraham, C. 72, 90, 95
intersectional analysis
    disability 124–5, 127, 131
    gender-based violence 125–6, 133, 134–5, 136, 203–4
    Hollywood films 135
    intersectionality, educational attainment 123–4
    rape 125–6, 134, 136
intersectionality 14–15, 17–18, 122–6
    assemblage and 141
    Butler and 130–1, 137, 141, 143, 147–8
    coining of term 5, 128–9
    concept of 122–3, 128–32
    decolonial feminism and 144–6
    domains of power 135
    identity and 147
    lived experience and 126–8
    metaphor of the intersection 138–42
    origins of 128–32
    political 132–4
    in practice 132–6

representational 133, 134–5
    scope of 136–8
    structural 132, 133–4
    subjectivity and 146–9
intersex bodies 34–5
Ireland, Republic of 208
Irigaray, Luce
    the imaginary and 61, 62–4, 66
    on nature 65, 70
    sexual difference and 58, 64–5, 66, 70

Jackson, Stevi 71, 81, 95, 173
Jagger, Gill 39
James, Susan 116
Jenner, Caitlyn 186
Jonason, Peter 26
Jordan-Young, Rebecca 29
judiciary
    gender and 72–3
    rape trials 62

Käll, Lisa 153
Kantola, J. 8, 9
Kaplan, C. 145
Karkazis, Katrina 36–7
Kavanaugh, Brett 226n8
Kay, Jackie 225n15
Kollontai, Alexandra 78
Koyama, E. 14

Lacan, Jacques 16, 45, 70, 155–6
    gender essentialism 53, 70
    I/ego formation 55
    the Imaginary 45, 54, 55, 59–62, 65, 66
    mirror phase 55
    the other 55
    the phallus 56–7, 58–9, 67
    public meanings 45, 58
    the Real 54, 57, 65
    sexual difference and 45, 55, 56–9, 64
    the Symbolic 54, 56, 57, 59, 65, 66
    symbolic essentialism 57–9
    three orders 54–6
    see also psychoanalysis
Lane, Riki 40
Le Doeuff, M. 107
legislation 2, 93, 178
Lego 6, 29, 153
Lenin, V. I. 77
lived experience 107–14
    bodily habits 58, 94, 111–13, 154
    life paths 113–14
    living bodily difference 109–10
    objectification 108–9
Livingston, Jenny 157
Lloyd, Elisabeth 25–6
Lombardo, E. 8, 9

Lorde, Audre 69, 127
Lugones, Maria 5, 59, 143–4, 146, 147, 207, 209, 219n5

McBee, Thomas 183
McCall, L. 145–6
McClintock, Anne 31, 61, 139–40, 166
McDowell, Linda 87
McKee, Lyra 208
McNay, Lois 166, 173
McWhorter, L. 147
Mairs, Nancy 68, 169–70
Marcus, Jana 195
Martin, Biddy 59, 165–6, 167–8, 173
Martin, Emily 32
Martínez Patiño, María José 36
Marx, Karl 71–2, 103–4
  economic determinism 76–7
  ideology 76, 94, 105–6
  materiality of the body 89
  relations between men and women 103–4
  see also historical materialism
Marxism 76–9
  Beauvoir and 97, 103–4, 120
  domestic labour and 77, 78, 79, 82, 83
  Lenin and 77–8
  reproductive labour 79–80, 82, 83
  the Woman Question 77, 78
Marxist feminism 76–80
  women as reserve labour 79–80
masculinity 1, 21, 30–1, 183
  Beauvoir on 106, 119
  class and 84, 206–7
  Gatens on 62
  gendered scripts 153
  toxic masculinity 204–7
materialist feminism 16, 90, 93–5, 173–4
Meijer, I. C. 170
menstruation 109
  sport and 110, 225n10
mental health problems 73
Merleau-Ponty, Maurice 97, 98, 111, 154, 196
mestiza consciousness 148
#MeToo movement 14, 134, 203, 206
migrants 137, 223n5, 225n11
  colonialism and 145
  right-wing populism and 8, 10, 13, 204, 208
  support for 201
  vulnerability of migrant women 10, 125, 145, 204, 208
  women care-workers 91–2
Mitchell, Juliet 53, 54, 82
Mohanty, C. T. 174
Moi, Toril 99
Monro, Surya 180
Moore, Keith L. 219n2
Morgan, Robin 209

Morris, Jan 182
multiple sclerosis 169–70
Murray, J. 7, 13
Murray, Pauli 183–4
Myrdal, Gunnar 97
myths
  Beauvoir and 17, 105–7, 113, 116, 120
  'the black rapist' 204
  changing 201
  of sameness 209
  see also imaginary, the

Nash, Jennifer C. 129, 136, 137–8, 149
Nataf, Zachary I. 195
nationalism 8–9, 10
nature/culture distinction 41–2
  entanglements 41–3, 199–200
  new materialism and 38–40
  sex/gender 38–40
Nelson, Maggie 188
new materialism 4, 41, 141
  nature/culture and 38–40
Northern Ireland 208
Nyong'o, Lupita 134

Obama, Barack 206
object-relations theory 220n3
objectification 108–9, 119
Oedipal complex/crisis 47, 49–51, 52, 56, 69
Ogando, A. C. 9
Ogunyemi, Chikwenye 114
O'Leary, N. 208
other, the
  Beauvoir and 100–2, 121, 156
  dimensions of otherness 117–19
  Lacan and 55
  woman as 100–2, 121, 156
Oudshoorn, Nelly 33
Oyewumi, Oyeronke 114, 143

paedophilia 11, 218n2
Paris is Burning 157–8, 173
parliamentarians 10, 72–3
Passarlay, Gulwali 223n5
patriarchy
  capitalism and 82–5, 104–5
  dual-systems theories 83–5
  historical materialism and 80–3
  race and 84–5
penis envy 44, 46, 50–1, 53, 63
Pérez, Emma 143
Perez, Maria 183
performance and performativity 58, 151, 152–3, 185
  see also Butler
performativity of race 163–4
Perry, Grayson 206

Peto, A. 9
phenomenology 97–8, 154, 196
   Beauvoir and 4, 97–8, 171
   feminist phenomenology 4
   queer phenomenology 171–3
   'woman' as situation 99–100
Phillips, Anne 205
philosophy of science 32
Poland 9, 10, 12, 218n
politicians 10, 72–3
poverty 73, 104, 136–7
power, distribution of 72–3
precariousness 158–60, 167, 171
pregnant men 197–8
primate studies 27–8
Prins, B. 170
Probyn, Elspeth 183, 189
Prosser, Jay 185, 186–7, 189, 190
psychoanalysis 16, 44–5, 70
   object-relations theory 220n3
   race and disability 67–9
   see also Freud; Lacan
psychological sex differences 16, 23–4
psychology, evolutionary 25–8
Puar, Jasbir 141, 142
puberty 109

Queer Nation 161
queer phenomenology 171–3
queer theory 4, 160–3, 184–5

race
   Beauvoir and 97, 101, 114, 117–19
   the imaginary and 61
   infant mortality and 125
   #MeToo movement and 134
   myth of 'the black rapist' 204
   patriarchy/capitalism and 84–5
   performativity of 163–4
   primal scenes 69
   psychoanalysis and 67–9
   rape and 126, 134, 136, 204
   see also intersectionality
Rana Plaza factory 91
rape 73, 166
   gang rape 202–3
   intersectional analysis 125–6, 134, 136
   male rape 81
   myth of 'the black rapist' 204
   patriarchy and 81
   power and 203
   race and 126, 134, 136, 204
   right-wing populism and 203
   sociobiological theories 25–6
   trials 62
   in war zones 202
   see also gender-based violence

Reagon, Bernice Johnson 209–10
real genders 156–8, 189, 190
recognition by others 18, 159–60, 191–2
refugees 101, 191, 201, 204, 208, 223, 225
religion 5, 86, 139, 223n5
   fundamentalism 9
   and right-wing politics 7, 9, 11, 201
religious practices 153
Respect ABQ Women campaign 135–6
right-wing populism 9, 114, 203
   gender essentialism 6–7
   gender theory and 11–12
   gender-based violence and 203, 204
   nationalism and 8–9
   rise of 7–10, 208
Rippon, Gina 20, 21, 22, 29
Rose, Jacqueline 176
Roughgarden, Joan 28
Roy, Arundhati 209

Salamon, Gayle 179–80, 191–2, 195
same-sex relationships
   criminalization of 224n1, 226n5
Sandford, Stella 96, 101, 110
Sartre, Jean-Paul 101, 115, 196
Schilder, Paul 48
Scott, J. W. 9
Semenya, Caster 36
sex differences
   animal studies 27–8
   behavioural 23–4
   the brain 6, 20, 28–30
   chromosomes 33–5
   evolutionary psychology 25–8
   genital 32–3
   history of research into 32–5
   inevitability of 64–5
   nature and 65, 70
   psychological 23–4
   sexed/gendered difference 2, 20–2
   sociobiology 25–6
sex/ gender distinction 1, 30–2
   nature/culture 38–40
   new materialism and 38–40
sexual difference
   animal studies 27–8
   behavioural 23–4
   the brain 6, 20, 28–30
   chromosomes 33–5
   evolutionary psychology 25–8
   Freud and 49–54
   genital 32–3
   history of research into 32–5
   inevitability of 64–5
   Irigaray and 58, 64–5, 66, 70
   Lacan and 45, 55, 56–9, 64
   nature and 65, 70

Index

psychological 23–4
sexed/gendered difference 2, 20–2
sociobiology 25–6
sexual difference theory
   Freud and 49–54
   Irigaray and 58, 64–5, 66, 70
   Lacan and 45, 55, 56–9, 64
   see also psychoanalysis
sexuality 18, 51–2, 63, 68, 78, 83, 85–6, 107, 110, 143, 161–2, 177–9, 180–4, 225n9
   asexuality 127
   bisexuality 51
   heterosexuality 1, 12, 52, 153, 156, 161, 162
   homosexuality 52, 135, 156, 162, 220n2
   lesbians, lesbianism 110, 127, 128, 130, 133, 159, 161–2, 172, 181, 183, 192
sexualization of children 218n2
Shaw, George Bernard 117
Shiva, Vandana 209
sites of agency 200–2, 207
social protection, access to 74
sociobiology 25–6
Soviet Union 78–9
Spain 9, 203
speculum 63
Spelman, Elizabeth 117
Spivak, Gayatri 66–7, 168
sport 35–7, 113, 201
   hormones and 36–7
   hyperandrogenism rule 36
   menstruation 110, 225n10
   Olympics 170
   sex tests 36
Stewart, Maria W. 130
Stoller, Robert 218n1
Stone, Alice 23, 33, 65
Stone, Sandy 185
Stryker, Susan 176, 181–2, 186
suicide 73
symbolic essentialism 57–9

Tate, Shirley 163–4, 165, 166
Taylor, Sunaura 169
theoretical shifts 4–6
Thompson, Raymond 193
Thunberg, Greta 208
Tomlinson, B. 131–2
toxic masculinity 204–7
toys 6, 20, 27, 152, 153
trade unions 84
trans people
   belonging 190–2
   bodily modification 38, 181, 188, 192, 195
   confronting nature 184–6
   crossing of borders 188–9
   expressive body 194–6
   feminism and 13–15

   gender homes 186–7
   gendered categories 178–82
   home 190–2
   local readings 182–4
   pregnant men 197–8
   queer theory and 184–5
   rights of 7, 13–14
   spatial metaphors 188–9
   trans bodies and biology 37–8
   trans narratives 186–7, 189
   transformative possibilities 196–8
   umbrella category of 177–8
   wrong body 192–4
Trump, Donald 8, 10, 138
Truth, Sojourner 31, 112, 130
Turkey 9–10, 114
Turner, L. 14

unconscious, the 46–7, 50, 51, 52, 67
unemployment 74
universalism 66–7

Valentine, David 177, 181–2
Van den Wijngaard, Marianne 34–5
Vigoya, M. V. 207
violence *see* gender-based violence

Wade, Cheryl Marie 68
Walby, Sylvia 83, 85–7, 93, 94, 133–4, 138
Walker, S. 12
Weedon, Chris 57
Weinstein, Harvey 203
Wells, Ida B. 130
Weston, Kath 122, 127–8, 149
Whitford, Margaret 63, 64
Whittle, Stephen 14, 188, 224n5
Williams, Serena 219n5
'woman' as other *see* intersectionality
'woman' as situation 99–100
Women's March on Washington (2017) 10
work
   care work 74, 91–2
   domestic labour 74, 77, 78, 79, 82, 83, 84, 174
   educational attainment and 72
   gender division of labour 84, 88, 92
   gender pay gaps 72, 74, 173, 201
   globalization 90–2
   unemployment 74
   unpaid work 74, 79, 85
   women in 72–4
   women as reserve labour 79–80
working class 31, 61, 84, 112, 114, 123–4, 206–7
Wright, Richard 97, 101, 117, 118

Xtravaganza, Venus 158, 166

Yoshikawa, Eriko 128

Young, Iris Marion 84, 112
Yuval-Davis, Nira 138, 140, 141–2, 144

Zavella, Patricia 135–6, 183